The Protest Is Still On

Selection of Articles in Political Economy

THE PROTEST IS STILL ON

Ashok Mitra

EMANCIPATION
KOLKATA
2007

First Published in India, 2007

Published by
Emancipation
49, N.N. Road, LIG, BL-C/8
Kolkata-700 011, India

ISBN 81-903443-2-3

Typeseter
Zenith Graphics
Kolkata-9

Cover Designed by
Saswata Dasgupta

Printed by
S.S. Print
8, Narasingha Datta Lane
Kolkata-12

Cover Printed by
G.S. Metadek Private Limited
Kaikhali, Chiriamore, Rajarhat
Kolkata-136

Publisher's Note

Emancipation would like to express its grateful thanks to Prabhat Patnaik, Mihir Bhattacharya and Sushama and Goutam Ghosh for their help in arranging this publication, *The Protest is still on*, which is a selection of articles from Ashok Mitra's column, 'Cutting Corners', which appeared in *The Telegraph* over a period of more than two decades between 1982 and 2006.

When issues concerning the development of the Indian Economy in the context of globalisation are generating such intense interest, we expect this collection will add a significant dimension to the on-going discussion.

Emancipation also thanks Samantak Das and Sujit Kumar Mandal for their kind help.

For Rudrangshu

who does not despise contrary things

Contents

Poison as prescription

It was the ancient Fifties. A venerable academic used to preside over the School of Economics and Sociology of the University of Bombay at its magnificent Churchgate campus. Once the annual budget of the Union government was presented on the last working day of February, the professor would, year after year, make the same observation on its contents: the budget was like the curate's egg, good in some parts, not so good in others. Given the predictability of his annual comment, the sobriquet, Professor Curate's egg, stuck to him.

An occasion for remembering that old story has been provided by the recomendations of the national commission for farmers. The commission has come down heavily on the concept of special economic zones. It has strongly disapproved of the eagerness in official quarters to compel farmers to surrender arable land for enabling the establishment of SEZs. There is no mincing of words on its part: "Prime farm land must be conserved for agriculture and not be diverted for nonagricultural purposes and for programmes like the Special Economic Zone."

While reaching its conclusion, the commission must have taken into account recent trends in farm output in the country, including the fact that per capita availability of food-grains today is less than what it was at the dawn of independence. The issue of employment and livelihood have not escaped its attention either. Despite the hoopla over accelerated growth in industry and services in the past decade, employment has been stagnating in these sectors. In the circumstances, the take-over of agricultural land—the source of livelihood for nearly two-thirds of the nation—for non-farming purposes is not only morally wrong, but it also hardly makes any sense in terms of sheer economic criteria either.

Nonetheless, the pressure persists. The globalization lobby, sold on the luscious dream of SEZs, have their agents at all levels of administration; they have also succeeded in penetrating the sanctum of politicians. The firm position taken on SEZs by the national commission for farmers is therefore encouraging. Projects of such nature, the commission is of the view, should only be assigned "wasteland and/or land afflicted by salinity and other abiotic stresses which reduce the biological potential of land for the purpose of farming".

What, however, follows in the commission's report is a gross anticlimax, reminding one of the analogy of the curate's egg. Distressed at the phenomenon of several state governments jumping on the wagon of SEZs, the commission wants the Union government to take the matter in its hands: the Centre must assume control over issues concerning agriculture all over the country, including policies with regard to land use. But land and agriculture are, under the Constitution, State subjects, occurring as Entries 14 and 18 in the State List in its Seventh Scedule. Not to be deterred, the commission has urged a fullfledged constitutional amendment, whereby agriculture would be transferred from the State List to the Concurrent List. Once that happens, the Centre would have the final say in all matters pertaining to the farm sector; anarchy in land use would automatically cease.

How should one assess the worthwhileness of this astounding recommendation? The Union government is obviously in the commission's judgement, more full of wisdom than state governments generally are and ministers at the Centre are more solicitous of the welfare of farmers than nondescript ministers populating state administrations. The assumptions are way off the mark. Why cavil at facts? The proposal for SEZs originated in the first place in New Delhi, conceivably on advice rendered by interested parties, foreign and domestic. It is the Centre, which has been dinning into the ear of state governments the fable of the economic miracle SEZs have effected in China while carefully failing to mention the scale factor that makes the difference: in conditions between the two countries.

In India, permits for SEZs are distributed like confetti, even for areas as small as 10 hectares; in China, the usual minimum size for an SEZ is at least a hundred times as large. And of course nobody chooses to mention the political surveillance the Communist Party of China exercises over the entire operations of the SEZs there.

The state governments have merely fallen into the trap set for them by the Centre in this matter. The principal decision-makers in the arena of economic policy in the Central administration are the office of the prime minister and the ministries of finance and commerce. While the ministry of finance might feel somewhat querulous about the possible revenue loss resulting from the proliferation of SEZs, all three entites are in fact keenly interested to see them sprout; their existence supposedly boosts the rate of growth of gross domestic product.

A further factor calls for equal attention. The Fiscal Responsibility and Budget Management Act has killed whatever scope for financial manoeuvrability the state government had earlier possessed. And yet, they have to pay heed to the clamour for development emanating from the grassroots. Desperately looking for funds to start new development projects, state governments fall prey to the illusory charm of SEZs. A constitutional amendment transferring surveillance of agriculture from the states to the Centre would not therefore save agriculture from the perils of SEZs. The remedy prescribed is about as dangerous as the disease.

It is possible to go a little beyond. The Union government has actually no *locus standi* to impose on the states any *national* policy for farming or farmers. If a state government, for example, wants to enforce a drastic policy of land reforms and passes legislation to take away from affluent peasants land in excess of, say, twenty acres, the Centre would have no business to thwart it in the name of a national farming policy; the Constitution does not give the Centre that right, and the recommendation of the commission to amend the Constitution for implementing such a policy contradicts the federal ethos which inspired the nation's struggle for freedom.

Why blame, though, the commission alone? Basic awareness of states' rights and provisions of the Constitution is often lacking even amongst those who preside over the state governments. Consider a recent instance. A state chief minister, call him A, is importunating an industrial tycoon to set up a major steel project in his state. His state does not, however, produce crude iron, while a neighbouring state has it in plenty. The chief minister of this neighbouring state, call him B, cannot be blamed if he would consider as his first priority the conservation of the raw material so as to start a steel project in his own state; entry 18 in the State List allows him this prerogative.

Chief Minister A is peeved no end, and wants the prime minister to order B to part with his crude iron. Nobody is seemingly around to tell A that, as long as the Constitution remains unchanged, the prime minister cannot do anything to help him out; even Entry 54 in the Union List, which permits the Centre to intrude into the jurisdiction of states in the interest of mineral development, is unlikely to be of any avail towards forcing a state to surrender its minerals to serve the interest of another state in case its own development is impeded thereby. Rather than committing the folly of calling for Central intervention, A should sit together with B and, on the basis of some *quid pro quo,* try to reach a mutually satisfactory arrangement.

Those ruling at the Centre would perhaps love to scrap wholesale the existing Constitution and replace it by a unitary framework of administration. That would only further multiply the country's already camplex problems. Expert-ridden commissions and state chief ministers should first brush up their knowledge of the facts of life before they venture to dispense advice and make wholesale recommendations on crucial national issues.

30th October, 2006

It always knows best

The World Bank is a rich, wise, serious-minded body. It always knows the best, it should not therefore be made fun of. What does one do then in the circumstance? A recent report prepared by the Bank has warned India about the grave consequences of raising the bank rate. A high rate of interest, in its veiw, stifles industrial growth since it raises the cost of production for enterpreneurs. It would therefore be, it says, an act of folly on the part of the Reserve Bank of India and the government in New Delhi to listen to stray counsel from bystanders and reverse the present cheap money policy; to do so would, by implication, adversely affect Indian efforts to maintain an eight to ten per cent rate of growth. There could seemingly be no greater calamity. The acolytes who have infiltrated the different strata of India's policy-making whould lose their face, as would the Bank itself.

The Bank's words cannot be brushed aside just like that. There is a problem though. For nearly four decades beginning with the early Fifties, this same institution, the World Bank, had been admonishing the government of India, in stentorian terms, on the rights and wrongs of economic policy. What it used to preach during those days is roughly as follows. India is an abysmally poor country. A poor country is in a position to save very little; it is, therefore, awfully short of capital resources so necessary for investment and growth. The limited capital that the country has must be put to the most effective use. This objective would be best served if the rate of interest in the country is set at a relatively high level.

A high rate of interest serves three purposes. First, it stimulates the expansion of deposits and the boosts savings. Second, it discourages projects, which have low productiveity, and hence low profitability, from competing for scarce capital funds. In the third place, high interest rates induce greater efficiency in the system. Since the rate at which money is borrowed is steep, those who borrow funds strain their utmost to raise their efficiency which would ensure them a satisfactory rate of return after the cost of production, including the cost of money has been taken care of.

For decades on end, the World Bank had served such fare. Those in charge of official monetary policy, had trained themselves to consider the Bank's advice as inviolable. Interest rates were accordingly set at dizzy heights. Investment activity in the country, as a result, became reserved ground for a select few private entrepreneurs who operated on a relatively large scale and had the necessary organizational ability to cultivate economies of scale; this allowed them to earn a decent rate of return even after paying through their nose for the money they borrowed from the banks. Both the limited nature of industiral growth during these decades and the severely skewed structure of that growth owed a great deal to the World Bank dogma concerning the appropriate rate of interest for a poor, capital-starved economy.

Middle-level and small-scale entrepreneurs were shut out of the industrial arena because they could not afford the high interest rates charged by banks. Aspiring young persons, eager to explore avenues of self-employment, were stopped in their track for the same reason. The plight was no different for millions and millions of the petty peasantry. The hard money policy, it is worth noting, was not much of a success in the pursuit of the goal of maximizing efficiency either. For the industrial sector became the monopoly of big industrial houses; under conditions of monopoly, even the World Bank would admit, production comes to a half before the point of full capacity utilization is reached.

It is a different epoch, and the World Bank is now chirping a different tune. The Bank is now a proponent of cheap money policy. Whatever it says is, to its poorer member countries, worth its weight in gold; the Bank is their principal lender. Politeness apart, they cannot quite gather the courage to remind the Bank what it used to say only a couple of decades ago. After all, great people and institutions revel in contradicting themselves. A new doctrine is on the anvil, and credit-seekers henceforth better fall in line. Whether a country has enough of savings is no longer considered as a *desideratum.* On the countrary we are being asked to proceed on the asumption that enough of loanable funds is available in the system and it is a question of stimulating the demand side alone.

A regime of low interest rates, the Bank is now cocksure, encourages entrepreneures to borrow funds on a generous scale and expand their activites; a nation wishing to accelerate economic development should therefore adopt a monetary policy which places the most emphasis on cheap money. The government in New Delhi and the Reserve Bank of India have been, in the more recent years, following this piece of advice with scrupulous reverence.

Is not there, however, more than what meets the eye in the wisdom the Bank is currently dispensing? It is conveniently silent on the issue of the inverse relationship between the rate of interest and the rate of growth in deposits. Low rates of interest discourage savings and deposit growth, while high rates do the opposite : if this dictum was true fifty years ago, it should also be equally true today. But the Bank, to all appearance is no longer overly concerned with the possibility that, with the enforcement of a cheap money policy in India, domestic savings would either shrivel or turn sluggish.

No need to worry on this score, the Bank will say; excess capital funds from rich countries, badly seeking a resting place, will arrive and take charge of the investment process activity over there. What the Bank fails to mention, owners of such foreign capital will thereby also expand their control over India's industrial and infrastrucural sectors. A low-interest-rate regime would serve foreign investors in another way as well; cheap money would enable them to keep their operational costs at reasonably low levels.

To commiserate with potential savers, who might be discouraged by low interest rates, will be however, somewhat beside the point. Low interest rates are a great civilizer; they induce citizens with excess funds at their disposal to travel toward the direction of the stock exchanges. Foreign institutional investors have, of late, marked out the Indian stock exchanges as their favourite hunting ground. They relish the prospect of a growing population of suckers in the Indian bourses; that would help them organize bull-and-bear runs with greater frequency and squeeze more and more profit from such operations.

A handful amongst the comfortably placed citizenry may, of course, feel querulous about speculating in the share market with their hard-erned money. An alternative choice is available to them. With globalization, the surging waves of consumerism have reached Indian shores; luxury consumption would take care of the excess income of those who are reluctant to indulge in share-market speculation. The World Bank has its friends among the transnational corporations which preside over the production and distribution, world-wide, of sophisticated luxury goods.

So, please be at peace, nothing has really gone wrong with the World Bank. The Bank is not bashful to be inconsistent. Behavioural inconsistency advances its global class interests. It is impossible to catch napping this *deus ex machina* for all seasons.

18th August, 2006

Deconstruct, then panic

Anno Domini 2001 is ancient times, and yet not so ancient. Early in that year, an official committee, worried over stocks of foodgrains laying with the Food Corporation of India reaching close to 50 million tons, hit upon a wonderful idea. The carrying costs of such a huge stock were allegedly, increasingly difficult for the government to bear; a portion of the stocks, the committee recommended, be dumped in the high seas.

The committee did not suggest releasing more foodgrains through the public distribution system at subsidized prices; it dared not make such a suggestion, for the World Trade Organizatrion would then have pounced upon it. Subsidized supply of food—or, for the matter, any commodity—in the view of this august body, goes against the interests of private operators, and thereby befouls the impeccability of the free trade concept. The committee could have recommended distribution of some of the surplus grains as charity to the country's needy population. After all, charity does not quite come under the purveiw of the WTO; in any case under Article 282 of our Constitution, the authorities, whether at the Centre or in the states, are entitled to offer a grant to anyone for any purpose. The committee however was not in a charitable mood. It did not even suggest that a portion of the accumulated foodgrains be fed to the rickety livestock roaming the wilderness of our countryside. No, the committee had fallen in love with the Indian Ocean: its recommendation focused on the unloading of surplus grains into the hungry, turbulent waters of the ocean.

The government did not quite dare to act upon the revolutionary proposal of the committee. One cannot fault it though for its various efforts over the past five years to ensure a rapid meltdown of the country's food stocks. And by government one means the continuum from the National Democratic Alliance to the United Progressive Alliance: in terms of class interests, no distinction is possible between the two regimes. The authorities did not quite visit the waters, but otherwise they have been extraordinarily active to do a Houdini of the FCI stocks, including those of wheat. While the local livestock were deprived, they allowed the export of wheat through private agencies, mostly to the United States of America, to feed American pigs. The price charged for such exports was less than what domestic consumers were asked to pay under the public distribution system. This was done *via* a stratagem: private parties to whom the stocks were initially released were offered a transport subsidy to sell grains overseas. On a rough reckoning, at least 13 million tonnes of wheat have been exported over the past quinquennium. The government did something else: it brought down drastically the procurement of wheat and other grains. The FCI purchased 20.6 million tons of wheat in 2001-02; procurement was gradually reduced to the level of 14.7 million tons by 2005-06. Annual wheat production in the country was more or less steady, around 72 million tons, in this period; so the lowering of procurement had nothing to do with the state of output. The FCI must have been told sternly; it was sin to procure foodgrains on its account. In many *mundis,* FCI agents turned into disinterested spectators as private traders bought up grains at prices less than the minimum support price stipulated by the government. These private traders also included representatives of multinational corporations like Cargill India, Conitnental and the India Tobacco Company.

The multifaceted efforts at reducing public stocks of foodgrains succeeded magnificently. By April of the current year, the deconstruction of public stocks of foodgrains was almost complete; the quantity of wheat lying with the FCI was down to barely 1.8 million tons. It is, in this situation, no surprise that the Centre is unable to meet its commitment to supply grains to sustain the rural employment gurantee scheme.

That is a bother because of all this talk about ensuring food security, but it has been accompanied by another development. Particularly because of the last round of increase in administred prices of petroleum products, the general price level has started spiralling. Inflation angers people across the board and thus affects the political fortunes of those in authority. The powers-that-be have therefore decided to turn the wheel a wee-bit the other way. Outbursts of fake consternation are suddenly frequent at the precarious state of foodgrain stock, particularly of wheat, at the disposal of the government. The Central cabinet gathered at an emergency meeting, reviewed the situation and took a number of decisions to bring down prices. Unlimited quantities—in the jargon, 'without cap'—of wheat, pulses and sugar are to be imported to replenish the government's foodgrain stocks and reconstruct the public distribution system. Excellent, but what is remarkable is that imports are proposed to take place not only on government account; the private sector is simultaneously being granted permission to import the aforementioned commodities.

This is, to say the least, bizarre. Commodity prices do not spurt on their own; they rise because private traders choose to raise them. In a situation of relative scarcity, it is in the interest of private traders to hold back supplies from the market, jack up prices and expand their profit. Itthen becomes the duty of the government, in case it is interested in disciplining prices, to augment supplies in the market, if necessary through imports. To allow private agencies to have a part of the planned imports cannot, therefore, but be counter-productive. Private traders do not constitute a philanthropic conglomerate. If they participate in the import business, it is not with the intent to use imports to level down prices. Bulls and bears play their respective roles in the commodity market too. It is in the interest of private parties to increase their influence in the commodity market *vis-ā-vis* that of the government. To invite private trade to come, be a sport and participate in the nation's price-disciplining activities obviously borders on the insane.

But there is an explanation to everything, including this one. Prices need to be rolled back to appease the public. The government cannot however ditch its class brethren in the trading fraternity. Trade, in the form of either export or import, gives rise to the possibility of a cut or commission at different points of the chain: let private traders too get a part of the proceedings. That they might not immediately release in the market the quantities they import is a small matter.

There is conceivably a bit more to it. If newspaper reports are to be believed, there was much discussion at the cabinet meeting on whether the public distribution system is at all an effective means to combat high prices and should not be dismantled altogether. Perhaps it was seriously suggested that, in this era of liberalization, we should dispense with the nuisance of public distribution and depend exclusively on the munificence of private trade to restore price tranquillity. The suggestion was not fully accepted, but a compromise has been worked out.

A comment in parting. Since independence, the national population has grown at least three times, the production of important foodgrains such as rice and wheat has gone up maybe five times, but the output of pulses, which are inferior grains providing protein to the poor, has registred an overall increase of barely 30 to 40 per cent; what do the authorities care if protein does or does not enter the bodies of the poor? It is, in that context, a great thing that some pulses are being imported too. Do not pay heed to remours, the government is not all that heartless.

7th July 2006

The part is not the whole

Exciting news. Tycoons presiding over international finance capital have taken to reading what was hitherto subversive literature; they have been bowled over by Marx. They, in particular, are ready to hail the *The Communist Manifesto* as the new *Bible.* Reasons exist for the feeling of dizziness on the part of the tycoons. The two principal ideologues of capitalism were in a sense both wet blankets. Adam Smith, the moral philosophy professor from Edinburgh, indeed spoke vigorously for the free market. But he did so for a somewhat disreputable reason: he disliked immensely monopolists such as master weavers who harassed and persecuted workingmen in their service. A competitive environment, he thought, would curb the excesses of the monopolist class. Our modern day capitalists, however, love monopolists; Adam Smith's stance is anathema to them. That is worse, Smith also forecast a most gloomy future for the capitalist system, for which the pointed an accusing finger at landlords and capitalists: "Rent and profit eat up wages and the two superior orders of people oppress the inferior one." Capitalists cannot disown Adam Smith, but they find it difficult to put up with what they call his idiosyncrasy.

The other great father figure of capitalism, David Ricardo, the London stockbroker, was only a shade better. With great skill, he built the theoretical framework of the free competition. In his opinion too, though, the prospects of capitalism were most uninviting. The effect of economic expansion, Ricardo concluded, would be a continuous rise not in rent and profit as claimed by Adam Smith, but in rent and wages; by inference, there would be a continuous fall in profits. And once the rate of profit dips down to zero, capitalists, Ricardo did not have the least doubt, would lose all incentive to carry on activities; the economy would reach a stationary state—hardly cheerful tidings for go-getter capitalists.

That apart, both Adam Smith and Ricardo were basically frogs in the well, Great Britain was the centrepiece of their attention. True, Ricardo did develop a theory of international trade, establishing the virtue of free trade in that it maximized gains for all participants. This advocacy, however, was within a narrow context. He was against tariffs such as the Corn Laws which raised the price of corn for the working class thereby both increasing their hardship and placing a constraint on the purchasing power they could spare for buying goods produced by local manufacturers. That was about all. Neither Smith nor Ricardo bothered to offer a vision of what untrammelled foreign trade could do to capitalism in the coming epochs.

Modern day votaries of capitalism, such as George Soros and Jacques Attali, are spellboud by the contrast Marx's writings presents. The first half of *The Communist Manifesto* is in fact a long poem of praise for the wonders the bourgeoisie, that is the capitalist class, has done to the world by replacing industrial production in small, isolated guilds by the modern giant manufacturing plants, exploiting to the hilt the marvel of division of labour. Consider, for example, the following passages from the *Manifesto:* "The bourgeoisie cannot exist without constantly revolutionizing the instruments of production, and thereby the relations of production, and with them the whole relation of society." "The need for a constantly expanding market for its products chases the bourgeoisie over the whole surface of the globe. It must nestle everywhere, settle everywhere." "The bourgeoisie has through its exploitation of the world market given a cosmopolitan character to production and consumption in every country. To the great chagrin of Reactionists, it has drawn from under the feet of industry the national ground on which it stood. All old-established national industries have been destroyed or are daily being destroyed. They are dislodged by new industries whose introduction becomes a life and death question for all civilized nations, by industries that no longer work up indigenous raw material, but raw material drawn from the remotest zones; industries whose products are consumed, not only at home, but in every quarter of the globe." Marx's accolade for international capitalism does not quite stop here. He goes further: "The bourgeoisie, by the rapid improvement of all instruments of production, by immensely facilitated means of communication, draws all, even the most barbarian, nations into civilizations. The cheap prices of its commodities are the heavy artillery with which it batters down all Chinese walls, with which it forces the barbarians' intensely obstinate hatred of foreigners to capitulate."

This is heavy stuff. No wonder the bosses of global finance are going through an exhilarating experience of serendipity; they can now quote chapter and verse from Marx's writings to vindicate all they had done to the world, are doing and propose to do in future.

Nothing is unfair in love and class war. Men like Soros and Attali can be pardoned if they indulge in a bout of *suppressio veri*; they hardly refer to the later part of *The communist Manifesto,* which has a different moral to tell. Marx praises the capitalist class because it brings thousands of workers under one factory shed and in huge workers' settlements. ("Modern industry has converted the little workshop of the patriarchal master into the great factory of the industrial capitalists. Masses of labourers, crowded into the factory, are organized like soldiers...Not only they are slaves of the bourgeois class and of the bourgeois State; they are daily and hourly enslaved by the machine, by the overlooker, and, above all, by the individual bourgeois manufacturer himself.") Little does the bourgeoisie realize that by ushering in industrial capitalism, it only digs its own grave. The working class, enslaved and oppressed by the capitalists, soon learns the magic of organized revolt. The creative urge of the bourgeoisie gathers the workers together, and thereby facilitaties rapid mobilization on their part. The aroused proletariat finish off the capitalists system. (Subsequently, in *Capital,* Marx formulated a theoretical construct, different form Ricardo's, yet reaching a conclusion identical with Ricardo's: the rate of profit will keep declining in a capitalist state until it reached zero, thereby providing a supplementary reason for the collapse of capitalism.)

Even global capitalism will have no respite. The working class organized across the continents in massive trade union formations will promote an invincible army of the international working class. Once working men of all countries unite, they will rise in revolt and put a stop to capitalism's strutting on the global stage.

Globalization has allegedly rendered such prognosis irrelevant. The elite, who today decide the destiny of international finance capital, keep quoting passages from Marx which suit them and are silent about the uncomfortable ones. This is only to be expected. What is however worrisome is that, in this post 1991 era, even some amongst those who formally claim to be devout Marxists slide into accepting the Soros-Attali version of the scripture. They tend to miss out what lay behind Marx's praise of the capitalist system: it is to be thanked because it makes it possible for the working class to transform itself into a mighty force of retribution which finally destroys capitalism.

A vision is not a half-way house. And an ideologue who believes in that vision has no business to assume that the mid-point is the final milestone. It is not his business either to take on the load of establishing capitalims; capitalists will perform that task according to their own lights. On the other hand, whatever the circumstances, it is the obligation of a committed Marxists to optimize the interests of the working class. Were they to believe it to be otherwise, whould they not rather join, openly, the bandwagon of the bourgeoisie?

29th May, 2006

Authoritarian utopias

The recent strike of State Bank of India employees would in the ordinary course pass into oblivion. But should it? A number of issues of wide social significance were embedded in the strike: they call for some rumination.

Two hundred and fifty thousand employees, spread over 9,000 branches, of the country's largest bank had struck work for one full week. The cease-work was total; it put in disarray large segments of the national economy. The SBI, after all, handles roughly 30 per cent of the aggregate banking transactions in the country. Clearance of cheques to the extent of Rs 500 crore was held up every day. Foreign exchange dealings were severely affected, as were exports. Since sales of stamp papers from trhe SBI were closed, chaos travelled in many other directions.

Aware of the consequences of a prolonged strike, the bank management, rumour had it, was willing to come to an agreement with the employees. But the ministry of finance was said to be adamant; autonomy in bank management obviously does not cover the aspect of industrial relations. The principal representation of the employees concerned the restructuring of pension payments for retiring employees. The last agreement on the matter was signed between the bank and its employees nearly 15 years ago. Economic circumstances, including the general price level, have changed markedly over this decade and a half, and the employees had been clamouring for a review of the retirement provisions.

It would be difficult to describe the demand of the employees as either unreasonable or unrealistic. The formula adopted some 15 years ago had allowed only employees with basic pay of less than Rs. 10,000 to draw pension at 50 per cent of basic pay; for employees at higher ranges of basic pay, the pension petered out to 40 per cent and less. The core demand of the employees was for making the pension a flat 50 per cent for all employees. The ministry of finance, however, applied pressure on the bank management not to give in; employees walked out *in masse*.

It was cynical waiting game for one full week. The authorities capitulated only after realizing that SBI employees could not be cowed down, and employees of the entire banking sector could join the strike in sympathy, thereby bringing the banking industry in the country to a total standstill.

SBI employees earning a basic pay of Rs. 21,040, it has now been decided, will henceforth get pension at 50 per cent of that amount, while those earning above that level will get 40 per cent for the incremental amount above Rs. 21,040 subject to a minimum of 50 per cent of Rs. 21,040. This is by no stretch any great concession; in the government sector, even the senior-most civil servant draws as pension 50 per cent of the basic retiring pay. What is more, the finance minister himself has gone on record that the SBI has the financial capacity to bear the extra burden the settlement is going to cost.

The attitude of the ministery of finance during the entire episode could be justly described as exceedingly curious. The demands of the SBI employees were not unreasonable given the prevalent culture elsewhere in the service sector. The SBI has been making huge profits in recent years and had enough resources to bear the additional burden involved in the demand placed by its employees. And yet, the government directed the bank to refuse to listenn to the voice of reason till as long as it could. The standard practice in the media is to haul the employees over the coals for any breach of industrial peace. In this instance, the guilty party is the governent which owns the SBI; it owes an apology to the nation for the dislocation of the economy its intransigence had caused.

The government would not quite spell it out, but its general stance is by now clear: even where employers have the financial capability, they must still oppose employee demands lest it spoils the market; concession to one group of employees could lead to similar climb-downs to the demands of other groups of employees, not just to one section, but over the entire range of commercial and industrial establishments. Such a development the authorities would maintain, might displease international finance capital, whom the government dearly wants to come and take charge of our economy. Workers in the country must always be on their best behaviour, otherwise foreign capital would not flow in. It is also for this reason that efforts are on for reforming the country's labour laws, thereby prohibiting strikes and facilitating the introduction of the 'hire and fire' principle.

The country's citizens elect a government through democratic elections. The government, however, has seemingly ceased to be sovereign; it has come to place itself in a corner where decisions are taken in the light of how international finance capital would react to them. Once the nuclear agreement is sealed with the United States of America, we might, it is apprehended in some quarters, lose a large slice of our prerogative of independent decision-making. Even earlier than that, we are already subject to external directives in crucial economic matters. These directives are not always categorically formulated. No matter, our decision-makers, itchy to have foreign capital of a magnitude of which the sky is the limit, don the role of forward planners and initiate measures which, they think, would please the foreign capitalist class. It could be pursuit of a will-o'-the-wisp. So what: the pursuit has its own pleasure.

There is of course a subsidiary argument mounted to resist the demands of employees in banks and insurance companies. These latter sections allegedly constitute an 'aristocracy of labour' who keep demanding higher and higher emoluments, while millions and millions of unemployed and under-employed countrymen are on the verge of starvation. This, the government, the India Incorporated and the complaint media are convinced, is a scandal; barricades must be manned, these wretched labour aristocrats must be mercilessly gunned down.

What is however not reckoned as a scandal is the spectacle of youngsters from affluent households, who have not even reached the age of 25, passing out of business schools being offered by industrial and commercial establishments fancy salaries starting from a couple of lakh rupees per months and ending in a stratosphere which boggles the imagination. The proliferation of such plutocrats does not appear to put a strain on anybody's conscience.

The standard response will be—what can be done, the business school graduates fetch the kind of money they do because it is a free market system; the mechanism of demand and supply is at work, the young boys and girls get what the market determines. But if this be so, should not the proposition equally apply in the case of bank and insurance employees? The SBI employees merely took advantage of the law of the market; they went on strike and paralysed the economy, thereby demonstrating their market strength. What is good for the business school goose should be equally good for the gender of lower-grade bank employees.

The authorities have to make up their mind. If they wish to quote the scripture of the free market, they cannot quote it in part; if they desire to please India Incorporated and international finance capital, they will have to accommodate the organized industrial class too. The alternative is to cross over to an authoritarian system where only the capitalist class, domestic and international, would be listened to and other voices severely suppressed.

It would be quite a surprise if such a system works, even for a week.

1st May, 2006

Beyond the round table

The day the prime minister convened in New Delhi, with much solemnity, his round table conference on Kashmir, the valley was observing total *bandh:* the people over there were mourning for the children slaughtered by the Indian army in Dhudipura village a couple of days ago. The display of sorrow, naturally, was not unmixed with anger, sorrow for the innocent children killed in such a grisly manner, anger that they could do so little to prevent incidents of this kind taking place over and over again.

The valley had come to a total stop. No matter, the prime minister had to have his round table. Ol' Man River Karan Singh was there, so too the young Abdullah colly, as were the usual establishment faces. It would be silly to pretend otherwise; they represent no more than a minute fraction of the Kashmir population. An immense pity, they themselves do not seem to be aware of this ground reality. What we the refore have in Kashmir today are two altogether separate universes of perception, one contradicting the other. The base, you may say, is walking in one directrion, the superstructure is going the reverse way.

True, the prime minister issued a regulation statement deeply regretting the unfortunate deaths in Dhudipura: his troops had committed a grievous mistake, they assumed children at play to be terrorists. Adding insult to injury, he announced lush monetary compensation to the families of those killed, as if money could substitute throbbing, pulsating life. Would these vacuous gestures recruit, for the prime minister's round table, even one honest patriarch from the valley, hangers-on excluded? Honestly, it does not seem so.

But Kashmir is not an isolated story. Some weeks earlier, in Kokrajhar in Assam, Indian army personnel had shot down in cold blood ten innocent villagers. The only plea proffered for the massacre was that the army contingent did not like the way these villagers were walking a path. Paraphrased, the explanation would roughly read as follows: we, because we represent the might of India, will decide which direction, you, slave citizens, are to leap at any particular moment; should we disapprove the specific quality of your jumpiness, we will shoot, period. In this instance too, the prime minister—or was it the home minister?—had sent his regrets and announced the grant of monetary assistance for the relatives of those whose bodies were shattered by government-of-India bullets.

These are not isolated narratives. Incidents of such nature follow a regular pattern across the North-east. Manipur has been particularly unquiet in recent months with streams of allegations of police and army atrocites against youth and women. An incident happens. The local population explodes in anger. The government expresses its regrets for the excesses that have been committed. The curtain comes down. The nation waits for the next episode and its locale.

This last sentence deserves to be severely amended. The nation is a segmented entity. Those who attended the prime minister's round table on Kashmir are not particularly exercised over incidents such as at Dhudipura. The droppers-in at the round table and the mourners in Dhudipura are two dissimilar worlds, with their own discourses. And this is the general truth for what passes for the Indian nation. Citizens in the Gangetic and Deccan plains live a closed existence. They are interested only in themselves. What happens in Kashmir or Assam or Manipur or in the forests of Andhra Pradesh, Bihar, Madhya Pradesh and Maharashtra hardly bothers them. Daily living is already complicated enough without their getting worked up over terrorism and insurgency: what is the government there for? This attitude is reflected one hundred per cent in the mindset of the media. The media do not own it as their responsibility to keep citizens residing in the heartland of India informed about the problems and agonies afflicting the people occupying peripheral areas such as Manipur or Kashmir.

Not that as Indians they do not feel a certain kind of pleasant sensation at the thought that Kashmir or Manipur belongs to them. Those who were under colonial subjugation only a while ago do not in their heart of hearts shy away from the dream of a colonial dispensation over which they themselves preside.

Facts, and reasoning based on facts, are of no avail here. Our government might have spent, since 1947, as much as Rs. 500,000 crore or even more to ensure the pearl of Kashmir for the Indian crown. The argument that the return of this investment is still somewhat indeterminate or that an outlay of this order could have superior alternative uses would not impress the feudal-imperial set. The imperial mind is knowledge-proof and Kashmir has to be an inalienable part of our great land.

We talk of the right to information and refer with smug satisfaction to this or that piece of recent legislation. How is it then that apart from some casual roving correspondents, few newspapers and electronic media have arrangements for regular reporting from the far-flung parts of the counry? How our co-citizens live and die in these parts is apparently not on anyone's agenda. A time therefore arrives when our agenda also ceases to be a part of the discourse of those living on the periphery.

Things are not much different in the case of those who are described as Maoists. It is close to six decades since independence. But the surcease of the colonial era has meant very little for the *adivasi* people. The British were not interested in development, and they chose to keep away. Those who came to control the Indian polity in the post-freedom decades are however activists, and of no mean order. Alienation of the Dalits from their land has therefore proceeded at a breath takingly rapid pace, with few reciprocal benefits accruing to those who are losing their porperty rights. When they protest, as they did in Orissa, they are greeted with a hail of bullets; Maoists are created where there were none.

To contain the Maoists, now reportedly well-entrenched in as many as eight states, there will be additional police formations, with occasional assistance from the army. More people will therefore get shot, resulting in more insurgencies. The government will make new budgetary allocations to wean away the poor from the clutches of the Maoists. These allocations will soon be reduced to boondoggles; land reforms will not figure in the official list of priorities.

The two discourses—the one at the base and the other that engages the superstructure—will not meet. It will be much like the Union budget presented on the last day of the previous month: it was replete with wisdom-laden paragraphs, but totally irrelevant to the situation of the ground. The discourse of the growth in gross domestic product has nothing for those whose exclusive concerns are for food and work. The disjunction between discourses is soon likely to assume a ubiquitous form. The prime minister will covene, from time to time, round tables to make happy persons who want to feel self-important; everything under the sun will be discussed at the round tables, but not uncomfortable items such as Dhudipura.

Unchanging India, unchanging the official passion for playing endless rounds of ring-a-ring-a-roses. This is possible only on account of a great expectation: sleeping dogs will continue to lie. Problems will arise only when such dogs begin to script their own discourses. Greater budgetary outlays to shoot the canine population may temporarily save the day. The day, though, could turn out to be of awfully short longevity.

20th March, 2006

Standing apart

Globalization has smashed all values to smithereens. Evangelists and idealists, however, still walk on the earth, determined to overwhelm humanity with love, goodwill and economic well-being. The multitude rushing to the stock exchanges or busy counting its profits from business process outsourcing may not have the time to listen to their preachings. The evangelists and idealists are not disheartened though; they are prepared for the long night.

Amit Bhaduri, one of the country's leading economic theoreticians, belongs to this rare breed of idealists. He stands a little distant from the madding crowd, and always keeps in mind the original purpose economics was supposed to serve: contributing to the wealth and welfare of humankind at large. An individual who describes himself as an economist, Bhaduri would say, must have no reservations about where the commitment of the science lies. His recent monograph, *Development with Dignity: A Case for Full Employment* (National Book Trust, Rs 45) bears testimony to this single-mindedness of his pursuit.

Bhaduri is humiliated by the phenomenon of massive unemployment and poverty in the country despite the near-sixty years since independence. It is, in his view, an intolerably absurd situation because means to eradicat these evils are not at all remote; a combination of "participatory democracy" and meaningful pro-poor measures can transform the state of things; all that necessary on the part of policy-makers and their advisers is to lose some of their inhibitions.

Bhaduri is aware of the danger of what he calls the stifling of individual initiative and proliferation of frivolous outlays if state-driven development activities are carried to excess. The consequences of unwholesome intrusion of foreign investment and dominance by private finance capital, however, worry him even more. He has no taste for the fetish of export-based economic development because it promotes little employment; he would, to accelerate growth, rather concentrate on expanding the domestic market. This task he links to what he considers the defining issue, a state-sponsored programme of full employment.

Bhaduri would like the roughly 34 million estimated unemployed in the country to be provided with work for 300 days in the year, at a minimum wage-rate of Rs. 60 per day, on development projects carried out under the aegis of the three-tier *panchayats.* The outlay needed for this purpose, according to his estimate, would be in the neighbourhood of Rs. 60,000 crore. Perhaps, to take care of those unemployed in urban areas, both the pattern of projects and the financial commitment involved would call for some adjustments. Even so, the broad contours of Bhaduri's plan are such that it would not really call for an overall outlay exceeding 4 per cent of gross domestic product.

Can we or cannot we spare this magnitude—amounting to approximately Rs. 80,000 crore, roughly six times the allocation for the employment guarantee scheme in the budget presented this week—to create full employment in the system? The most tautly argued—never mind if it is at the same time the most polemical—chapter in Bhaduri's book bears the title, "The 'Government-Can't-Do-It' Syndrome of Public Finance". He does not believe in wearing kid gloves. His introductory observations read as follows. "Economists thend to discuss public finance and government at budget, restricting themselves by assumptions only to issues, which are amenable to their technical analyis. The fact that the assumptions are blatantly unjustified in most cases, and the issues selected are often not relevant, hardly matters to them."

He pours scorn on the Fiscal Responsibility and Budget Management plan to be such that it does not face any encumbrances from outside the country. Were the Union and state governments together unable to make enough economies in their budgets to come up with the required amount, he would go for large-scale domestic borroweing by the government of India from the nation's central bank. Since the government owns the major part of the equity of the Reserve Bank of India, raising money through issue of securities should be, according to Bhaduri, child's play; the interest burden too could be met by issuing further securities.

Bhaduri would have his repartee for those who shudder at the fiscal irresponsibility they think is implicit in his proposal: the United States of America sustains itself by gargantuan borrowings from abroad: the International Monetary Fund and the World Bank keep mum. It should be no different in our case, more so since the borrowing would be only from internal sources. In any event, should the full employment programme get going, there would be, Bhaduri is confident, enough additional output generated to take care of the additional purchasing power that would circulate in the system. He, in fact, goes further: the additional market the full-employment programme would create, would ensure self-sustaining economic development for the country. Besides, financing the programme exclusively through domestic borrowing "would weaken the tie between the Indian stock exchange and the institutional investors and would leave the government with greater space to follow a thorough-going employment programme."

Bhaduri dots some i's and croues some t's so that full employment might co-exist with the dignity in living. Each tier in the panchayat system must have full fiscal autonomy; decision-making should be fully decentralized; the right to information must be made available to each and every citizen; the progress of the various on-going schemes should be monitored via periodic reporting of physical progress and open-air rendering of accounts of money received and money spent.

Once the orthodoxy preached by the Fund and the Bank is shed, there can perhaps be few quarrels over the rationality of the Bhaduri plan. The problem lies elsewhere. Neither the Indian economy nor the Indian polity is a *tabula rasa.* There are entrenched interests who nurture the belief that annoying the proponents of the Washington Consensus is against the country's long-range interest. That apart, given their obsession with the single-point goal of growth in gross domestic product, they have, they would claim, better use for a sum of Rs 80,000 crore annually than wasting it on creating jobs for some useless loafers.

Bhaduri is an idealist, but even an idealist cannot afford to fail to recognize the reality of class interests: no sense of indignity troubles the narrow circle of people who indulge in luxurious living while very large sections of their countrymen are without a minimal supply of food, clothing, shelter and educational opportunities.

Bhaduri should know all of this. A quarter of a century ago he wrote a seminal paper, which demonstrated that increased defence outlays by a poor country are of no avail for increasing defence capability *vis-a-vis* a real or imaginary enemy: each increase in defence outlay by one country leads to a corresponding increase in the same outlay in the enemy country, and the process continues *ad infinitum.* Nobody has bothered to draw any lessons from that most revealing Bhaduri exercise. Last year, India's defence outlay was, at one go, raised by Rs 27,000 crore, while the outlay for agriculture actually shrunk by Rs. 3,000 crore: nobody made a squeak. Members of parliament would be scared to death at any suggestion to lower the outlay on defence, along with that for deterring national and international terrorism, so as to help finance a full employment programme along the line suggested by Bhaduri.

It would, nonetheless, be not only unseemly, but also unjust, to end on such a discouraging note. Saints and idealists know now to stick to their resolve, which in the long run does indeed change the world. Amit. Bhaduri must continue knocking on closed doors. That is what his conscience will dictate him to do: that conscience, to say the least. should command the respect that is its due.

3rd March 2006

Right off the rails

With free market economics in full command, the planning commission has naturally fallen into disuse. That the ninth five year plan has now been completed by the commission after two fifths of the plan-period is over does not evoke any derision either. The operational word is tedium. The Commission is there, just like a dump of rubbish at some corner of the village common.

But, then, the commission has now been burdened with a new deputy chairman. The point of installing a new deputy chair man will be lost if the august body does not bestir itself into some activity. A press note has therefore been released encapsulating the supposedly novel thoughts that are gaining currency within the commission's portals. One principal suggestion the commission has offered is to extend the scope of privatization so as to cover the country's railway system.

Private entrepreneurs are not as ignorant of the realities of the life as the planning commission seemingly is. You can put full page advertisements in the leading newspapers of the world, including the *Washington Post, The New York Times, Le Monde. La Prensa* and the rest; hardly any customer will be around to buy the Indian Railways, or for that matter, any railways in any part of the world. Railways call for huge and "chunky" investments but fetch an extremely low rate of return. This has emerged as a global phenomenon. Even the giant of a monopoly such as the Indian Railways is able to register a surplus of only a modest proportion compared to the capital stock that has gone into it. The railway network has in fact survived in this poor country inhabited by poor people only because of heavy cross-subsidization of passenger fares made possible by hefty levies imposed on the freight of goods.

There is clearly a limit to such cross subsidization; if it is pursued beyond a point, the railway system runs the risk of losing the custom of goods traffic to road haulers. Without backup from the state, which has been in a position to influence the cost of road haulage *via* regulation of excise and other duties, the Indian railways would have experienced enormous difficulties in balancing its accounts.

The most crucial issue is however the investment that has been sunk into the railways by the government of India in the 100 years preceding independence. You can be a member of the planning commission even if be reft of any knowledge of history. Daniel Thorner's classic work, *Investment in Empire,* will be, it can be taken for granted, foreign to the commission, which is a great pity. Thorner discusses, in meticulous detail, the processes of the step by step construction of the Indian railway system by the British rulers.

It was a costly venture, a time consuming venture, but the British knew the long term benefits likely to accrue if investments in the railways were carried on without bothering too much about the short run problems of funding. A major portion of the surplus squeezed out of the empire was purposely ploughed back into the railways. No private company, be it a Bird or be it a Heilgers, would have dared to come forward in the relevant period with venture capital of the magnitude needed to develop the railways in any part of the country. Given the abysmal poverty of Indians, a fair rate of return on the outlay was out of the question, at least in the intial phases of the experiment.

Successive viceroys and the secretaries general of India chose to take a long view. The model they chiselled to bleed India while depended upon the penetration of transport and communications into the countryside so that raw materials could be bought cheaply and moved with expedition from the country's deep interior and, analogously, finished British industrial products could be transported to every part of the country and sold at high prices, all through the courtesy of the Indian Railways.

The perseverance with investment activity finally paid off, the Indian rail network became a self-reliant institution, and it could even begin to make a contribution to the general budget. A separate rail budget was itself an innovation; it provided proof of the key role the Indian Railways had come to perform in the Indian economy.

In the post-independence period, the emphasis has been to build around the system the British had set up by recourse to a few strategic devices, such as laying new lines, conversion of narrow gauge to broad gauge lines, electrification and deselization, and so on. The claim has in fact been posted that the two pillars that have sustained and developed national unity and integrity in the post-freedom phase are Indian Railways and the Life Insurance Corporation of India. The rhetoric is not all that vacuous; the reach of both organizations has been such as to bring the different parts of the country together.

Now it is a new agenda in the wake of a new discourse, that of liberalization and free market economics. The insurance sector in India has already been opened up to private capital. The judgement has perhaps also been reached within the planning commission that there was little rationale in doing things by halves; the railways might be privatized as well. The problems in the wake of the attempt to sell of the country's rail system are however likely to be daunting. Private ownership of railways has died out even in the countries of classical free enterprise, for instance, the United Kingdom and the United States. Barring a few exception, railways in these countries now happen to be a luxury service for ehe edification of the very rich who do not mind being soaked. Elsewhere, wherever the railways are in operation, it is because the governments of the countries concerned are anxious to provide a crucial infrastructural service to the community at large.

It would be difficult to sell off the Indian Railways as one integer. The total value, at current market prices, of the capital stock of our rail system—rolling stock, tracks, land and buildings—will run into hundreds of billions of rupees. No tycoon will be in the vicinity to assume charge of the burden, especially in the context of the recent general decline in the world economy.

What is still conceivable is adoption of the standard practice rundown families follow while disposing of their pots and pans. The sale takes place in lots. The Indian Railways could ponder over the prospect of selling a bunch of rolling stock to party A, selling some length of railway tracks to party B, selling real estate around these tracks to party C. There need not be just one single party A or one single party B or one single party C either. Rail property in different parts of the country could be sold to hundreds and thousands of customers in bits and pieces.

It is possible to quote a precedent to go by. At the end of World War II, when chaos descended on the then Burma, every successive hundred meters of railway track, the story goes, was sold to different parties by whoever was in effective power in a particular region of the country. A train could proceed further only after making a compulsory halt at intervals of these one hundred meters and paying up the rental—may be a thousand kyats—to the claimants of the franchise. Rest assured, once the holistic approach sponsored by the planning commission and elliptically endorsed by the railway and finance minister through their budgets this year really takes off, anarchy *a la* Burma will spread all over the country. That is a denouement which, for all one can conjecture, unites the fundamentalists at home with the world be investors from overseas, many of whom favour puny sized underdeveloped economies for the reason that subverting the rulers of small countries is a less onerous task.

The plot is bound to thicken in the course of the next few months. This hapless nation can only wait with bated breath.

2nd March, 2006

Battered by VAT

It has turned into a pattern. Those who have coaxed a majority of the states to surrender their constitutional right to levey sales tax and, in lieu, introduce a Centrally-directed value-added tax with effect from this year, meet every now and then in New Delhi under the benign patronage of the ministry of finance. The *raison d'étre* of such meetings is to assure themselves, and, in turn, the nation, that this substitution has been a thundering success. Appreciating the subtle nuances of language does not come easily to the ordinary householder. It is therefore quite a dilemma for him/her to decide whether what the drum-beaters of VAT are indulging in is prevarication or dissembling, or both.

Take the latest statement issued by these eminences. They have gone on record that the states which crossed over to the Vat system have done remarkably well: between April and December, 2005, the revenue accruing from VAT to these 23 states has gone up, it is claimed, by 14.3 per cent over what collections from sales tax were in the corresponding period of the previous fiscal year. Is that not clinching proof of what a wonder VAT is? Those participating in the celebrations have made an additional point. The success of VAT is so pronounced that perhaps there would be no need for utilizing to the full sum of Rs. 5,000 crore set aside in the Union budget to compensate the losses incurred by the joining states in the first year of introduction of the new system. The amount of compensation doled out till now is only Rs. 1,026 crore.

Questions nonetheless near their head. Even assuming that over the first half of 2005-2006 the VAT-joining states have experienced a 14.3 per cent rise in revenue, what about the performance of the non-joining states? Can those who congregated in New Delhi last December for the self-congratulatory session offer evidence that the increase in sales-tax collections during the first half of this year over those in the corresponding period last year has been less than 14.3 per cent? As long as this query is not answered in the affirmative, the superiority of the VAT system cannot be logically established.

The pall-bearers in New Delhi cannot avoid facing another query. The sales-tax collections in the entire country in 2002-03, 2003-04 and 2004-05 were Rs. 86,073 crore, Rs 98,377 crore and Rs 1,12,066 crore respectively.

Work out the arithmetic; over the last two fiscal years, the increase in sales-tax revenue was, in any case, around 14 per cent or a bit more. The introduction of VAT has obviously not made any differnece till now to the overall trend of collections from commodity taxation. The point can be proved even for individual states. In West Bengal, for instance, sales-tax collections in 2002-03, 2003-04 and 2004-05 were respectively Rs 4,191 crore, Rs 4,946 crore and Rs 5,836 crore. Whle, the annual increase in sales-tax revenue recorded in 2003-04 and 2004-05 was as high as 18.1 per cent in both years!

Since discretion is the better part of bragging, the so-called empowered committee, which met in New Delhi in December, did not disclose separately the VAT performance of West Bengal in the first half of 2005-06. But this must have been disappointing, for already a sum of Rs 88 crore has been paid out to the state as compensation against revenue loss. What is particularly worrying is that hefty amounts of compensation have already been disbursed by the Centre to such important states as Maharashtra (Rs. 259 crore), Karnataka (Rs. 251 crore), Andhra Pradesh (Rs. 193 crore), Kerala (Rs 181 crore) and Bihar (Rs. 47 crore) as well. In each of these states, the rate of increase in collections under VAT must have been lower than what it was during the first half of the last fiscal year. The scheme of compensation ordained by the Union government, let us remember, is 100 per cent in the first year, 75 and 50 per cent respectively in the second and third years, and nothing from then on. Given the trend of collections that is emerging, the state governments signing up for VAT have to realize what a frightful prospect awaits them.

The assertion that the VAT experiment has been so successful that only a paltry figured of Rs. 1,026 crore out of the total allocation of Rs. 5,000 crore for the year has been disbursed as compensation is a prize example of obfuscation. In any case, the sum of Rs. 5,000 crore was set aside as compensation to cover all the 30 states in the country. However, seven major states, including the state with the largest population, Uttar Pradesh, the state with the largest size, Madhya Pradesh, and the most economically advanced state in the south, Tamil Nadu, have refused to join the VAT game. Had they joined, they also would, in all probability, have needed to have been paid heavy compensation. That apart, the statement carried in the press regarding payment of compensation of only Rs. 1,206 crore is silent about whether this disbursement is against losses suffered during the first month or the first quarter or the first six months of the fiscal year.

Two further points deserve clarification. Several state governments, in contravention of the declared two-rate structure of VAT—12.5 per cent and 8 per cent—have excluded petroleum products from the purview of the new system and have continued to impose sales tax on these products at the rate of 25 per cent or more. Should pressure be mounted—it has actually already been mounted—to bring taxation on motor spirits within the VAT fold and slash the rate of tax down to 12.5 or 8 per cent, the state governments are bound to lose heavily. To quote again the instance of West Bengal, of its total collections from sales tax of Rs. 4,191 crore, or 21.3 per cent, was from imposts on motor spirits. In the following year, out of the total sales-tax revenue of Rs 4,946 crore raised in the state, an amount exceeding Rs 1,200 crore, or close to a quarter of the total, was from patroleum products. Were this lucrative source of revenue-raising to disappear or be drastically reduced, the state government would be in a worse financial mess.

The other question mark is with respect to the revenue from Central sales tax, imposed at the rate of 4 per cent on so called 'goods of national importance', and collected and retained by the state governments in terms of an agreed formula. New Delhi is determind to phase out this tax in the course of the next couple of years. This would mean a loss of revenue of around 12 per cent of aggregate revenue from commodity taxation for almost all the states.

It is, cann't we say, a strange phenomenon that is developing in the country. The political clout of the Union government *vis-ā-vis* that of the states is weakening each day. In contrast, its economic power is growing apace, thanks to the thoughtlessness exhibited by some state governments; doing off with the sales tax is a gross example of how the states are contributing to their economic self-destruction. The Centre might consequently feel bold to keep imposing on the states' priorities that are vastly different from the needs and sentiments of people at the grassroots. This would be a recipe for national disaster.

One or two state governments had made a commitment to review their decision to join the VAT system after taking into account the experience during the first years of its operation. That first year is about to end. Is it not time for these governments to wake up before it is too late?

3rd February 2006

Impolite predictions

The extent of Amartya Sen's learning and the depth of his understanding of issues are now part of contemporary legend. What, however, deserves mention in the same breath is his civilization. His politeness is immaculate. He would listen, with gentle patience, even to comprehensive garbage gushing out of the mouth of a company of fools.

Which is why one read, with both surprise and a deep sense of gratitude, a comment Sen made during his recent visit to the country. He did not stand on ceremony. If the economic trends unfolding in the country continue in the manner they have of late, half of India, he is reported to have observed, would resemble California, while the other half would be reduced to sub-Sahara. Sen knew what he was talking about. He has lived in California, and has, for long years, done detailed research on the human condition obtaining in the sub-Sahara region. For want of food, nourishment and minimal health facilities, men, women and children live in dehumanizing poverty and die like flies in that part of Africa. The United Nations keeps going through the motion of organizing relief to the region, but all this adds up to nothing. The rest of the world takes it as granted that the situation in sub-Sahara is something beyond the capability of redress through collective human effort. A natural calamity such as the tsunami can be tackled; the sub-Sahara calamity is supposedly beyond repair.

Amartya Sen and flamboyance do not go together. He must have been provoked to such an extent though by the kind of economic policies and measures which are taking shape in India that he, for a moment, chose to forsake civil society politeness; he spoke his mind. True, with globalization taking splandid wings, segments of the Indian economy are experiencing an exhilarating pace of growth.

The Sensex is about to cross the 10,000 mark. A booming stock exchange, the Union finance minster has pontificated, is synonymous with national prosperity. The industry bosses have endorsed this point of view; so too the media. It is a return to the Bharatiya Janata Party's feel-good aura. The nation's foreign exchange holdings are bursting at the seams. The prime minister is determined to have more foreign direct investment not just in industry and agriculture, but in the services sectors as well, including in wholesale and retail trade. Hints to this effect have already been dropped at the World Trade Organization's recent ministerial session at Hong Kong. The IT sector, besides, is galloping ahead, and contributing to the mind boggling zilch in the country's leading urban complexes.

When distinguished Indians living abroad, such as Sen, arrive on short jaunts, specimens of the feel-good lobby capture them, accord them jazzy receptions and look forward to some conventional words of congratulatory cheer from the visiting eminences. For whatever reason, this time Amartya Sen disappointed them. In case present conditions persist, he told them bluntly, while they might succeed in rendering one-half of India into an arcadia replicating the charm and prosperity of California, another half of India might get reduced to the state of sub-Sahara, characterized by hunger, squalor, misery and the stink of a million deaths.

Sen's words were not palatable to his particular audience, nor to officialdom nor to the media. What he said did not therefore receive the attention they deserved. Truth does not always prevail in India. That should not worry Sen; he can afford to speak what he considers to be right. And there is a silent majority of scholars in the country who will agree with him.

However, particularly since Amartya Sen happens to be the author of *The Argumentative Indian,* may one be permitted to voice a minor query? Is he sure that, if things proceed as they are proceeding, it is only one-half of India that would be reduced to the state of the sub-Sahara region? For, consider the general state of affairs. With stock exchanges on the high, citizens with money to spare, do not care to put it in savings that could help capital formation in industry and agriculture; they rush to gobble up the advice of their stock-brokers. To augment capital formation, the government therefore seeks FDI at terms howsoever detrimental to the nation's interests. Agriculture in particular has suffered the most in the past decade, the rate of growth of farm output has fallen behind the rate of population growth. Yet, roughly two-thirds of the nation are still dependent on agricultrue for their survival. As the process of growing income inequalities has not come to a halt either, roughly 90 per cent of a the agrarian community must have experienced a further worsening in their economic conditions over the decade. Should the writ of the WTO be made to prevail, they would be even more immiserized in the immediate future.

The tragedy does not quite come to a surcease here. Foreign investors have told the prime minister point blank; they not only would prefer to take over retail and wholesale trade in the country, extend their grip over insurance and banking activities and have a piece of lucrative defence production; they would, in addition, like to send their surplus lawyers and accountants to build a career in India.

Consider the consequences if all, or even, some of these demands are conceded. The informal sector, carrying the load of disguised unemployed in the language of Maynard Keynes (1883-1946), perhaps currently provides some sort of livelihood to as many as one hundred million in the country: selling vegetables and fruits in the market, hawking odd bits and pieces of clothing in small neighbourhoods, merchandizing titbits of food items at street corners, running tailoring establishments and engaging in similar modest activities. Once the foreigners walk in, the profession of all these people will be gone. Besides, as call centres spread their tentacles in different directions, employment opportunities are bound to shrivel in big, small and middle scale industries. It is inherent in the pattern of jobless growth that development is accompanied by a shrinkage of work opportunities, and employment gets concentrated in the hands of. a very small minority, the great majority of the nation's motion pushed towards the hellish state of joblessness, penury and destitution. In contrast, perhaps less than 5 per cent of the population will be rolling in luxury yielded by sharemarket shenanigans and IT benevolence will be scaling to dizzier heights of prosperity.

Which is why one has a feeling that, even while in a forthright mood, Amartya Sen's innate politeness did not quite desert him. The future landscape of India, he fears, will consist of one-half California and one-half sub-Sahara. One is tempted to have his statement slightly amended: the India of tomorrow would be only one-tenth California, nine-tenths would he sub-Sahara; we might then slip down to the status of being one of the poorest five amongst member-countries of the UN.

This column has to conclude with a lament. The country is yet to get rid of its colonial hangover. The sort of comments Amartya Sen has made has, in fact, been made, perhaps using a different terminology, by humbler economists resident in the land. They could be, and have been ignored. Amartya Sen cannot be, because of the global regard and attention he commands. He, however, visits the country only occasionally. One remark by him during one such cursory trip is unlikely to change the order of things. How much one wishes that men like him would return home on a permanent basis and make an everyday muisance of themselves.

23rd January, 2006

Bountiful happiness

As if the nightmare of collapsing dominoes that haunted John Foster Dulles in the Fifties is coming to frightening reality half a century later but not in Asia; in Latin America. In country after country, the United States of America's proconsuls are having a torrid time, soulmates of Fidel Castro are making a habit of emerging triumphant in presidential elections: Luiz Inacio Lula da Silva in Brazil, Hugo Chavez in Venezuela and now Evo Morales in Bolivia. The outcome of polls in Argentina and Ecuador have not been hopeful either. The disaster in Bolivia is particualrly galling. For long, this country was considered by the Central Intelligence Agency as its home base: Che Guevara, if we would care to remember, was captured, tortured and killed here by CIA men.

Adversity, besides, does not come alone. Almost coinciding with the moment in which Evo Morales was thundering anti-American invectives in this victory oration before milling crowds at La Paz, Harold Pinter, the ailing British dramatist, took the prim world by surprise: his Nobel Prize acceptance speech *via* video from London was as much unexpected as unprecedented: a ballistic missile of extraordinary proportions, pillorying the debasement of human civilization US political bosses have brought about.

A species of nature's compensation is, however, at work. All is no lost for the US. At least in another corner of the world its fortunes would appear to be taking an excitingly better turn. India is fast emerging as one of its staunchest allies. At the conclusion of a recent meeting with the US secretary of state, India's foreign secretary beamingly assured all and sundry that the nuclear agreement between the two countries was on 'the right track'. Even more cheerful news, India's prime minister has reiterated his resolve to toe all the way the American line on economic reforms; he has pledged to work for the easier entry of foreign investment in the country, including in the retail trade sector, he is for further relaxation of direct tax rates, he is determined to amend, as expeditiously as possible, the country's labour laws.

This last assurance will not only lift official American spirit, it will please equally the *mélange* known as India Incorporated. The heart of the prime minister they now know, is in the right place; all that needs to be done is to extricate him from falling victim to seasonal leftist intimidation. Why, cannot

India be like the US; why cannot they hire and fire workers at will as in the US? Why must they continue to suffer from the nuisance of strikes and put up with the insolence of trade union goons? The prime minister's half-promise will enthuse them to redouble their efforts to get scrapped the odious provisions in the country's labour laws.

Since class interests are involved, passion gets injected into the debate. Attempts to disseminate such information as that both the formation of trade unions and the right to strike are acknowledged as integral parts of the American legal framework too tend to be greeted with near-disbelief. Even in the American milieu, it is actually far easier to sack a stray executive than to get rid of a band of workers who are registered members of a trade union that is affiliated to the giant labour conglomerate, AFL-CIO.

Rationality plays hooky particularly in discussions concerning the information technology sector. On a rough reckoning, annual net earnings of this sector on account of BPO activities must be touching $20 billion or thereabouts. For a country in India's circumstances, this is a lot of money. Those presiding over the IT industry have, as a result, developed the notion that they deserve to be treated with the softest of kid gloves by the authorities. They expect not only to be provided with suitable land at throwaway prices and adequate infrastructural facilities at low cost. In addition, they demand, apart from the lightening of the tax burden, zero tolerance of such hanky-panky as strikes and trade unionism. There is the rule: under the country's laws, neither industrial disputes nor trade union activism can be forbidden *a priori* in any industry, not even in a 'continuous process' industry. No exception is possible for the IT sector.

A fresh plea has since been put forward by the admirers of India Incorporated: Let IT sector be treated as a public utility—an essential service—and a convention be strictly followed to keep it outside the purview of strikes. As matters stand, however, public utilities too cannot be kept out of bounds if a ferment of industrial unrest grips the economy. The railways are, for instance, generally regarded as an essential service all over the world. That convention not withstanding, even in the US, the subway system in New York came to a total stop as recently as last month because the workers walked out. Workers of the London underground did exactly the same thing on New Year's eve.

The latest position stalwarts of the IT industry have adopted is no less curious: granted that organizing trade unions and cease-work cannot be formally prohibited; it must, however, be left to the employees of the IT sector to decide *on thier own* whether they are to form a union or indulge in industrial agitation; no outsider must be permitted to intrude.

Such a demand too is both unrealistic and contrary to law. Outsiders have always been an adjunct to the trade union movement in all countries and in all sectors. Jyoti Basu started his political career in 1940 by organizing the workers of what was then known as the Bengal and Assam Railway. He was not an employee, but a rank outsider. B.T. Ranadive and S.A. Dange built the Girni Kamgar Union in Bombay into a massive organization of militant textile workers; non of them had ever worked in a cotton mill. The country's labour legislation, in fact, provides for a certain proportion of office-bearers of a recognized union to consist of outsiders.

There is little point in flinching from hard datum: roughly one million workers are currently engaged in the country's IT units. Even assuming that each of them is on the average paid roughly Rs. 3,00,000 annually—a guess on the high side—the total wage bill comes to $3 billion, barely one seventh of the net profit owners of the industry are reaping. The employees, who do all the donkey work, might well aspire for a bigger slice of the cake. In the claustrophobic conditions in which they work, it is only natural that employees in the IT units will be somewhat inhibited to organize a union to fight their cause both for a higher share of the profits the companies are making and for better working conditions. Outside advisers, it is plausible to argue, ought to be around to help them in the task.

The IT bosses had never had it so good. While piling up profits, they have also persuaded state authorities to spend enormous sums to improve the infrastructure pertaining to the industry. This has led to a depletion of public funds to shore up the living conditions of the immiserized population in the neighbourhood. The messy controversy that has of late reared its head in Bangalore is focussed precisely on this issue. Those lording over the call centres apparently could not care less how the poor in their immediate environment fare. The most prominent of them has gone on record with an extra-ordinary statement: "97.5 per cent of the earning of this [that is his] company comes from countries like the United States, Germany and Japan, and they do not care what your problems are." By "your problems', the IT czar obviously implies this nation's problems: since 97.5 per cent of his earnings is the bounty of foreigners, he too, it seems, is prone to think as the foreigners think and care not a hoot for the problems afflicting this country.

The era of the comprador is coming to an end in Latin America. Have no worry, it is being ushered in India.

6th January 2006

Courting imbalance

Times change, contexts alter, economic controversies, however, have a way of renewing themselves. The phenomenon of global poverty does not abate, but the modalities for tackling the problem undergo what is described as a paradigm shift. One particular instance is the debate over the relative emphasis to be given to industry, agriculture and the services in the total scheme of things. As World War II ended, economists got greatly excited over Wassily Leontief's *tour de force,* the input output analysis. Leontief drew attention to the potential for removing hitches in the process of economic growth if inter-sector balances were scrupulously maintained at each point of time. In his interlocked system, the output of one sector provides the input of other sectors, and this is true for all sectors in the economy. Given this peice of wisdom, planners could distribute investment over the different sectors in such a manner that, at the margin, the demand for and the supply of each economic activity will match perfectly; the outcome would be most efficient economic planning for the country as a whole. Before he migrated to the United States of America, Leontief had worked for some time with the Soviet Gosplan, and his analysis was enriched by that experience.

In the late Forties and the early Fifties, the economics of Leontief-type material balancing became the rage among economists; the first batch of planners in the recently liberated underdeveloped countries were agog with the rich possibilities of applying it in their investment planning. Hypothesis however has a habit of invoking counter-hypotheses. Within a few years, another economics don from an American university, of central European extraction, Albert O. Harschman, appeared on the scene with a new theory of economic growth. His was a prescription for unbalanced development. The view he advanced was straightforward. A poor country is short of savings, and therefore of capital funds necessary for growth.

Most poor countries are, in fact, heavily dependent for resources either on rich foreign governments or on international financial agencies such as the World Bank. The limited resources available for investment in these countries' growth must be put to maximum use. First thing first: the acutest need for poor nations is satisfactory growth in agriculture and industry. The output of the farm and manufacturing sectors ensure food, clothing and other such basic necessities of life—as also exportable goods against which the country could import commodities the domestic availability of which is short, for instance, machinery and equipment.

Hirchman's theory was biased against the concept of material balancing in the planning of growth. He would pour all available investible funds into the farm and manufacturing sectors; services could take care of themselves. A trace of grandfatherly wisdom was discernible in the economic discussions he initiated. Once you have produced enough of rice wheat and coton and sugarcane, once you have produced enough of textiles and footwear and other such essential consumer goods, please do not have a care, transport somehow will become available to reach the products where they are in demand. The roads may be in a miserable condition, full of potholes, and sometimes almost non-existent, the trains may run only fitfully and rolling stock may be awfully short, communications between two trading points may be skimpy, the ports may be at a primitive stage of development, but these impediments and inconveniences are no matter, once the supply of the basic goods is there and the demand too, the twain are bound to meet. Exportables will somehow manage to reach the ports and be carried to distant shores, maybe by wobbly boats; internal trade will grow, maybe by harnessing a greater number of horse and bullock carts. Houseing for workers in the factory sites may lag behind, telephone lines may often be down, but let no sleepless nights be spent over such deficiencies. Once industry and agriculture get booming, the rest of the development process is certain to ensue; perhaps at the end of five years, perhaps after a decade. Unablanced development, with primacy placed on agriculture and industry—Hirschman did not have the least doubt—will lift the economy much faster than if some of the investment funds were diverted to build nice roads, state-of-the-art telecommunications systems or extraordinarily competent modern ports.

As in literacy debates, economic controversies too come to an *interruptus* at some vague point or other. Such too was the fate that overtook the debate over balanced *vis-à-vis* unbalanced development. One conceivable reason for the death of this particular polemics was the fading away of central economic planning in country after country, following the collapse of the Soviet Union and its associate states. The Leontief co-efficients have still much use in microeconomics, such as operations research exercises for individual firms. But Albert Hirschman is very nearly a forgotten name.

Should it be so though? Is the problem Hirschman sought to draw attention to a non-issue? After all, the vast majority of the member countries of the United Nations remain abysmally poor, they continue to suffer from lack of development fudns. With the shift in global political circumstances, both state initiative at the domestic level and government-to-government aid for improving the lot of impoverished masses in the poor countries have declined. Correspondingly, responsibility for promoting economic growth has passed on in large measure to international finance capital. Private capital from outside, while currently filling the larger part of the picture, has however its own priority. Since foreigners bring in bags of money, they insist on having the greater say in articulating the details of development programmes in these countries. Tycoons from overseas are not particularly interested in balanced or unbalanced models of growth. Their focus is on maximizing the rate of their private return.

Hirschman would have felt most uneasy. These foreigners are much less interested in investing either for agricultural or for manufacturing growth. Their interests centre on wholesale and retail trade, six-or-ten-or-twelve-line speedways, health plazas, hotel complexes, golf courses, and so on. These will cater to global tourism, attracting a large influx of affluent people from all over. The activities generated will have, though, little of employment content, especially for local people.

What is taking place is, ironically, a different kind of manifestation of unbalanced development. Hirschman would have frowned on it. The service sectors are geting all the investment funds, industry and agriculture are being banished to a corner. The local authorities are handing over, with alacrity, farm land at throwaway prices to rich foreigners in the honest belief that the good Samaritans from overseas will usher in rapid industrializatrion. All that the country will actually get in return is at best a string of call centeres, at worst rows and rows of massage parlours passing as a health park.

Hirschman's theory is dead. But a few plucky ones are trying to let it come alive again in an extraordinarily perverse manner. You may remain underdeveloped, unbalanced investment of a purposive sort will nonetheless ensures plenty of casinos and cabaret joints for visiting foreigners and the home-bred filthy rich. One remembers an instance Hirschman once quoted to exemplify the absurdity of turning the concept of unbalanced investment upside down. In a newly-laid township, with few people yet settled in, a boulevard has been built, running for miles on end; practically no traffic moves along it, either during the day or at night, but thousands of parking meters have been installed along both sides of the boulevard. The country suffers from chronic famine, and the rate of illiteracy is 70 per cent.

Where the mind is unhinged, apparently the economics is too.

29th December, 2005

Slave, scab, pipedream

Despite their legacy of Rembrandt, Frans Hals and Van Gogh, the Dutch are a severely practical people. The minister of justice in the Netherlands has, not surprisingly, hit the nail on its head. Since the purpose behind outsourcing is to get work done at nominal cost, why, the prisons under its control are the ideal setting for it; the prisoners are as good as bonded labour and will have to complete at token wages whatever assignment they are given.

Bonded labour and outsourcing have in fact often meshed into each other. Consider the opening up of the American continent. The Pilgrim Fathers were followed by steady waves of men, women and children who arrived in North America to escape religious persecution or the ravages of famine in Europe. That was one of the biggest events in the 17th and 18th centuries. Virgin tracts in what later came to be known as Dixieland were waiting to be colonized. There was, however, a shortage of manpower. Inputs of labour were called for before the great United States could emerge lush in prosperity.

The hund was on. The white settliers were too few in number. Besieds, the work called for was of a daunting nature. Some outside source of labour had to be found. The solution of the problem was soon at hand. Impoverished, immiserized workers were purchased, wholesale, at throwaway prices in the dark continent of Africa and shipped to the United States. Outsourced labour, forced to migrate, arrived as slaves and were put to work in the southern territories of North America. The lands were cleared and levelled, and went on to produce unbelievably rich harvests of wheat, corn, cotton and tobacco. American industrialization was based on the surplus yielded by American agriculture, and American agriculture was, overwhelmingly, the product of imported slave labourers. The labour force, originally outsourced, was, *via* migration, rendered into an internal input.

That annual of colonization and colonialism was repeated, in miniature scale, in the middle decades of the 19th century in the shipment of cheap Indian labourers, first to Mauritius and subsequently to the West Indies. Scholars have chosen to describe this shipment of indentured workforce as a new kind of slavery. Immiserized peasantry, mostly from Bihar and the United Provinces, were recruited on a long-term basis at laughably low wages and sent away across the seven seas to pioneer sugarcane cultivation in Mauritius and engage in both bauxite extration and plantation activity in and around the Caribbean Islands. Once again, a key input, picked from an outside source, was internalized through the process of migration.

The slaves imported from Africa into the United States were paid bare subsistence and notheing beyond; they were under bondage to their masters. In the case of indentured labour brought in into Mauritius and the West Indies, some wages were offered, but the workers were still contractually bound to their employers. It could be—and was actually—argued that, left in Africa, the slaves would have died of hunger or been consumed by anarchy. Similarly, indentured labour who migrated to Mauritius and the West Indies, came to enjoy, it was climed, a much higher level of living compared to what was the fate of their cousins left behind in the desolate north Indian villages.

Centuries have rolled by, industrial societies have advanced spectacularly, technologies are transformed, services are increasingly displacing material production in the composition of national output. On top of all this, industiral nations are in fierce competition with one another for survival in the global market. Cost-cutting has accordingly emerged as a major issue of concern for them. The answer to their prayer of efficiency is once again outsourcing. However, unlike in the past, the emphasis now is not on shifting the outside source—low-cost labourer—inside the country, but on leaving it where it belongs. Were such cheap labour to be imported into the country notwithstanding the huge transfer costs, it could be sucked in no time into the local milieu, get unionized and therefore no longer remain cheap. Rather than that, such workers are encourged to stay back home and be organized in call centres. Let god be thanked for e-commerce, work will be "outsourced" from the rich Western countries to these "offshore" workers. A fantastic increase has taken place in business process outsourcing, for example, in India over the last 10 years, the rate of expansion exceeding 100 percent per annum. Processes that are being outsourced include response to credit card enquiries, preparation of invoices, payrolls and cheques, reconciliation of daily accounts, writing medical transcriptions, processing applications, billings and collections, demand and sales forcecasts, actuarial analysis, and so on.

Countries like ours have lapped it up. Call centres have come up at furious speed in the major metropolitan areas. Computer-savvy young people, with a background of relative affluence and fluency in one or two foreign languages, have found a haven in these centres. Despite certain constraints at the workplace, the wages offered, while perhaps only about one-twentieth or even less of what is paid in Europe or America for a comparable job, are substantially higher than what the young BPO cadets could expect to fetch in the local labour market.

It would be indecent to spoil the party. Some peripheral comments nonetheless ought not to be held back. The aggregate number currently employed in the Indian call centres is estimated to be around 3,50,000. Even were this number to mount to one million in the course of the next five years, that would still be barely 0.25 per cent of the total working force in the country. It will therefore hardly do to go over board. Moreover, the BPO is a totally city-based activity; the millions and millions of unemployed and underemployed in the countryside are beyond its ken.

The other point, crying out for attention is the somewhat precarious nature of the employment provided by the call centres. It is the mirror image of a dependency arrangement. Were the political climate in the United States and the European Union to turn sharply against outsourcing, it could be a swansong for the BPO units. Intense debate is already on in the Western world on the economics and morality of outsourcing: the tussle is between employers keen to economize on costs on the one hand and the trade union movement unhappy with the loss of potential work opportunities resulting from outsourcing on the other. The Republican Party in the United States, given its symbiotic relationship with leading business groups, has not stood in the way of BPO. But a Democratic Party regime might be much more ambivalent. The prospects are even more dicey in Europe, where the overall rate of unemployment is eight per cent and the rate of economic growth just nominal. Unemployed workers, who related their state of joblessness with the contracting out of work to low-wage countries, can be kept pacified with dole of a relatively generous size only if the economy grows satisfactorily. If it does not, there is bound to be trouble ahead.

For nations, at present benefiting from BPO activities, there is a somewhat bizarre socio-political spin-off of the goings-on. The outsourcing network has nurtured a new generation of comfortably placed citizens deeply thankful for the bounty the advanced Western countries have gifted them. Whether this development protends a newer kind of slavery—with the slaves not removed from their native land—is a theme that is fodder for dialectics. It would perhaps be equally contentious to describe the BPO recruits as international scabs. Even so, the hypothesis of a breathtaking BPO-based expansion of employment and income in the poorer countries would seem to be a comprehensive pipedream.

11th November 2005

The moving finger

The script follows its own inexorable grammar. The International Atomic Energy Agency has voted in September. It will, for routine's sake, take another vote in November. It does not really matter whether India chooses to reverse its vote in this second round, or stays neutral. Since the European Union is this time solidly with it, the United States of America has the seal of approval of the IAEA for whatever it intends to do at the next stage.

At the United Nations security council, things are going to be much smoother than what they were during the imbroglio over Iraq. At the time the blatant aggression was planned against Saddam Hussein's mythical weapons of mass destruction, France and Germany constituted a formidable pair of Doubting Thomases. This time the snooty Europeans have been caught in the American trap. Having sponsored a resolution to the effect that Iran's impertinence in persisting with its nuclear power programme be reported to the security council, France and Germany will have neigher logic nor face to stall the proposal for punitive measures against the Iran regime. The proposal will be duly vetoed by Russia and China. That too is, however, well anticipated in the script puncitiliously authored by George W. Bush's henchmen. The UN will be immobilized by the veto. The clarion call from the US president will nonetheless ring out: this was the appropriate moment for the international community to assume responsibility.

There are innocents abroad who assume that, following the outcry over the invasion of Iraq and the nightmare that country has subsequently been reduced to, the US—once bitten twice shy—will be extraordinarily cautious before attempting a similar military solution in Iran. Nothing of the sort. The American strategy in west Asia is a tight integrated package. To the architects, of this strategy, the entire west Asia is a homogeneous zone presenting a common battlefield. Those holding the reins of power in the countries included in the zone are congenitally anti-American, they must be sent packing one after another; there is no other way to ensure American near-monopoly over the region's oil supply. As per the script, Afghanistan was number one on the agenda; Iraq followed. The third country to be enlightened on the facts of life happens to be Iran. After Iran, it will be rest assured, the turn of Syria.

That apart, Bush is now a veteran of at least two, according-to-him, enormously-successful wars. He knows how to consummate his heart's desires.

In the past, cloak and dagger operations against a country reckoned as enemy of the US were managed by the Central Intelligence Agency, with the state department having a large say in the preparation of such operations. The US has now decisively entered the imperial age; maintaining international relations on an even keel has low priority. The state department is therefore downgraded, the department of defence has assumed centre-stage. The war against terrorism is henceforth the outstanding issue in foreign relations. The Pentagon is in supreme charge and will be given a free hand in the conduct of this war. The nuisance of, for instance, congressional approval for waging covert activities against a foreign country has been successfully circumvented by a series of presidential 'findings'. These findings furnish the defence department and and its various wings with full authority for military strikes against hostile concentrations in alien territories; concentrations which, in the judgment of the Pentagon, affect the security of the US. An Extraordinary Strike Group, over which the defence department has total command, has been set up for the purpose. This group will receive fullest logistical support from the army, the navy and the air force. It is supposedly capable of mounting a massive aggression against the enemy at a moment's notice in any part of the world. There is no question any more of divided responsibility and the associated handicap of multiple centres of decision-making which made wuch a mess of the Bay of Pigs operation four-and-a-half decades ago. From now on, foreign invasion, by whatever name it is called, will be planned and executed exclusively by the defence department; the state department will have practically no say. In fact, the successive installation of two secretaries of state, Colin Powell and Conodoleezza Rice, both black—or at least of mixed ethnic background—has coincided with the state department's loss of clout. Whether there is a causality involved can be left to academic researchers to mull over.

Whatever it be, donald Rumsfeld and his defence department, the script says, will henceforth call the tune. Once the diplomats have played their role and the IAEA and the security council palavers are over, the admirals, the air marshals, and the generals will take over. A pretext—such as Iran's alleged instigation of guerrilla activities in Iraq—will be found, a number of softening up operations by the Special Expeditionary Force, lanched from the Persian Gulf or the Arab Sea, will follow, ostensibly in search of hidden caches of enriched uranium or other fissionable material or concealed warheads and delivery systems. Maybe over a period of a couple of months, Iran will receive the treatment, with the usual quota of wholesale killings and destruction. At the end of this phase, troups will enter Iran from perhaps four directions—from Afghanistan, from the southern waters, from Iraq and from, who knows, this or that central Asian republic where the US has of late been allowed to establish military bases. The revolution devours its children; the counter-revolution too does exactly the same things. The taliban were set up in Afghanistan by the US in the Eighties to get rid of the Soviet invaders; the relationship turned sour and the taliban had to be destroyed by the Americans some 20 years later. Similarly, the *mullahs* under Ayatollah Khomeini were encouraged in Iran in the Fifties by the CIA to checkmate Mossadeq and his Nationalist Fron hell-bent on nationalizing foreign-owned oil companies; the *mullahs* having gone astray—first by ejecting the Shah and subsequently succumbing to wild Americanism—must now be destroyed by the same good Americans.

Given this context, the ire the left are nurturing against our prime minister, who saw to it that we voted the straight American line at the IAEA, is neither here nor there. As product of the long civil service tradition, the prime minister knows the way contemporary history has arranged its script and who the global master is. Besides, he has by now also learnt how to ignore the bark of the left. Even though the latter has threatened to support the prime minister's government from now on only on an issue-to-issue basis, it has not said that it would actually oppose and *vote against* the government on the same basis. So who is afraid of Bhai Vir Singh Marg?

But the dilemma of India's officialdom is hardly the heart of the matter. The coming American invasion will turn Iran into a heap of mass destruction, as happened in the case of both Afghanistan and Iraq. Most of this will be vindication of Samuel Huntington, but will the US succeed in entering the orbit of either tranquillity or contentment? The guerrillas, by whatever name they are called, have taken over Iraq and Afghanistan. Do not bother to lay a wager, they will do so, in no time, in Iran too, The script does not deviate.

31st October, 2005

No values, just greed

Is it all ideological, an expression of deeply held values, the ire votaries of economic liberalization exhibit toward public sector entities? There can of course be the point of view that a government, any government, has no business to stray beyond the confines of defence and law and order; the social contract entered into by citizens does not entitle the authorities to interfere with the processes of agriculture, industry or services, or, for the matter, those of education, culture and literature too. All such incursions, it will be maintained, constitute infringement of individual freedom, citizens must not be prevented from unfettered decision making in the different walks of life. To do so is to stifle their creative genius.

A subsidiary argument is often added, based on the belief—in some instances, conviction—that the public sector is organically less efficient than the private sector: if the criterion of efficiency is maximization of the rate of return, it is private enterprise which is always likely to excel. A government entity is subject to many operational constraints, including political ones, that affect uninhibited profit realization; no such constraints hamper private enterprise. And, if it is a question of transparency, private firms triumph all the way; their activities are an open book and subject to the rule of law, whereas government undertakings work under a veil of secrecy, skeletons are not allowed to come out of the cupboard.

Is there not more than meets the eye in the on-going debate? Since the United States of America is supposed to be the fountainhead of private enterprise, a reference to a controversy raging in that country should not be considered as beside the context. Apart from his war on global terror, President Bush has set his mind on another target: the overhaul of the country's social security system currently under public aegis. The system, in his words, is in a "crisis". It is however awfully difficult to locate the nature of the "crisis". Pension payments under the US social security system are made out of collections from the payroll tax. Till now, the annual yield from the payroll tax has consistently exceeded outgoes. The surplus in 2005 is likely to be around 180 billion dollars. According to the most conservative estimates, this surplus would continue till 2028, and the total accumulation is to reach 3.5 trillion dollars. The reserves of the social security fund might run out only as late as in 2042 because of a growing bulge in the proportion of old people in the total population. This projected event is still some four decades away. George W. Bush's claim of a crisis in social security therefore seems to be a wild exaggeration. With some adjustments in payroll tax rates and prudent investments, there might be no crisis even in a distant future.

Bush and his associates will not go along. They are keen to disband the government-managed social security fund and hand it over to private groups. This eagerness to scuttle social security certainly has some ideological roots. Those who strongly believe in the economic philosophy of no free lunch would have little sympathy for people who depend on government hand-outs in their old age. The latter, they would argue, must make their private arrangements for survival during retirement; the government must not encourage them to look toward it. This argument is however based on shallow reasoning, for when citizens contribute to the payroll tax, they are actually providing for their future, it is no free lunch. The real reason for targeting the social security system lies elsewhere. The Republican administration is under strong pressure from lobbies that are its natural allies. Private investment firms and brokerage houses are casting covetous eyes on the billions and billions of dollars of collections from payroll tax. Were all this money to come under their command, the stock exchange would soar and soar, and profits registered by tycoons would scale hithereto unheard of heights of prosperity.

Ideology is bunkum, class interest has impelled Bush to plan for the dismemberment of the social security network. Those arguing in India for the progressive disinvestments of the public pension fund as well as of the profit-making public undertakings are perhaps not behaving any differently. Public enterprises such as the SAIL units, the Oil and Natural Gas Commission and Bharat Heavy Electricals were built in the early decades of the post independence period when the private sector was nowhere in the picture. Raising the kind of money needed to construct heavy industry units was then beyond the capability of private entities. That apart, the gestation period was long for such units, and the rate of return was relatively low in the initial stages. One remembers an occasion in the Sixties when the free enterprise lobby led by Minoo Masani wanted the Bokaro steel plant to be located in the private sector and assigned to the Tatas; J.R.D. Tata hastily came out with a statement expressing his inability to gather resources adequate for such an ambitious enterprise. He was quite categorical: the government should take charge of the plant.

Since the struggling years are behind and these *navaratna* units in the public sector are showing lush profits, the disinvestments lobby has chosen to bestir itself. It was all right for the government to toil and trouble so as to ensure the profitability of these units; but not to sell them off now to private parties, who could sit back and enjoy the easy-flowing profit, will supposedly be a sin. It will also be difficult to prove that if Bhel or ONGC were placed in private hands, profit-making will be any greater. Besides, public sector units are subject to a number of public scrutinies such as by parliamentary committees and the comptroller and auditor-general, from the rigours of which private units escape. In any event, recent American economic history is a greater educator: hanky-panky in private enterprises is, to say the least, no less rampant than in public units.

The case for disinvestments of the country's public sector units therefore cannot be based on the criterion of either efficiency or transparency of operations. The campaign for privatization merely reflects a heightened greed on the part of corporate sharks. It is little use pretending that many amongst those currently at the helm of the country's administration do not suffer from a natural sympathy for the corporate world. It is even possible to identify one or two ministers who were till the other day lawyers in the service of private corporations, including transnational corporations. Not everybody in our times has the guts to say, in the manner of Dwight Eisenhower's first defence secretary, Charles Wilson, who was formerly president of General Motors, that whatever was good for General Motors was good for the United States. That does not however mean that a handful in the Union Cabinet in New Delhi do not hold identical sentiments in private: whatever is good for Tycoon A or Tycoon B is, they honestly believe, good for India.

Given this frame of mind, it is hardly surprising that these ministers place their own interpretations on the common minimum programme and try the sneaky way to ruin profit-making public enterprises. No question of any burden of ideology or values here; the disinvestments minded ministers are solely driven by the urge to augment the profits of their class brethren in the corporate world. Here too, George W. Bush has shown the light, as he has done in several other areas.

22nd August, 2005

Cellphones in lieu of rice

The left is in a bind. The government has gone ahead and decided to sell in the market 10 per cent of the equity of the profit-making public sector enterprise, Bharat Heavy Electricals Limited, and this despite the forthright declaration in the common minimum programme that no such impropriety would be embarked upon. The left is equally unhappy at the government's tardiness to implement something that is very much there in the CMP: a national employment guarantee scheme.

The factors underlying the problem are not difficult to unravel. The CMP is only a number of pledges. The Congress, which heads the government, has to pay formal obeisance to it. The party however has another agenda, mostly implied or hinted, set for it by the Bretton Woods institutions. To ensure undisturbed parliamentary majority for the regime, a gesture of loyalty has to be displayed to the CMP. On the other hand, the Congress, in thraldom to the globalized ambience, must conform to the test of the grammar laid down by the World Bank-International Monetary Fund duo. The left had committed a tactical mistake right at the beginning. It went on record that, under all circumstances—that would include even when the United Progressive Alliance government deviated from the CMP—it would not vote out the regime since the alternative would mean the retrun of the Bharatiya Janata Party to power. Sonia Gandhi's loyal troops therefore feel reasonably safe to concentrate on craving the favours of the Bretton Woods twins. The latter want disinvestments of public sector undertakings; they also dislike the idea of the government of India's frittering away of money on what they consider to be wasteful boondoggles such as an employment guarantee scheme.

Under relentless pressure from the left, the government finally introduced in parliament a rural employment guarantee scheme. It is an extremely truncated version of what was promised in the CMP. It provides assurance of work only in the rural sector and only for one hundred days in the year. Even this abridged scheme is yet to be formally operational, notwithstanding the completion of one full year by the government. The blame for this delay the regime is laying at the door of the BJP. One of the BJP bigwigs happens to be the chairman of the parliamentary standing committee attached to the ministry of rural development: the rural employment guarantee bill, it is being alleged, is held up by this standing committee, what can the poor government do? One can however quote dozens of instances where the government has proceeded on particular legislative measures without bothering about a parliamentary standing committee's recommendations or non-recommendations. The failure till now to implement even the abridged scheme is therefore not simply on account of procedural difficulties. The government's heart is not in the matter.

Those keen on the rural employment guarantee scheme are sure of their facts. Agriculture is still the livelihood for more than three-fifths of the nation's working force and thus provides sustenance for more than two-fifths of the nation. Both farm production and farm employment, data officially released suggest, have declined in the post-liberalization period compared to what they were in the preceding decade. The rate of growth of agricultural production in the Eighties was roughly 3.2 per cent, while the rate of growth in employment was 1.2 per cent. In contrast, in the Nineties, while farm output grew, but at the reduced rate of 1.7 per cent per annum, farm employment, instead of growing, actually declined at an average annual rate of 5.3 per cent. The woes brought on in the Indian countryside in the wake of the official decision to abide by the conditionalities attached to membership of the World Trade Organization have their own story to tell, Daily reports from practically all parts of the country about rural distress, often culminating in starvation deaths, have by now ceased to cause any ripple. The media consider such reports as not globalization-friendly, and have a way of absentmindedly disposing of them.

The irony lies elsewhere. Millions and millions of people are without work and therefore without purchasing power to buy food. At the other end, something like 20 million tonnes of foodgrains lie unutilized in government godowns. The cost of carrying year after year a stockpile of this order is mindboggling. Reports emanate from time to time of a portion of this stockpile becoming unfit for human consumption. The authorities nonetheless continue to be adamant: no expansion of the public distribution system enabling supply of grains to the famished population at subsidized prices. They have been equally reluctant to relaunch food-for-work programmes which had met at least with limited success in preceding decades.

Against this background, a rural employment guarantee scheme, carefully planned and carefully executed, could, it is said, serve, simultaneously, four different objectives (a) provide food for the hungry; (b) reduce the load of rural unemployment; (c) lighten the burden of carrying cost for foodstock lying with public agencies; and (d) create new rural assets. The gains seem to be so overwhelmingly obvious that the issue of relatiive scarcity of resources should not stand in the way. An annual outlay of Rs. 30,000 crore or thereabouts on the rural employment guarantee scheme will certainly generate more social contentedness than a similar amount spent on buying armaments or luxury passenger planes from overseas. As far as it is possible to perceive, the objection to the programme is not on grounds of lack of finance. It is almost ideological, with a coating of class bias. It is based on the supposedly moral precept of there being no free lunch in life; thereby disfavouring free or subsidized food even to the dying. Orthodoxy of this kind has not prevented the authorities from sending to the United States of America foodgrains at highly subsidized prices for the consumption of the pigs over there. American pigs must have been reckoned as deserving of more sympathy than poverty stricken men, women and children back home.

On this issue, quarters close to the Bretton Woods institutions have consistently played the role of staunch agnostics. Instead of squandering thousands of crores of rupees on the employment guarantee scheme so as to strengthen the demand side of the rural economic system they would like the authorities to concentrate on the supply side. Besides, whatever is done to strengthen the supply side will, according to their belief, be to the advantage of class interest proximate to the powers that be. Their concrete proposal is to divert the money provisionally earmarked for the employment guarantee scheme for projects to build more and more highways and feeder roads to link the highways with the Indian countryside, improvement in this manner of the rural infrastructure, the nation is being assured, will facilitate the movement of foodgrains and other farm products to urban areas—and to ports too, thereby helping exports as well. Such strengthening of the infrastructure will also help industrial goods, including imported industrial goods, to penetrate into the countryside and find a market among the comfortably off in the rural sector. Forget the poor, they do not directly belong to this agenda. But as long as transport picks up, trade too will and as trade flourishes, rural prosperity will take off. Once that happens, the trickle-down factor will activize itself, the poorer sections will accordingly experience an increase in income and employment.

A further suggestion is also on offer. Part of the money saved by scrapping the employment guarantee scheme may be deployed to encourage the manufacture and distribution of cellular telephones. Cellphones are regarded as an important resource for developing instant communications between town and country, also with the great outside world. A spectacular advance in communications in this manner will vastly add to rural welfare, so much so that one should not worry about providing the rural poor with foodgrains: handing over to each of them a cellular telephone is a preferred alternative.

It is on the basis of such fastidious prescriptions that an important plank of the CMP is sought to be scuttled.

10th June 2005

Calamity imperialism

Poor Vladimir Ilich Ulyanov. He died eighty years before the tsunami took place, he could not possibly anticipate the infinite variety the final stage of capitalism, imperialism, is capable of displaying.

Anyway, it will not do to underrate the abiding relevance of that pearl of wisdom: some people's adversity is some other people's opportunity. The tsunami, in the view of no less a person than Condoleezza Rice, has emerged as a "wonderful opportunity" for the United States of America. The countries laid low by tsunami are mostly devastatingly poor. Ravaged by the awesome natural calamity, they have cried out for relief and succour from rich foreign nations and international agencies. The US, and such organizations bossed over by it as the World Bank, were ready with their funds and schemes.

Beggars cannot be choosers. Countries seeking relief were in no position to pick and choose from offers, gifts and other forms of aid dangled before them. The tsunami affected countries were provided help, but the terms of such help have been set by the imperial power, the US and its cronies. The latter have kept to the fore two separate objectives: first, using the modality of relief to extend imperial power over the ravaged territories; and second, arranging the content and pattern of assistance in a manner as would optimize the benefits from it for the imperial power. Most of the money flowing in the name of tsunami relief has been intended not so much for the succour of people in the tsunami-affected lands as for swelling the returns to multinational corporations as well as non-government organizations and of consultants, technicians and other so-called experts overwhelmingly from Western countries.

One example will perhaps suffice to clinch the point. In Sri Lanka, Indonesia and Thailand, donor governments and international agencies have pressed for legislation preventing poor fisherman's families along coastal belts ravaged by the tsunami to rebuild their homesteads; rehabilitation has taken the form of converting old fishing villages and beaches into polo grounds for tourists and vast watery arenas for corporate fishing, both serviced by private hotels, airports and highways, the construction of which is being financed by tsunami money coming from foreign sources. According to one calculation, nine-tenths of every tsunami dollar treks back as income and profit to the donor country; the actual effective aid is a homage to tokenism.

The tsunami is, of course, a calamity caused by nature. People from the less fortunate parts of the world are well conversant with another kind of calamity that is the artefact of human agencies. Consider recent events in Afghanistan and Iraq. The infrastructure of these countries have been totally destroyed by American aggression. Roads, bridges, irrigation systems, power installations, hospitals, schools, oilfields, airports, harbours, nothing has escaped the wrath of the invading troops. Here too, the imperial power is fired with a double-barrelled objective. The first aim, fairly obvious, is to liquidate native politicians who are cheeky and do not kowtow to the imperial overlord. There is, however, a second, somewhat lesser, goal. Once the targeted country is comprehensively destroyed by war, the imperial power takes the initiative to re-build it. Unutilized capacity in the imperial economic system spells the prospect of large-scale unemployment and social discontent. One way to obviate such risks is to try to create opportunities for absorption of men and matérial in foreign operations.

An imperial war, duly won, serves its purpose in an enchanting manner. The conquering nation, the US, undertakes the task of reconstruction. The human urge to put back to shape a destroyed land is only subsidiary. The principal aim is to provide work and income to unutilized manpower and productive capacity in the imperial backyard. Transnational corporations arrive on the scene. They rebuild hospitals, schools, roads, factories. They re-lay oil pipelines. they take charge of the distribution of essential commodities. They rope in NGOs from back home to organize medical assistance, in the process often ensuring the collapse of the existing government hospital system.

Much of this is, in fact, an extended version of the "pump-priming" suggested by John Meynard Keynes seven decades ago. Daunted by the spectre of economic depression accompanied by massive domestic unemployment, Keynes had recommended activities like digging holes and refilling them, there by spending government money to create fresh employment opportunities. The income accruing to those newly engaged in hole-digging-cum-refilling operations, Keynes hinted, will be spent quickly in the consumer market, and boost effective demand. This rise in effective demand will have a "multiplier" effect over the entire system. The depressed economy will no longer stay depressed. It will grow buoyant and gradually approach the level of full employment.

Condi Rice knows her Keynes. Whether it is the tsunami or the aftermath of the Afghanistan and Iraq wars, the post-calamity developments highlight "pump-priming" on an international scale. Instead of digging millions and millions of holes and refilling them, the imperial nation in one instance deploys tsunami assistance to multiply economic opportunities for citizenry back home; in the other instance, it picks a distant, wretched country, first to destroy it and then to rebuild it, for the same purpose. If nature is reluctant to gift a calamity, step forward and create a calamity: destroy a foreign country and then engage in its reconstruction. Imperialism, the highest state of capitalism, thereby adds a new feather to its cap. This new achievement is best described as calamity imperialism.

Let us, nonetheless, face reality. Neither unprovoked wars nor disasters such as a tsunami can be an everyday affair. The imperial power and its agents, therefore, have to fall back on other devices to further their objectives. The essential point is to create situations which can lead to a weakening of regimes in poorer lands. A common ploy is to engineer a permanent shortage of funds at the disposal of such regimes. For example, fiscal and monetary advice of an otiose kind can go a long way to destabilize the socioeconomic structure of the country the imperial power wants to destroy.

Monetary chaos and fiscal instability can make a shambles of a polity, and its demoralized rulers can be gradually conditioned to capitulate to external influences. Assurance of immediate cash assistance to cover up financial difficulties can be a great allure. One major reason the US administration, the World Bank and the International Monetary Fund are so keen that governments of poor countries practise balanced budgets eschew deficit financially and switch over to dubious fiscal measures such as the value-added tax, is the near-certainty that, under these dispensations, the lack of resources will become increasingly more pronounced, thwarting the fulfilment of basic needs of the people, as a result provoking widespread social and political discord.

Once that happens, the local government will have nowhere else to go and will succumb to wily external pressures. The federating states in India will, for example, be particularly vulnerable when faced with such a situation. The Centre will be either reluctant of incapable or offering them the funds they desperately seek. The states will then turn conceivably to either agencies like the World Bank and the Asian Development Bank or directly to the US government.

This is not such a far-fetched proposition; the process has already started. A number of state governments in India have gladly accepted technical and financial assistance from the US administration to improve their basic infrastructure, including that of local bodies. What can ensure is easily foreseeable. Once foreigners take charge of our municipalities and *panchayat* institutions, the nation's sovereignty, whether economic or political, will, who can deny, take a beating.

There, however, is the rub. The nation is in such a cynical state of mind that issues concerning sovereignty are being widely regarded as a huge joke.

30th May, 2005

Mixed up values

Obfuscating saturation advertisement in the media, lavishly financed by taxpayers' money, has hailed the occasion. Congratulatory statements have been issued on behalf of the World Bank and the International Monetary Fund. It has nonetheless been a wobbly beginning for the value added tax. On the date of its supposed introduction—the first day of the new fiscal year—only 18 of the 30 states and Union territories comprising the country had signed in. The list of non-joiners includes the economically most important state in the north, Uttar Pradesh, as also the economically most important state in the south, Tamil Nadu. The country's largest state, Madhya Pradesh, too, is keeping out of the new tax system. With half the country not joining, it is a picture of total confusion. Traders are on the warpath for their own reasons. But the worst sufferers, should the new tax system be still persisted with, will be those engaged in small-scale industrial activities. They will go to the wall unable to compete with VAT-advantaged giant-sized industrial concerns; the prospect of a substantial swelling of unemployment is hardly negligible.

In contrast, the denizens of big industry are happy beyond measure. Their kingdom is about to come. The VAT regime paves the way for a unified commodity market in the country untrammelled by varying tax rates for the same commodity in different states and with a simplified two-rate system for the entire range of commodities. In the process, the new regime promises to throw out of the window the principle of progressive taxation featuring in modern societies since the second half of the 19th century. The VAT rates structure, as ordained by New Delhi, will ensure that a nonmotorized bicycle and an American-type luxury limousine are taxed at the same rate.

The more interesting aspect of the innovation in the tax system is however the legislative procedure followed to usher it in. A draft bill was suggested to each state by the Union ministry of finance. The states accepted this draft with minor emendations to accommodate local factors. The bills were then moved in the respective legislatures for consideration and passing.

It is an integral part of legislative procedure that the objects and reasons for a proposed bill must accompany its presentation before the legislature. The following paragraphs are excerpted from the text of the objects and reasons for the VAT bill as submitted by a particular state government. This text is more or less identical in the VAT legislations passed in all the joining states.

"The Chief Ministers of States and the administrators of the Union Territories have unanimously resolved in a meeting by the Union Finance Minister on the 16th November, 1999, to bring out major reforms in the method of taxation of commodities in the country by replacing the existing scheme of sales tax with the Value Added Tax (hereinafter referred to as the VAT) scheme. In pursuance of such agreemtnt, all State Governments and Union Territories have, already initiated necessary steps towards introduction of a legislation on the VAT under the guidance of the 'Empowered Committee of the State Finance Ministers on Sales Tax Reforms'..."

"3. The existing sales tax structure has unduly increased the tax burden on a commodity by taxing both inputs and outputs and thus, is creating a cascading burden of taxation resulting in adverse effects on the economy. The VAT scheme will be helpful to eliminate the tax burden by setting off the tax paid on inputs against the output tax payable. The VAT scheme will, thus, encourage industries, trade and the people. It also results in augmentation of revenue through widening of the tax base and ensuring better tax compliance."

"4. The Bill seeks to introduce the taxation of commodities by way of the VAT scheme in lieu of the existing scheme of sales tax."

"5. The Bill has been framed with the above objects in view."

The facts emerging from this statement of "objects and reasons" have no ambiguity about them. The Union finance minister convened a meeting where state chief ministers were present; the decision was taken at that meeting to abolish sales tax and substitute it with the VAT in all the states and Union territories, pursuant to this decision, bills enabling introducting of VAT were placed before the respective state legislatures. Each bill was duly passed. The state governor subsequently gave his assent to the bill, and it became a part of the statute.

Therein lies the problem. The country has a Constitution. It is a written Constitution. Under Article 246 of this Consittution, there is such a thing as the seventh schedule. This schedule consists of three separate lists, the Union list, the state list and the concurrent list. The Union list covers subjects that come under the purview of the Union government which has the prerogative to legislate on these subjects and to preside over their administration. The state list includes items over which a state government has exclusive jurisdiction, including the authority to legislate. The concurrent list covers subjects over which both the Centre and the states have administrative as well as legislative jurisdiction, but in case there are Central laws or administrative decisions taken by the Centre, these will prevail over any state legislation or any administrative decision taken by a state. The prerogative to impose sales tax comes under the exclusive jurisdiction of state governments in terms of entry 54 in the state list of the Constitution. What the Constitution has given only the Constitution can take away. State governments, either singly, or collectively, cannot abrogate on their own a dispensation bestowed upon them by the Constitution. Nor can the Centre, by issuing an executive fiat, obliterate this entry from the state list. Even a unanimous decision of the Centre and all the states will be unable to remove or replace sales tax from the state list unless a constitutional amendment is carried out to that effect.

The same kind of difficulty will arise, it can be argued, with VAT. No state government is entitled to introduce VAT since tax on value addition does not occur in the state list of the Constitution.

In this case, there is a way out though. Under Article 248 of the Constitution, the Union government is empowered to legislate on residual matters not mentioned in any of the three lists. The Centre therefore can, at its own initiative, propose a value added tax and have it enacted by parliament. It may even distribute the entire proceeds of such a tax among the states. But this particular route has not been chosen. Instead, the states have been urged to initiate on their own measures to introduce the VAT scheme in lieu of the existing scheme of sales tax, never mind the Constitution. For years on end, the Washington Consensus has been urging the Union government to opt for an all-India value added tax which will curb the independent tax-levying power of the states and transfer this authority at the Central level. Pursuant to this prodding, the ministry of finance has coaxed and cajoled the states to fall in and agree to cross over to VAT.

The problem will still not go away. External forces which these days have a substantial says in deciding India's economic and fiscal policies may have little or no respect for our Constitution. They may not even be aware that we operate on the basis of a written Constitution. But should our own policy-makers be oblivious of the Constitution? Reforms may be a beautiful event, but, as long as we have a written Constitution, even a beautiful event must pass the test of constitutional propriety.

What is surprising is that at no stage those in charge of piloting the VAT legislation or its vetting have seemingly concerned themselves with the constitutional issue. It could be an instance either of ignorance or of indifference, or, who knows, of total disdain. The World Bank and the IMF have asked us to introduce VAT, how dare you raise the silly issue of the good-for-nothing Constitution?

This may appear as convincing logic in some quarters. The only problem is that, should the authorities themselves spurn the nation's laws and

Constitution, others are likely to gather inspiration from the example set. These others will include not only revolutionaries of the People's War Group genre, but also run-of-the-mill murderers, forgers, bank embezzlers, rapists—and arsonists, besides those who specialize in burning the Constitution.

15th April 2005

Trigger-happy

Three separate incidents recently took place in different parts of the country: they nonetheless form a pattern. Militarymen occupying a compartment in a mail train hurtling along the plains of western Uttar Pradesh throw out of the bogey five innocent civilian passengers, who meet instantaneous death. On Republic Day last, an army contingent, marching along Hoja near Guwahati, find themselves hemmed in by a crowd of romping villagers; the troops get nervy at such undesirable confrontation and shoot down ten of the unarmed villagers. A slip of a girl, barely twelve or thirteen years of age, encroaches on the property of a power-generating plant in West Bengal—to cut grass according to her neighbours to pilfer coal according to the authorities of the power station—a security guard cuts her down.

Each of these incidents should be an affront to those who place civil liberties and sanctity of life and living at the core of a democratic society.Insensitivity, however, has entered the soul. Following some temporary localized furore,public misgiving over these killings has died down-as if shooting down citizens in this manner is a normal part of existence. In any event, what is loosely described as civil society has over the years travelled through a certain learning curve:horror stories of violation of human rights in Jammu and Kashmir, the depredations of Border Security Force personnel along the Bangladesh border, rapes and killings in Manipur by members of army battalions. Army and security forces being on the rampage is now regarded in wide areas of the country to be as inevitable as natural calamities; they are accepted with equanimity. Those in charge of the nation's defence and security are regarded as belonging to a very special category; their occasional dalliances—which could even include pillage and murder-are not expected to raise any eyebrow.

But let us think a while. Is not the growth of a social psyche of this nature a direct outcome of the obsession over security of late plaguing governments in country after country, India being no exception? In a way, this marks a note-worthy triumph for the American administration; its philosophy of terror has come to receive almost universal acclaim. Authorities in diverse lands have trained themselves to perceive terror and security risk in every bush. Outlay on security increases year after year. Both defence equipment and defence personnel keep expanding at a seemingly inexorable rate. The populace is being made aware that security has over-riding priority, considerations of security precede the interests of the people. In case, for ensuring the security of the nation and that of the nation's leaders, civil liberties have to be curtailed, the people are supposed to accept such a dispensation without demur.

The parliament loves to indulge only in frivolities. There is, besides, an aura of hush-hush around budget allocations for defence and security. To question these allocations is, it is hinted, close to treason. It therefore happens that appropriations for security and defence measures are passed without a debate. These outlays rise with every year; no questions are asked from any quarter. All questions are reserved for the occasion when the government is urged to spend money on a rural employment guarantee programme or for midday meal schemes for children.

Where the issue is security, supply creates its own demand. The proliferation of security arrangements fosters a culture of security-fetishism. The prime minister and his/her kith and kin must be blanketed by security monitored by the Special Protection Group. Such prerogative belongs to former prime ministers and their families, near and distant, as well. Cabinet ministers and ministers of other ranks too enjoy near-identical privilege. Members of parliament and politicians of lesser breed do not like to be left in the lurch. Soon, a lobby develops. Entitlement to security provisions emerges as a hallmark of social snobbery. The rat race commences in right earnest: who can beat whom in the splendour of security arrangements emerges as an issue of life and death. Inevitably, pomp of security puffs up good-for-nothing politicians and similar species.

There is an inverse effect of this obsession over security. Army and security staff deputed to security duty or for surveillance in sensitive areas acquire inflated ideas about their usefulness to society. If the be-all and end-all of a politician's daily perambulations is security entitlement, personnel in charge of security gradually get their heads swelled up and soon tend to nurture grand illusions about their own importance. In their assigned spheres of responsibility, they begin to behave as entites who are the final arbiters of law and justice: people do not matter, only they do, and they can do whatever they like. Once they reach such a state of mind, they reckon they have the right to throw out at will civilian passengers from train compartments, to mow down innocent villagers moving in a group and to take the life of a teenagerd girl indulging in her little pranks.

Things have now descended to a level where security is no longer quite aimed at ensuring the life and limb of the people—ordinary people; the latter, rather, are there to satisfy the whims of the defence and security apparatus. Perhaps politicians—and other such extra-ordinary specimens—who have turned security to the holiest of holy cows have lost their bearings as rational human beings. It does not distrub their aesthetics either that, in this still horrendously poor country, thousands of crores of rupees are spent in the name of their personal security. Perhaps their senses have been so dulled that they are not the least concerned that because they, the chosen ones, are traversing from one spot in a city to another one—a distance possible to cover in two and a half minutes—all traffic within milles of the route is suspended, and pedestrains are rudely stopped in their tracks, may be for a full half-hour; as they pass in a bullet-proof car, four or five surveillance cars precede it, and the same number of cars follow, each car blaring obscene hooting sounds, the accumulating sound pollution breaching all norms.

Only a few decades ago, a statesman of stature had called upon his comrades to mingle with the people as fish mingle in water. Was that a levity not worthy of consideration, or are we now living in a different planet? It is not the contention that terror is an absent, unreal category in any country these days. But if arrangements to cope with the threat of terror grow into a monstrosity which negates civilization, certainly it is time to stop and ponder. Consider Sweden, where an incumbent prime minister was shot one evening even as he, after watching a film at a neighbourhood theatre, emerged in the street. Security for important people in that country has been beefed up following that killing. But such security is still demure as well as unobtrusive, the flow of civic life is the least disturbed. Or imagine, through some magic, Mahatma Gandhi is reincarnated in our country and he remembers the fate that overtook him on January 30, 1948. One can lay a wager he would still, refuse, furiously, the government's importuning to accord him Z-class security.

21st February, 2005

Money to burn?

If a country's prosperity is defined in terms of the foreign exchange assets it holds, India has never had it so good. Foreign exchange holdings at this moment exceed $ 130 billion. Compare this to the horrendously low $1 billion, held at the midpoint of 1991. Cataclysmic changes were then introduced in India's economic policies to cope with the situation. That kind of nightmare is seemingly over for ever and it is henceforth jingle bell, jingle bell, jingle all the way.

There is ample reason to argue that the inflow of foreign exchange is not going to stop in the immediate future. International speculators are currently in love with India. They are allowed to bring in funds and take them out whenever they like. A slice of these funds they park with Indian banks and earn a comfortable rate of interest, a rate substantially higher than what is offered, for instance, in the United States of America. Most of such short-term funds are, however, deployed in the country's stock exchanges. No capital gains taxes are to be paid: foreign institutional investors therefore make a beeline for the bourses in Mumbai, Chennai, Hyderabad, Delhi, Kanpur and Calcutta. As much as 40 per cent of the transactions in the share markets are attributable to foreign speculators: with this much of clout, they dictate the proceedings in the bourses. It is to the interest of the foreign institutional investors that share prices keep soaring, to dizzy and dizzier heights. Once they decide the time has arrived for profit gathering, they sell the shares and take their earnings for remittance abroad.

The story spreads across the continents; India's stock exchanges provide such rich gravy. More and more international speculators crowd into our share markets, and the country's foreign exchange holdings continue to scale more and more gigantic heights. Those presiding over the country's affairs can relax: no memory of the pre 1991 days should henceforth disturb their psyche.

Perspectives nonetheless differ from party to party. According to many monetary and foreign trade specialists, foreign exchange reserves covering a country's imports for roughly six months is enough to take care of contingencies if, for some reason or other, short term payments difficulties arise. To hold further foreign exchange assets is, they feel, a luxury the country can do without. The deputy chairman of the Planning Commission appears to endorse this view. A reserve stock of $10 to $50 billion, in his judgement, should be adequate for the management of balance of payments: the rest of our foreign exchange holdings are almost idle hoards.

In the view of the deputy chairman, a major part of our surplus foreign exchange holdings should be used up for developing the contry's economic infrastructure. The country lacks state-of-the-art facilities such as roads and bridges and harbours and airports of international standard. To attract foreigners into India's industry and agriculture, we must, the deputy chairman is convinced, transform the state of our infrastructure, both qualitatively and quantitatively. Perhaps, he has in mind airports like JFK in New York and O'Hare in Chicago and roadways like the German *autobahn* and the New Jersey Turnpike. Were we so bold as to deploy our excess foreign exchange to develop facilities similar to these, there would be no stopping the country's rapid economic development.

There is a problem though. Our foreign exchange holdings—the bulk of them do not actually belong to us. We have not earned them through, for example, exporting our merchandise and services. These holdings are with as becuse foreign parties who won them have temporarily placed them with us. They are a part of the global footloose capital flows which have entered India in quest of high returns either from stock market speculation of from investment in bank deposits. Sooner or later, the owners of such capital might want their money to be repatriated overseas and in foreign exchange. In case we use up these holdings to develop replicas of the JFK airport and the New Jersey Turnpike, we will have no foreign exchange left to foot the bill of repatriation.

The deputy chairman will therefore have to be disappointed; the governor of the Reserve Bank of India has told him as much. But the phenomenon of surplus foreign exchange holdings will persist. They are a nuisance, but not for the reason the deputy chairman thinks. The foreign institutional investors who walk in freely into our stock exchanges and speculate with their free-wheeling funds are actually a hindrance to the country's economic growth. In their search for quick profits, they often heat up the share markets. Because of their manipulations, share prices rise and rise. The ordinary Indian householder is enchanted: profits can be earned and income can be doubled, tripled and quadrupled so easily, by merely placing money in the share markets. The lure is irresistible: those with even the meagrest means rush to the stock exchanges and buy, buy, buy.

Thereby is enacted a tragedy, For a poor country, which India remains, the major task to ensure development should be the foregathering of savings, which can be turned over for investment, by those who can afford to save. However, given the false climate we have been trapped into, honest citizens do not think any more in terms of savings, they, insted, scrape together whatever resources they can put together and plunge into share speculation. The government follows the lead and comes to believe that the nation's economic health is co-terminus with the wellbeing of the bourses.

The deputy chairman of the Planning Commission is right. We have to curb the unhealthy bulge in our foreign exchange reserves. But, to do so, we must see to it that the group of master speculatiors—those who goad others to speculate—are shunted out of our precincts. This can be done through two easy means. First, we re-impose controls and restrictions on the inflow of foreign funds so that foreign money, which is not invested in production activities but is devoted exclusively to speculation, does not get easy entry into the country and its exit is made equally difficult. Second, we impose a heavy tax—not a token one—on share market transactions besides bringing back a heavy dose of capital gains taxation.

These are obvious soiutions to the riddle of surplus foreign exchange funds. Easy solutions do not though always satisfy specific interest groups. The lobby for running down foreign exchange reserves to import material, equipment and expertise to build beautiful and expansive shopping plazas, tourist extravaganzas, dazzling expressways and dizzy skyscrapers will therefore continue to be around. The argument that the foreign exchange reserves do not really belong to us to spend is unlikely to cut any ice with them. Who knows, perhaps, there is more than meets the eye in this demand to eat away the exchange reserves. Once the reserves disappear following the government's yielding to pressure to deploy them for developing the nation's economic infrastructure there is bound to be another acute foreign exchange crisis, forcing the country to sign a further deed of transfer of its economic sovereignty to foreigners.

And will it be impolite to point out that to spark faster growth in the country, we need infrastructure, but infrastructure that is integrally linked to rural reconstruction—irrigation channels, drainage, land reclamations, rural roads, primary schools, village health centres and not exhibits of zilch and glitter. The Planning Commission bigwigs will again be disappointed: rural reconstruction calls for very little spending of foreign exchange.

21st January 2005

Reforms gone haywire

The word, "comprador", of 16th-century vintage, has its roots in the Portuguese language.It has, however, travelled far and wide since.It originally meant a native house-steward,at least so suggest the dictionaries. Gradually, in the heady colonial days, comprador came to connote a native servant employed as head of the native staff, and as agent, by European commercial and business houses. In the course of the past century, particularly in the context of Latin America, the expression has assumed a more pointed significance.A comprador is now an individual who not only acts as agent representing foreign interests, but who,in addition, almost as a matter of principle, places the interests of foreigners above those of his native country.

Political economy in Latin America is full of rich debates concerning traits and symptoms of compradorism as well as stages and phases of the comprador epoch.The reverberation of these debates has not quite reached India.This is understandable, for Indian scholars have greater respect for pucca Western strands of thought.That does not mean though that the practice of compradorism has lagged behind here.The decade of the Nineties is for India about as important, one is almost tempted to say, as the final decades of the 18th century were for the advent of the Romantic era in Europe. Indians have learnt in the course of this decade that to be gracious to foreigners is the quintessence of economics; that is to say, the interest of foreigners must precede national interests. Which is why in 1994 the American consultancy group, Enron, was allowed to float a power-plant company in Maharashtra whose equity was to vest one hudred per cent with the Americans, while the bulk of the investible funds needed for it were to be provided by Indians.

The Indian authorities also agreed to sign a power purchase agreement which accepted as commonplace the notion that the Enron corporation would sell power to the natives at a price much, much higher than the price paid for per unit of power produced by plants installed by Bhopal's Bharat Heavy Electricals in several places in the country. Intense debate took place in parliament over the wisdom of the deal struck with Enron, but all questions raised by doubters were brushed aside.

Foreigners, the nation was informed, know better; foreigners are *ipso facto* efficiency personified, and we must, for efficiency's sake, pay them through the nose. There was some gossip that, to facilitate the adoption of such a stance by the ministry of finance and the ministry of power in New Delhi and the state government of Maharashtra, some money had passed hands. Even if the gossip had some basis, that was, however, an integral part of comprador culture. Native agents are—foreigners take it for granted—entitled to some *bucksheesh* for services they render, services that most of the time go against the native country's interests. It is a different matter that Enron was soon found out to be, in the United States of America itself, a crooks' opera, and the projected power plant at Dabhol came to an ignominious end.

The recent hullabaloo over the legitimacy or otherwise of subsides for oil and gas supplied to domestic consumers tells a story which has a grotesque overlap with the Enron incident. The terms of the power purchase agreement signed with Enron amounted to offering a hefty subsidy to the foreign firm. Such a subsidy was then considered to be a noble act. A different tune is now being sung over the persistent public demand that the domestic price of oil and gas supplied to domestic consumers be subsidized through a reduction in import and excise duties. Such slashing of duties is akin to subsidy, which the public is being told, is sin; one must not charge for a product a price lower than its cost, such practice allegedly retards economic efficiency.

It is all great fun. Those in authority are aghast at the suggestion to subsidize domestic consumers. There could be greater signs. Forget Enron. Barely a couple of years ago, exactly such a sin was committed by the government of India when, following directives from the World Trade Organization, it lowered import tariffs on 500 odd farm products, including wheat, cotton, tobacco, copra and rubber. In effect, by lowering the tariffs, the Indian authorities offered subsidies to foreign producers and exporters so as to enable them to lower their prices and thereby eject the home produces from the Indian market. In consequence, hundreds of Indian farmers experienced indescribable hardship; some of them were driven to commit suicide. Tariffs were lowered and subsidy offered to foreigners at the cost of Indian farmers; the government was not at all concerned if, in the process, domestic interests were adversely affected; comprador ethos was in uninhibited flow: sin is no sin if committed to further foreign interests.

The dictum has gradually attained respectability. Subsidies are all right if they promote foreign interests; they are otherwise if they promote a domestic cause. Lowering excise duties on oil and natural gas is resisted by the authorities because such a reduction will offer relief to domestic consumers. This, according to the authorities, is impermissible; domestic consumers are not foreigners.

Come to think of it, the country's taxation policy, already incorrigibly pro-rich, has gradually undergone a comprador tilt as well. This is only natural, since taxes and subsidies are aspects of the same phenomenon: a tax is a negative subsidy, a subsity is negative taxation. Since 1991, while direct taxes have been continously lowered for companies, including foreign companies and upper income groups, indirect taxes have been raised. Lowering direct taxes is equivalent to offering subsidies to affluent citizens and foreigners. On the other hand, a stiffening of indirect taxes, the incidence of which falls mostly on the relatively poor, is akin to lowering subsidies for the poor.

Indian economic policy has therefore evolved into a compound of two principal objectives: first, promoting the interests of foreigners against those of the native crowd, and second, furthering the interests of the rich by putting an increasing squeeze on the poor. This is economics made easy, and is being religiously put into practice by the craftsmen at work in New Delhi.

Examples of how far the government has proceeded in the pursuit of these twin goals are indeed galore. Consider, for instance, the Central Electricity Act 2003. Subsidy, the act echoes, is sin; cross-subisdy is equally so. The state electricity boards have been enjoined by the act not to charge affluent consumers at rates higher than costs and use the proceeds of such higher charges to offer lower rates to poorer consumers. Cross-subsidy of this nature is supposed to be bad economics. The act, passed last year, has the vociferous support of the government of India and its various institutions, including the Planning Commission.

Nobody seemingly bothers to consider that abolition of the principle of cross-subsidy is really a wholesale repudiation of the structure of progressive taxation, the centrepieces of public finance in the Western world since the middle of the 19th century. According to the doctrine of progressive taxation, the rich have the ability to bear a higher rate of taxation compared to the poor, and therefore deserve to be taxed at a higher rate. Receipts from tax-payers in upper-income ranges, taxed at higher rates, have, over the past 150 years, provided the funds in country after country for essential social services specifically aimed at ameliorating the conditions of the poorer classes. The Central Electricity Act 2003 and its proponents have gone on record defying this basic canon of public finance. And we are supposed to accept all this in the name of economic reforms.

29th November, 2004

Taking on nature

Democratic freedom should include the freedom to dream. There is however a problem. Some people's dreams can turn out to be some other people's nightmares; democratic freedom, we could be told, also includes the freedom to suffer nightmares. And not only that: in some instances, the nightmares may well descend on real life.

The human race benefits because, every now and then, visionaries spring from within its fold and dream what, in the beginning, appears to be an idle, innocent, nondescript dream. One such dream, of recent vintage, is the vision to bring together the water flowing through all the rivers in the country by building a great, complex, equity creating interlinking system. Why should some states be regular victims of floods while others are afflicted by drought, some states be served, courtesy the bounty of nature, by an array of turbulent overflowing rivers, while some other states remain content with narrow, shallow-bedded rivulets which dry up in the summer months? Whatever the economists might claim, ours is still a basically primary goods producing country with more than three-fifths of the population dependent on agriculture as their source of livelihood. India is a union of states; to vest this unity with due significance, economic development, including agricultural development, must be harmonized among all states. Attainment of this goal should be the central objective of national planning. In pursuit of the objective, a group of noble persons have come up with the idea of pooling together the waters from each and every river in India, big and small, irrespective of whether they flow from north to south or in the reverse direction, from west to east or *vice versa,* or whether they whimisically criss-cross the country, or any parts of it, or behave in an even more haphazard manner.

The essential point to keep in mind is simple: whatever the length of the individual rivers or the course they follow, the flow of water is most unevenly distributed among the regions. As a result, farm output, the frequency of cropping and the cropping pattern vary sharply in the different parts of the country. Admittedly, the anarchy in the availability of water is not *per se* against nature, since nature itself has bequeathed this state of things. But it certainly does violence to the concept of equity and equality so effusively elaborated in our Constitution. The natural lie of the nation's rivers is held to go against the directive principles of state policy which form the core of that august document.

The aforementioned noble people set their minds to correct what they considered to be an outrage of nature. They drew attention to the most ambitious hydraulic engineering widely featuring in the country, such as the multi-purpose river barrage works, including the great Bhakra-Nangal project. The principle of water regulation therefore was, they argued, already very much in place. What the wise men were now suggesting was, in their view, only an extension of the kind of activities already going on in the country: join the Ganges with the Cauvery, join the Tungabhadra with the Kosi, join the Narmada with the Brahmaputra, and so on. Let there be a grand design to distribute the total water available to the country equitably over all its territories. Let there be a national decision-making body at the apex to decide how much of the total water is to be made available to which state on which day of which week of which month of which year. True, this giganic operation was not going to be a cheap affair. According to preliminary estimates, it was likely to cost the nation plus-minus Rs. 5,00,000 crore, which is roughly one-third of the country's gross national product. There is, however, no reason to be upset, the outlay will be spread over a ten-year period. This amount of time will in any case be needed to sort out the technical, topological, geological, environmental, social and economic snarls that the execution of the stupendous project will call for.

The project will involve not only a massive movement of water systems. It will also necessitate movement of earth, rock, forests and settlements, and of course will involve the movement of millions and millions of people. It will mean brushing aside the barriers of limited sovereignty enjoyed by state governments, district administrations and *panchayat* bodies: they will cease to have authority not only over the movement of water in the rivers within their nominal jurisdiction; but also over the location of the people constituting their electorate. Their control over the land masses delineated as under their command could, if necessary, be derecognized so as to serve the cause of the great dream of one India—one river system.

Idealists weave the dreams. It is however politicians, administrators, engineers, contractors and promoters of diverse descriptions who execute the dreams. More often than not, these latter categories demand a commission or a cut for their labours. Many of them are agog with excitement: the gravy to flow from out of the total kitty of Rs. 5,00,000 crore will mostly travel toward their direction. True, it will be only over a ten-year period. Even so, a sum of Rs. 50,000 crore each year is not to be scoffed at.

But there are several other problems, and they will not go away. The country has had enough of trouble arising out of the Narmada Valley project, which too has involved re-allocation of human settlements and churning of a large number of social, economic and environmental issues. The Rs. 5,00,000 crore mega dream will be in magnitude easily a thousand times greater than the dimensions of the Narmada project; the dimensions of the problems the execution of the dream are likely to engender will be, rest assured, more than a thousand times more formidable. The ecological challenges alone are mind-boggling. That apart, given the various divisivenesses already plaguing the nation, the political convulsions to ensue in the wake of the first endeavours at interlinking of rivers are altogether unpredictable, some actually fear a collapse of whatever little cohesion there is still left in the nation. Capping all will be the challenge of moving millions of men, women and children from old river basins to new settlements, may be a thousand miles away, and finding for the populations thus uprooted from old moorings new livelihoods. All things considered, such as the circumstances in Jammu and Kashmir in the north, the explosive situation in Assam, Manipur and Nagaland in the east, and insurgent groups bestirring themselves in several other parts of the country, the wisest thing, one would have thought, will be to bury this particular mega dream for some while. What is intriguing is the report that this dream is also shared by the incumbent president of the republic. He has apparently chosen to don the garb of an activist in the matter and has gone public with his views. The Union council of ministers is expected to aid and advise the president on sensitive issues. It should do so with immediate effect in this particular matter; otherwise the danger lurks of not just a breach of propriety, but of much more.

A doubt, besides rears its head here : should not the noble thinkers, before embarking on mega dreams, give more modest ones a chance? Taking on nature itself, no less, is a testimony to the dreamers' imagination, but what about such lesser ventures that call for only a few administrative decisions to ensure better inter-regional equity; for instance, a more liberal allocation of bank advances for economically retarded states, or a directive that, for the next ten or twenty years, three-quarters of total Central investments taking place in the country must go to states with per capita income less than the national average?

29th October, 2004

The golden age

Whether the deputy chairman of the Planning Commission dragged him to the New York Stock Exchange or he went of his own volition is beside the point. The fact of the matter is that our prime minister was very much there, addressing the glitterati of American capitalism. The prime minister made one particular pitch; over the next ten years, he badly needs for India 150 billion dollars of foreign direct investment, the good capitalists of the United States of America must help him out. Managing the left inside the country, he assured his audience, was no problem; once the Indian economy proceeds swimmingly given the splurge of FDI, the country would shine for ever, the minor irritations would be forgotten by all quarters.

The prime minister must have done his homework. The amount of FDI he mentioned as crucially necessary to engineer a spurt in growth has to be taken seriously. Who knows, India's modest economic performance even in the post-liberalizartion phase could perhaps be because of the failure of foreign capital to rush in. Those who preside over foreign capital love an ambience where everything moves on a fast track. India has not till now provided such an ambience. In China, ther rate of growth has averaged 9 to 10 per cent annually in the recent period, so that the market for practically all varieties of goods and services is expanding by leaps and bounds. Foreign investors realize the profit-making opportunities such a situation presents; they do not have to be entreated to travel to China; they, on their own, make a beeline for that country.

Conditions are much more daunting in India. During the major part of the past decade, the rate of economic growth has here wobbled around 4 to 5 per cent per annum. The market has, in consequence, been rising at a rate much tradier than in China. FDI in fact stayed stuck at roughly $2 billion each year for most of the decade. Some improvement in FDI flow has taken place only in the last two fiscal years reaching $4.7 billion in both 2002-03 and 2003-04. Even so, it seems to be a sort of a vicious circle; foreigners would not come in unless economic prospects, according to official assessment, cannot improve unless foreign capital comes in greater quantities.

Taking the prime minister's words at their face value, the country needs in the course of the next decade an extra 8 to 10 billion dollars of FDI every year over what it has been getting of late in order to achieve a spectacular take-off in economic growth. Unless FDI of this order fructifies, things, he hints, would remain gloomy.

This is precisely where doubts arise. Without successful pursuit of American tycoons, the country, the prime minister is sure, will have no salvation; foreigners therefore have to be offered ingratiatingly attractive terms. Obviously, had we our own additional resources for investment, we would not need to be importunate with foreigners. But the country's decision-makers are known to have all facts at their fingertips. It is therefore permissible to assume that they are not unaware of one interesting datum: in the five-year period 1999-2000 to 2003-2004, India has imported a total of $25 billion of gold; the magnitude of such imports in the last fiscal year was as high as $6.5 billion. It is a free-for-all economic system we have been operating since 1991. The import of gold, either for conspicuous consumption in the form of jewels or as hoard, is without subject to any constraints. We are supposed to be a poor, underdeveloped nation, short of savings, which necessitates our prime minister to go out with a begging bowl beseeching funds from Western capitalists. But circumstances could change dramatically: provided the leakage of domestic savings in the form of gold imports stopped and these savings were instead directed into investments in areas of national priorities. The prime minister is a hunting for 8 to 10 billion dollars of additional FDI each year. By promulgating an order suspending gold imports, he would have at his disposal domestic resources covering the bulk of the requirement.

We are once more confronted by an issue crusaders of economic liberalism have placed on a moral pedestal: the government must not interfere with the freedom of choice on the part of the people. If they want gold rather than development, the authorities have no business to meddle in the matter. There can however be other moral problems as well. Those who hanker after gold are generally also those who have already enough of development. Should there be no extra investment in the coutnry, they would not be bothered in the least. At the other end, though, huge masses of the poor, the undernourished and the underprivileged are bound to benefit if, instead of importing gold, we use the nation's savings for adding to our capital stock, particularly in economic and social infrastructures. The problem of working out the strategy for growth is not therefore a mere matter of lobbying or not lobbying for foreign capital, often at terms that reduces the nation's sovereignty. It is equally a class question. The rich, who mostly do the savings, may not be prepared to allow these savings for purposes of national development that will more overtly benefit the poor. In other words, the prime minister has to humiliate himself and the nation in foreign fora because the wealthy sections will not permit their savings to serve the cause of national priorities.

Here, then, is the irony of the situation. The prime minister is the prime minister because the poorer sections have voted for a combination of political groups and parties who have agreed to have him installed in that position. His supplicant role before foreign investors is, on the other hand, causally related to the selfish attitude of the non-poor, who must have their luxuries, never mind what it costs the nation. (The pattern is invariant. The banks lend money at cheap rates so that more and more of cars, refrigerators and music systems are purchased by the affluent; but there will be horror if the banks were asked to advance funds to develop the country's infrastructure at similarly low rates.)

An incident during the early days of the "economic reforms" comes to mind. One opposition member of parliament wanted to draw the then finance minister's attention to an anomaly in the framework of the government's economic policy: he, the finance minister, wanted to have more savings in the system so that the pace of economic growth got speeded up; at the same time, he was providing huge incentives to the consumer electronic industry which could not but erode savings. The finance minister—the current prime minister—rose to reply to the opposition member: whatever his detractors might say, he was determined to encourage consumerism in the country; he had daughter who was a hard-working professional woman, her only relaxation was to watch the television in the evenings on her return from work; he would be a heartless parent to deprive the daughter of this little enjoyment; he would actually endeavour so that every daughter in the country came to possess a television set. The issue of economics was sidetracted; so what, there was thunderous thumping of desks reverberating across Samsad Bhavan.

This about sums up the Indian development dilemma. We prefer jewels and motor cars and television sets for our children today, the country's poor can fend for themselves. As for the future, as Doris Day sang long ago, that is not ours to see.

15th October, 2004

Dear money

Intense flutter in establishment dovecotes, the inflation rate has exceeded 8 per cent per annum, it threatens to scale even higher levels, something needs to be done. The greater worry is over the impact of rising prices on the forthcoming assembly elections in Maharashtra and elsewhere. People are so unreasonable, they get angry when prices rise and tend to vote against those in power, a few measures must be taken to salvage the situation. Not surprisingly, the issue of cheap money policy has once more come to the fore; perhaps a review is called for.

The problem has not emerged overnight. Ever since a deliberate decision was taken to bring down interest rates, the average bank deposit rate has lagged behind the rate of inflation. This has resulted in a continuous erosion in the real worth of whatever savings the majority of the nation are able or inclined to chalk up. Pensioners and other constituents of the middle class, along with fixed-income earners and wage workers who too have been hard hit, have registered their protest. Till recently, the authorities were not overly concerned. But, with prices sharply shooting up, there are now signs of an intensified awkwardness. Whatever the assurances held out by ministers and their minions, a further rise in prices seems inevitable: as long as the Americans are determined to stick it out in Iraq. The turmoil in the international oil market is unlikely to abate. The consequences are going to be grim for heavily oil importing countries such as India. Should the dogma of low deposit interest rates persist, domestic difficulties could only aggravate.

For policy-makers, the dilemma is real. Low deposit rates make for low lending rates, which, it was till now assumed, stimulate investment. Capital formation has been sluggish in the Indian economy in recent times. It has been so in the United States of America too. But there is a difference. Technological progress has been so rapid in the US that existing capital stock is more than adequate to produce the goods and services the nation needs. In fact, demand satiety in that country has led to the phenomenon of plants and factories scaling down activity from five days to four days in the week; in some instances factories hitherto working for four days have switched over to a three-day work schedule; workers have been asked to stay at home in the remaining days, with their emoluments fully protected.

In this kind of uncertainty, entrepreneurs naturally shy away from fresh capital investment. This however creates a crisis in the labour market; the roll of the unemployed lengthens. To quieten social discontent, fresh investment has to be coaxed into the economy. Monetary policy has been put to use for the purpose. The advice has gone out: lower and lower further the interest rate for bank lending, thereby inducing enterpreneurs to borrow more and expand their operations. Billions and billions of surplus funds are lying idle with the banking system; the US administration has been keen to put such funds to work through the mechanism of a cheap money policy.

Globalization, off and on also known as neo-colonialism, gives birth to copycat economics. Since the Americans have lowered interest rates, for dear life we too must also do so in India: such was the decision taken at the highest level half a dozen years ago or thereabouts. Bank deposit rates were slashed from 10 per cent and above to around 5 per cent and above to around 5 per cent. Identical situations, even if in different countries, it was maintained, necessitate identical treatment. Industrial recession haunts the US, it haunts India as well. Therefore, so went the prescription, follow the leader: to encourge investment and growth, force down interest rates in our country too in the manner it has been done in the US.

A basic flaw vitiates the argument though. In the US, there is no dearth of savings, the per capita income is in the neighbourhood of $30,000 or more per annum, the banks are awash with savings; the problem is to find outlet for such savings. In India, in contrast, given the pervasive poverty, savings are low. By bringing down interest rates, savings are not stimulated, but discouraged, thereby affecting investment. Low lending rates fail to give a boost to capital expansion for yet another reason: the lack of purchasing power of the nation's overwhelming majority keeps the demand function depressed. Entrepreneurs are no fools. Low interest rates do not induce them to expand their activities; the prospect of a healthy rate of return from new investments is, they know, circumscribed by the size of the market.

But perhaps there is more to it than meets the eye. In a class-riven society, the monetary establishment too panders to upper class dreams. Low interest rates are accordingly intended to serve another objective as well. A citizen with some savings at his disposal has the option of placing these savings either as deposit with the banks or for share market speculation. The economic history of several countries actually suggests an inverse relationship between economic growth and speculative gains; speculative activity takes a backseat when production surges forward on the wings of fresh capital formation sustained by rising bank deposits. Speculation, on the other hand, emerges as king when production slumps.

Pushing by fiat the interest rate down so that it falls below the rate of inflation may therefore be an excellent stratagem to advance the cause of favoured groups. Faced by the prospect of shrinking income and earnings, desperate citizens may choose to play Russian roulette in the share market; the banks in any case offer a piffle. Whatever the befuddled ordinary citizens lose in the bourses would line the pockets of the fat cats. The lobby favouring cheap money could, in the circumstances, continue to rule the roost.

Unless, of course, a shift in monetary theology takes place at the *sanctum sanctorum* itself. Reports are filtering in that precisely such a shift is taking place. While industrial recession persists, the American economy is nonetheless coming under increasing pressure, in the sense that prices of sensitive goods are going up inordinately. What was unthinkable till yesterday has therefore been permitted to enter the list of thinkables: monetary experts in the US have begun to urge a tightening of money supply to cool the economy; the bank rate is about to be raised. Therein lies subaltern hopes. Once the Federal Reserve system in the US raises interest rates, the Reserve Bank of India too is boud to spring to action and order the banks to raise deposit rates appreciably. As precursor, the cash-reserve ratio has already been raised.

What the authorities will do with lending rates is a different matter though. True, dear money policy may be defended on the classical ground that it weeds out the inefficient from the market. Affluent categories could, however, continue to obtain money from the banks at favoured rates because they supposedly served this or that national cause, such as export promotion, or promotion of tourism, and of course the sacred arena of information technology. The poor and the disadvantaged sections however are likely to continue to receive the short shrift, with the lending rate pitched high for them. This was necessary, it would be said, to cover the "risk factor"; providing finance to the impoverished classes, who does not know, is a risk venture. The truth is somewhat to the contrary; it is a claque of industrial and commercial tycoons who have till now failed to return an amount aggregating to as much as Rs. 200,000 crore they had borrowed from the commercial banks. They are bound to be treated with kid gloves while the poor are shown the door. This is high finance ordinary mortals are not expected to understand.

20th September, 2004

That sinking feeling

The gentleman is inconsolable. He is, he says, a "small" investor, and has lost as much as Rs. 120,000 in the post-election mayhem in the stock exchanges. For this great ill-fortune, he places the blame squarely on the left, whose offensive against privatization and disinvestment, he does not have the least doubt, was the cause of the market calamity.

Consider though the dilemma confronting the left. They fought the elections on the plank of opposing privatization and disinvestment which, in their judgment, have been the principal cause for the loss of jobs and growing immiserization of hundreds and thousands of countrymen belonging to the middle and working classes in the recent period. They fought the Lok Sabha polls on the basis of their anti "reforms" manifesto, and have achieved stunning success: close to four-fifths of the candidates they put up have got elected to the Lok Sabha. This rate of success is the highest amongst all political parties; for both the Congress and the Bharatiya Janata Partry, the rate is as low as one-third, or even less. If, as the gentleman alleges their obstinate reiteration of the theme of anti-privatization has been responsible for the downslide in the share markets, should the left go back on their commitments, betraying the mandate they have received from their supoorters? But will that not make a mockery of the democratic process?

Democracy is supposed to be a political system where the views of the people are reflected through periodic elections, and those elected are expected to honour the views endorsed by the people. The choice could not therefore be starker for the left: either they honour their pledge to those who voted for them and demand a surcease to the dismantling of the public sector, or they show deference to the susceptibilities of gentlemen such as our poor "small" investor, for whom soaring share prices are the be-all and end-all of existence. The left, how mean, decided to maintain their democratic integrity; our poor "small" investor is aghast.

Is there at least not some ground for probing the credentials of those who describe themselves as "small" investors? Taken at his word, the gentleman referred to in the opening sentence of this column lost Rs 120,000 due to share market upheavals immediately following the declaration of the poll outcome. Assume that he incurred all this loss on May 17 last—the Black

Monday—when the market took the deepest plunge; at one time, almost 800 points were shed off from the Sensex. In percentage terms, this decline of 800 points meant an erosion of share values to the extent of something like 15 per cent. Be generous; and make the further assumption that, because of the goings-on during that day, the shares held by our gentleman actually lost as much as 20 per cent of their value. Does this not however imply that the aggregate value of the shares he held was in the neighbourhood of Rs 600,000? Besides, it would be altogether incredible that a gentleman who could afford to lock up funds of the order of Rs. 600,000 in the stock exchanges, would not own other assets too, such as some bank money and one or two house properties. It would be a gross travesty of the dictionary meaning of terms and expressions if a genleman of this background is to be given the sobriquet of "small" investor. In any event, in a country where roughly a third of the population is perpetually hungry, where child mortality and female nutrition rates, as well as the standard of literacy, are about the worst in the United Nations listing, and so-called economic reforms have aggravated the living conditions of the poorer sections of the community, to assign greater priority to the share market woes of our selfcentred gentleman would be immoral—and indecent—by all criteria.

That apart, whatever his plight, the gentleman should not curse the left. Rather, he should begin by cursing himself. The left did not goad him into investing in the share market; he propelled himself toward that direction, perhaps influenced by allures held out before him by brokers and similar other species. Moreover, the left could not have worked the kind of havoc that was wrought on our bourses on Black Monday. They have no instruments at their disposal which could allow them to dictate terms at Dalal Street or India Exchange Place. That kind of clout is possessed by only the big operators who dominate the financial sector, the biggest of such operators are the foreign institutional investors, who have by now taken charge of all our stock exchanges. These major players are in a position to buy shares in bulk when prices rise an sell the same share later in the day; alternatively, they sell shares in bulk when prices are falling and buy back the shares later in the day. They are the architects of both bull runs and bear squeezes. Our "small" investors merely follow their lead.

What happened on Black Monday bore the imprint of a major bear operation launched by the big operators, including the FIIs. They were out to frighten the daylights out of the political establishment: concede too much to the left, and we will befoul the share market, which will affect the country's economic stability. The unfolding events of the days had the hallmark of a massive act of blackmail, accompanied by a threat to repeat the blackmail every now and then. If only the government would gather the courage to institute an enquiry into the detailed proceedings of that day, much of the truth will be out.

The authorities may yet have their own reason for not ordering such an investigation. Meanwhile, a further clarification is perhaps well in order. The loss our "small" investor suffered on Black Monday could have been just a paper loss: if he did not get overly panicky and unload his shares once prices started crashing, he might still have saved himself from suffering any major mishap; share prices recovered quite a bit later on the day itself and, despite some minorihccoughs, have since regained a measure of "stability". Why lament over a loss that might not in fact have occurred?

Back to *Julius Caesar.* The fault does not lie in the stars—nor in the shenanigans of the left—but in the behaviour of the "small" investors themsleves. You will come to my parlour: said the spider to the fly! The fly obliged. "Small" investors in their droves moved to the stock exchanges along with their savings. They had the option to keep these savings in term deposit with the banks. Such deposits were fully assured, but the return was low. By bringing down the rate of interests the banks are permitted to offer, the government has seen to it that the ordinary citizen discarded the savings habit and flocked to the share market. This was supposed to be in consonance with the grammar of economic reforms. Low interest rates, it was argued, will encourage entrepreneurs to borrow more and invest more in productive activities. What has come about is precisely the reverse; low interest rates have stifled savings and given a boost to the speculative forces active in the bourses. What fool will keep money in the banks to earn a measly five or six per cent return when investing in shares might yield, overnight or in the course of the day, as much as one hundred per cent return, or even more? Contrary to capitalist wisdom, for poor countries awfully lagging behind in basic investments in agriculture, industry and infrastructure, obsession over the state of health of the share markets is antigrowth and therefore anti-people. Money spent in speculation is money that cannot be invested in growth; it is high time to call the bluff of the big market operatives, including FIIs.

But such harsh truth does not go down well with the society's creamy layer. If only, during the past five or ten years, the lucky dogs at the top themselves chose to shine a little less and cared to bring a teeny-weeny cheer to the daily living of the nation's overwhelmingly poor, the electoral verdict would presumably have been somewhat different and their *bete noire,* the left, would have stayed in the wilderness.

11th June 2004

Follow the market

Those were its proselytizing days, in the Sixties. The World Bank used to display before bemused governments of poor countries resorting to price controls a sparkling pearl of wisdom: do not deride the blackmarketeer; instead, honour him. The price he charges reflects social reality; it is because the supply of a commodity is awfully short in relation to its demand that the blackmarketeer sets the price high; this encourages additional output and thereby close the demand-supply gap. On the other hand, when the government, by imposing price controls, puts the squeeze on profit margins it deters further output and additional supply. It is therefore the blackmarketeer who is the purveyor of genuine social welfare. The market is king, the blackmarketeer scrupulously obeys the dictates of the market.

The officially sponsored and officially sustained Indian Institutes of Management have been major promoters of the free-market doctrine in our country. Following globalization, their prestige and influence have grown exponentially. What they teach is in accordance with the wavelength of the Washington consensus, and the Washington consensus shapes the destiny of the world. The IIM graduates are naturally in great demand. Spokesmen of the IIMs have now made it a habit. On the eve of the academic session each year, their spokesmen do a press-briefing to inform countrymen how successful their boys and girls have been in today's intensely competitive market; even before they obtain their formal certificates of graduation, they are snapped up by the corporate sector, and some of them by major multinational companies. And, what do you know, their starting emoluments are a minimum of six or eight or ten or twelve lakh rupees per annum; those picked by the global companies, at least some of them, earn as much as one million dollars annually in their Newfoundland, their America.

The majesty of the market is the ruling idea. It engrosses society. Admission to any of the six IIMs is the dream of every boy and girl in the country, at least every boy and girl from aspiring families. All told, IIMs offer only 1,500 seats each year, while the number of applications easily exceeds 150,000. A common admission test is held to select the top one per cent of the candidates and weed out the rest. Competition, fearsome competition, is the name of the game. Those who fail to enter the portals of the IIMs are obviously a frustrated lot. To console them, ersatz management schools have sprouted all over the country offering crash courses of doubtful value at fancy prices. There is no dearth of takers for these courses too. Water finds its own level; backwater also does.

Let us however return to the problems encountered by seekers of admission to any of the IIMs. Market signals are not for spurning. An IIM graduate, evidence says, fetches the highest price in the job market, so much so that even many Indian Institute of Technology graduates, after receiving their B. Tech or M. Tech degrees, gladly spend another two years to get the imprimatur of an IIM graduation.

The demand for admission into the IIMs is high. The demand for a modality which either ensures or heightens the chance of admission to an IIM is therefore equally high. Demand creates its own supply. In the circumstances, some enterprising people assume the responsibility to arrange for such a modality, they organize a racket to leak the papers for the CAT organized by the IIMs, and charge for their service what the market rate will be. According to gossip, the market pirce quoted per one leaked paper is as high as four or five lakh rupees.

Everything was hunky-dory till recently. Suddenly, a kink has developed. A number of the smart entrepreneurs who were at work leaking the CAT papers have been caught at one or two centres this year. The discomfited Union minister for human resource development has taken the initiative to cancel the test taken at each and every centre. This has caused chagrin among candidates who appeared at the centres where the leak did not take place. As of now, confusion abounds.

What is still difficult to understand is the feigned sense of outrage in genteel society at these goings on. If one embraces the market principle, one must go the whole hog, no scruples should be allowed to encumber the rake's progress. The racketeers who arranged for the CAT leak have followed the teaching of the World Bank mentioned earlier to the minutest detail. The bank hailed the blackmarketeer because the blackmarketeer's acts and activities, according to its judgment, mirrored social reality. But why stop with the blackmarketeer? Why not include others as well in the pantheon of market-loving gods and goddesses? The law of the land may suggest that the persons who engaged in the business of leaking CAT papers are guilty of criminality. The law of the market however does not say so. The racketeers involved where merely responding to a challenge posed by the market. Admission an IIM is as good as admission to El Dorado. A leaked CAT paper facilitates admission to the IIM. There is therefore a fantastically high demand for a leaked paper in the market. The racketeers took the initiative to arrange for the supply required to satiate the demand. Have a heart, the price they charged—four or five lakh of rupees or whatever—was market determined and hence sacrosanct.

It is a moot issue. We cannot embrace globalization and the doctrine of the free market, and yet be choosy. Having scrapped price controls and done away with other restrictions on the market, it is no longer in our domain to be squeamish. The legal system the nation has inherited is also a moral system. That structure of morality is in conflict with the signalling system laid down by the market forces. Let us be blunt. The issue is not just the narrow specific happenstance of the "scandal" of the CAT leak, it really is a tussle between the old morality and the new ethos.

To consider another instance. The government at the Centre is not, apparently, the least concerned about development. Apart from *Hindutva,* it has its focus on China and Pakistan. It would like to spend all the money it can collect on defence, including nuclear defence, and security. In order to augment its own resources for such purposes, it has been advised to flout constitutional norms and conventions and deny the state governments their fiscal dues. Propelled by the same motive, the Centre prints money at zero cost and charges fantastically high interest when lending the money to the states. The states are in consequence in dire trouble. The government in New Delhi is a distant entity. The state governments, in contrast, are next door to the people who howl for food and apparel and literacy and shelter and jobs.

The pressure is nearly unbearable on the state administrations: they must either fulfil the people's aspirations or death to them. Frightened out of their wits, they run hither and thither, in search of funds which could be put to use to enlarge health and education facilities and create income and employment opportunities in industry, agriculture and infrastructure. Advice flows freely to the states' politicians and administrations: do not stand on ceremony, it is a hard competitive world, pursue the potential investors and other money-givers wherever they foregather. In case you find a group of potential investors congregating at a golf course on an indolent afternoon, please agree to act as their caddies for the afternoon; as you cart around their sporting paraphernalia, do tell them how investmentworthy your environs are and superior to other environs, they may take pity and offer you a few crumbs.

But suppose these would-be-investors, mostly foreigners, love to spend most hours of their weekend in a massage parlour, which no doubt has a more sophisticated French sobriquet, *maison* this or *maison* that. Would you also invade this parlour with your brochures and videotapes, even if such leisure activities as the parlour specializes in are illegal in the country? This can pose a problem. It can actually be a moral problem too. But whatever it is, should you fall prey to it, or obey the law of the market, since otherwise you will be unable to survive? No question. The advice will be: be a good boy, and fall in; you must not tinker with the market; rather, change your law.

28th November 2003

Tidings from Cancun

In the wake of the stalemate in Cancun, the Indian commerce minister, always confident and suave-looking, offered a judgement: the major lesson from Cancun, he observed, was that economic issues, whether at the national or the international level, need to be considered in isolation of political issues.

How naïve can one be, or seem to be? What, after all, are the positive achievements of the World Trade Organization ministerial meeting in the Mexican resort city? For the developing countries, the principal outcome is not just the rejection of the proposal to continue the inordinately high farm subsidies now prevalent in the advanced industrial countries. The latter group of countries have been told in no uncertain terms that reciprocity is the heart of the matter: if Europeans and North Americans are reluctant to cut down drastically their farm subsidies, as far as the poor countries are concerned, no further progress with trade liberalization is possible on their part either.

The second success story, which has not received the prominence it deserved in media reporting, is the virtual stalling of the agenda set up half a dozen years ago at Singapore. Governments of the developing countries had then abjectly caved in and accepted, as prime subsequent tasks of the WTO, the initiation of measures towards liberalization of investment policy, competition policy, public procurement and the services sector. Were this agenda insisted upon, their macro-economic management would in effect be handed over by the poorer to the richer nations; with the Washington Consensus determining the contours of domestic as well as international economic policy. The passionate brawl in Cancun over agricultural subsidies, which blanked out all other themes, put paid to Western ambitions in this respect.

Consider the factors which helped the poorer countries to record these triumphs. At the core of the success was the presence of the solid phalanx of anti-globalization demonstrators, laying a siege at the conference venue for days on end, thousands and thousands of protestors from the different continents. It was political drama of the most intense type, ringing out the clarion call: "injustice shall not pass". Lee Kyung Hae's martydom signified a noble, heroic climax to the proceedings.

The breadth of the protest movement, and its organizational vigour, unnerved as much the representatives of the rich countries as the intending

Judases amongst governments of the poorer nations. The global protest has ceased to be an occasional international nuisance, it has evolved into a great ethical phenomenon, before which both the greedy crowd and the feebleminded stragglers could only cower. Without question, this is the most significant global development over the past decade; politics is in command, and has taken charge of economic issues.

The second political factor at work is of equal import. For the first time, China functioned as a strategic member of the WTO. It made its weight felt. This meant a qualitative difference to the in-house parleys: China's has been in recent times the fastest growing national economy, with an increasingly major share in global exports. Yet another factor helped to tilt the scales at Cancun: Brazil has now a national government presided over by an incorrigible left idelogue, and is no longer a pushover. China, Asia's biggest nation, and Brazil, Latin America's biggest, became the prime movers of resistance to Western blandishments; the respect they drew facilitated the cementing of the concordat of the poor. This too is a development of immense significance. India could not dare to break ranks; even the ordinarily prime Indian mandarindom, befuddled by the turn of events, is unable to predict how the international balance of power is going to shift in the immediate and not so immediate future.

For there is a further exogenous explanation of why the American administration and its friends failed to shatter the unity of the poorer countries. Post-Iraq, the United States of America, while still the world's mightiest political and economic power, is in real danger of being reduced to the status of almost a paper tiger. The number one crony, Tony Blair, is fighting for his political life; the report of the Hutton commission might well prove to be his swansong.

What is more daunting, American public opinion has suddenly begun to swing wildly against George W. Bush. The number of body bags shipped from Iraq is regularly increasing, leading to widespread public disaffection at home. Even the portals of Washington's stodgy National Press Club, the *sanctum sanctorium* of the US establishment, is no longer a safe haven for the US defence secretary, or, for the matter, the president himself; doubts are being freely expressed over the re-electability of the president in the elections next year. Even the frog feels superior when the elephant gets bogged down in a marsh. Not surprisingly, fainthearts have come to gather courage, the US government has been unable to persuade the majority of the 148 member-nations of the WTO into rubberstamping the draft resolution it sponsored.

What does all this add up to? Quite obviously, success in economic causes is a basic product of political pulls and conter-pulls. And it is only a beginning, a very mild beginning. Within the Indian delegation too, political considerations emerged to the fore. The Federation of Indian Chambers of Commerce and Industry-Confederation of Indian Industry lobby must have dearly loved to strike a deal with the Americans, since that might have helped to push up India's exports to the US from the current level of around four billion dollars to something doubie of that over the next few years, and thereby countered the ongoing industrial recession in the country. Poor farmers, who will be at the receiving end of any such side deal with the US, however, make up a much larger slice of the Indian electorate. Crucial elections are in the offing; the Bharatiya Janata Party-led regime had therefore little choice but to join the China-Brazil *entente.*

Political calculations nonetheless, change ever so swiftly every now and then. Poll arithmetics can be made to swim this way or that by coalition permutations and combinations worked out by political parties; the farm lobby could lose its clout over New Delhi's government following the emergence of a new situation. Besides, no Judas today does not guarantee no Judases for tomorrow. Should Hindu fundamentalism take over the BJP lock, stock and barrel, the ruling thought may veer towards the dream of a grand American-Israeli-Indian armed conglomerate. There could be other developments worldwide, and the solidarity of the poor nations might turn out to be a transitory episode.

But, then, prognosis on such issues is awfully difficult. Habits do not dissolve overnight. American citizens, having got used to relatively cheap consumer goods from China, India and Brazil, could be unwilling to give up merchandise coming from these countries; their votes too count in US elections. This possibility may still not calm the nervousness of the New Delhi regime. It may start worrying over the consequences of an adverse impact of retributive measures launched by the American administration. It may also decide not to take seriously the point of view that clamping restrictions on importables from the poorer countries through tariffs and quotas could make the US itself a major defaulter of WTO rules.

Those determined to surrender national sovereignty to external forces may choose not to be detained for long by the realpolitik of global trade. The danger remains of an Indian capitulation, if not within the next few months, may be after the Lok Sabha elections next year. The necessity of vigilance—on the political front—therefore cannot be wished away.

A couple of concluding thoughts. First, for close to forty years, India has refused to have any meaningful conversation with China. In retrospect, this has been a major blunder. China's annual exports to the US stand at close to 125 billion dollars. These comprise an impressive array of mostly consumer goods which the Americans would hate not to be continuously supplied with at the present reasonable prices. China also holds exchange reserves exceeding 700 billion dollars that are swelling at the annual rate of 100 billion dollars.

It will be wise on our part to forget past animosities, and attempt to arrive at an arrangement with our northern neighbours so that some of the more abrasive moves of the Washington Consensus can be effectively resisted through joint action. This will also enable us to stay on the right side of the Arab world. Secondly the Western discommfiture at Cancun can certainly be availed of to propose a re-appraisal of the existing staffing structure of the WTO secretariat. It currently acts as an articulator of the interests of the highly rich, industrialized Western countries. It must be changed so as to be in accord with emerging global realities.

19th September, 2003

Dog day afternoon

Smugness overwhelms. The Reserve Bank of India, bathed in self-importance, has raised its estimate of the rate of growth in gross domestic product in the current year. Reason: the state of the monsoon, now performing better than earlier assumed. The RBI need not have bothered, even a boy or a girl at the primary level, just initiated in arithmetic, could have done a similar revision in the GDP estimates. The accolade for the RBI is nonetheless deafening: it is as if any day the president would announce a special Bharat Ratna for the RBI governor for doing such a good turn to the nation.

There is fierce competition even in the race for naiveté. After being in the doldrums for quite some while, the sensitive index is suddenly behaving in a manner which suggests a tiger has been put in its tank; it has crossed 4,300 and might soon leap beyond 5,000. The India Incorporated circuit are exhibiting a Pavlovian response; given the evidence of the sensex, they too are sanguine, there is no stopping Indian economic growth.

The logic is simple, market sentiments reflect the psychology of entrepreneurs as well as of buyers; the spurt in the share market heralds the strengthening of the forces of both supply and demand, the economy is consequently bound to move forward.

But dozens and dozens of instances can be quoted from 20th century British and American economic history where buoyancy in the share market did not lead to buoyancy in economic activities; the actual development was precisely to the contrary, production of goods and services turned sluggish, investment was lowly, and economic recovery was a will-o'-the-wisp.

The explanation for the seeming puzzle was simple. As share prices picked up, entrepreneurs, who were going through a dull phase, decided to cross over to investing in the stock exchanges rather than engaging in new investments; householders with money to spare also preferred to speculate in the share market rather than go for greater purchase of consumables. History bears witness to a similar relationship in the reverse direction as well: when bears take charge of the stock exchanges. speculators burn their fingers; scared by such a development, investors, reluctantly or otherwise, engage in investing in new economic activities and thus contribute to GDP growth.

India Incorporated, like the government in New Delhi, have been incompetent prognosticators in recent times: their post-liberalization bragging of a major breakthrough in the economy has been repeatedly belied. They are in danger of being proved wrong once again. The latest cheery news from the bourses may actually divert funds away from new investment into share speculation, causing a further setback to industrial production. Whimsical weather could then combine with the zigzaggedness of investment intentions and hold back the nation's economic prosperity.

Yet another phenomenon is worth probing. In the course of the past half a dozen years, the major stock exchanges in the country have been by and large taken over by foreign institutional investors. Close to $ 40 billion have freshly entered the Indian system during these years; the overwhelming part of this flow has not added to domestic capital formation, and, instead, travelled to the share markets. Ground exists for inferring that it is these foreign funds which have smothered the stock exchanges in a great bear hug, and kept share prices depressed, since the late Nineties. The foreign investors have by now purchased a sufficiently large number of shares of Indian companies at rock bottom prices. This has been however only the first half of the total operation they have in mind. To complete their design, they will perhaps henceforth use their clout to engineer a bull run in the stock exchanges.

The securities and exchange board of India is no match for the resourcefulness of FIIs. The latter therefore will have their way and could, over the next few months, try to inject a fervour in the market; share prices might soar and soar. Once the FIIs reach the judgement that enough was enough, they might then begin unloading. They will thereby make a killing, the profits they reap could amount to several billion dollars. The investors from overseas might simultaneously decide that these profits deserved to be repatriated while the going was good and free convertibility was still available for short-term fund. In such an eventuality, India could well be the scene of a rerun of the 1997-98 debacle which overtook South Korea, Taiwan, Hong Kong, Thailand and Indonesia.

The half-empty *versus* half-full bottle joke about the distinguishing mark separating a pessimist from an optimist is a cliche, but a pessimist is at least right 50 per cent of the times according to the statistical theory on normal probability distribution. The facts are in any case uncomfortable. We have gradually played ourselves into an impossible corner in economic matters, form which we can be extricated only with the intermediation of external forces.

Two such forces are predominant. First, although farming activities contribute barely a quarter of our total domestic product, agriculture still provides the sustenance for more than three-fifths of the Indian population. As a result, the national economy, despite the so-called five-year plans and despite the more recent free market genuflections, continues to be a gamble on the monsoon. In the second place, in the industrial, including manufacturing sector, expectations as well as performance remain heavily dependent on the exogenously determined factor of availability of foreign funds. Direct foreign investment does not enter, or registers only a perfunctory presence; Indian industrial production therefore lags behind. The share market, captured by foreign finance, too plays the dance of the marionette.

Foreigners connive, the shares fall; foreigners inject vigour, the shares take off toward the direction of Mars. The only difference differentiating the past from the rude present is that, in the past, we had only one Almighty, the rain god, determining our destiny; now there are two of them, the rain god and the investing deities arriving from foreign lands.

That the India Incorporated circus is really Impotence Incorporated is revealed by the data recently released by official quarters on total investment that took place in the country's industrial sector in 2002-03. Domestic investment in all the sectors taken together is less than Rs. 10,000 crore. Since the GDP is currently hovering around one million crore, not even one percent of the GDP is being set aside for industrial capital formation.

This by all accounts is an extraordinary situation. India, it would appear, is in danger of being reduced to the status of a dependant economy, such as Brazil once was—a huge economic apparatus whose engine of growth is positioned outside the system. And while Brazil over a long period was dependent upon only North American investors, we are subjugated to the moodiness of the monsoon, and have combined this with a systemic bondage relationship with foreign investors: till as long as direct foreign investment does not come, India will not grow till as long as foreign investors are in control of India's share markets—these will be prone to grotesque volatility, again holding back economic growth. All that apart, till as long as Indian agriculture is not liberated from the vagaries of the monsoon, the country will continue to languish.

Unless of course, anarchy altogether changes the script. Organized anarchy, or anarchy which subsequently learns how to organize itself, gets known as revolution. Anarchy which shies away from revolution gets described as progressive degeneracy. In a climate dominated by degeneracy, it is dog day afternoon, the likes of Praveen Togadia, Nitin Parikh and Pappu Yadav wielding the stick.

5th September 2003

The great train robbery

Parliamentarians and state legislators indulge in their regular frivolities, walk-outs alternate with inane shouting bouts on the floor of the house. Meanwhile, the Great Train Robbery in the form of substitution of the sales tax system by the value-added tax is about to reach its denouement. Nobody seemingly cares. It is now left to the degree of political pressure nervous traders can generate to determine whether the proposed cross-over, which is an outrage, is going to be a settled issue.

It has been quite a grand design. The World Trade Organization places country governments on notice: every member-country should, by 2005, enforce a uniform VAT applicable to each corner of the country, they have also to ditch that abomination, sales taxation, with varying rates of sales tax in different parts of the country, which impedes economic integration so necessary for capitalist expansion. All member countries will have to, post-haste, submit to the WTO fiat. The United States of America will, of course, be the exception. The US, being the US, is beyond the pale of the United Nations rules and international agency diktats,

India is not the US. It has therefore to comply with the WTO directive. Even otherwise, the two main political parties in the country, the Indian National Congress and the Bharatiya Janata Party, believe in the concentration of authority, including fiscal administration, in the hands of the Centre. Any measure which adversely affects the economic viability of state governments—and correspondingly benefits the Centre—is a welcome development for both parties. A VAT they will welcome with hugs and kisses.

There is a stumbling block though. The sales tax is an item entered in the state list in the seventh schedule of the Constitution. Neither the Union government nor the states can, on their own, get rid of the sales tax system without amending the Constitution. Introduction of the VAT poses a similar problem. The authors of the Constitution had envisaged a certain balance in the distribution of fiscal power between the Centre and the states. To disturb that in any manner without a constitutional amendment is clearly a preposterous proposition.

At the same time not obeying the WTO is inconceivable. New Delhi therefore set up a stratagem, a stratagem to cheat the Constitution. The

Union finance minister convened a meeting of state chief ministers on November 16, 1999. The finance minister and his official were at their charming best. The Centre is not intervening, but it is for the states to recognize what a great boon it will be if the clumsy sales tax system, with a rates structure varying from state to state for each and every commodity, were replaced by the VAT featured by country-wide uniformity in tax rates. That will render India into one integrated market, entrepreneurs and industrialists will be saved the bother of developing different investment and production strategies for different states; in consequence, a furious economic spurt will ensue. thereby actually resulting in much greater accrual of revenue in the state government coffers.

The states fell for the bait; at least their ministers did. A so called empowered committee of state finance ministers was set up inside the ministry of finance in New Delhi; it was serviced, and hence dominated, by ministry of finance officials; the mind at work was that of the Centre, the hand that wrote was of the states. The states were persuaded to believe that it was a canard to allege that the Centre was guiding the committee's decisions. No sire, the Centre is not twisting our arm, we are twisting it ourselves. Everything was apparently hunky-dory in the begining. The change-over, it was tacitly agreed, was to take effect from April, 2002. The date was subsequently shifted to April 2003, and then further pushed to June. The early optimism faded; things were not proceeding altogether smoothly, while the WTO deadline was only two years away.

For the constitutional hurdle loomed large. Close to thirty states have to enact legislation to scrap sales taxation and introduce the VAT. The latter tax instrument, given its country-wide ambit, is to be, in all senses and purposes, a Central legislation, and an altogether new entity. The Constitution does not however give any authority to either the Centre or the states to chop or change its, that is the Constitution's, corpus just like that, without a constitutional amendment. When in November 1999 the state chief ministers, under the tutelage of the Union finance minister, agreed to replace the existing sales tax by the VAT, the thought of the constitutional hurdle must have worried them. The sales tax is a tax on the sale of a commodity or service; the VAT is an impost on the value added at each point of production of a commodity or a service, and is without any direct nexus with sales. It is not a sub-species of sales tax, but a different animal altogether.

The Union government knew it would be impossible for it to pass a constitutional amendment for scrapping sales taxation and inserting the VAT in either the Union or the concurrent list; such an attempt will immediately make obvious the larceny that was on. The compliant "empowered" committee was therefore advised by the ministry of finance to take the route of subterfuge. The legislation the states will embark on will be intended to replace the old sales tax by the new VAT, but the exercise will be described as a change in the method of sales taxation, a task well within the jurisdiction of the states, and not necessitating a constitutional amendment. The dishonesty could not be more palpable.

If the new tax were merely to effect a change in the method of sales taxation, the nomenclature of the proposed legislation would have been the Sales Tax (Amendment) Act, and not the VAT. Sales taxation is the exclusive prerogative of the states, while the new legislation will take away this prerogative from the states and substitute it by a tax which will in practice be controlled and regulated by the Centre. That this will be the reality has been confirmed by the statements of the Union finance minister in Parliament. Under the pretence of acting as a "facilitator", the Centre has taken charge of the whole business of implementing, nation-wide, the VAT.

It is going to be the deciding voice in such crucial matters as commodity classification, rate fixation and identification of taxable items, and order the states accordingly. The ministry of finance has already evolved a set of parameters in these matters and the states must scrupulously conform to these in their drafting of the VAT legislation. Till now only one state, Madhya Pradesh, has conformed to the Centre's directives and its legislation has received presidential assent. Seven other states, which too have presented their VAT legislation for the president's assent, have failed to meet the Centre's specification, assent has been withheld in their cases. They have to fall in line, so too the 20 other states who have yet to pass the statute in their respective legislatures.

All this is turning out to be a messy affair. To circumvent the Constitution and yet fully respect the WTO writ separate legislation is necessary for each state. The state legislations need to be drafted in a uniform manner, definition of terms and expressions must be identical for all states, so too the rate of duty for each and every commodity. As the deadline approaches, most states have begun to wake up to the dangerous possibilities latent in the VAT, although the realization is yet to sink in that, once the change-over occurs, the states will be reduced to the state of total vassaldom to the Centre.

This is then the Great Train Robbery of which the political parties, who foam in their mouth in season and out of season in the cause of states' rights, appear to be blisssfully unaware of. It will be an irony of some sort if the planned stealing is finally thwarted more by small time tax dodgers concerned about the privacy of their account books than by those who dream of a decentralized India where the states come to full bloom after wresting greater powers and its sources for themselves, and the Centre left with only a few delegated rights.

But suppose the Centre succeeds in crushing all opposition and threatens to initiate the new measure right from the next month—or the next year—what about the judiciary? Should it not please sit up and expose the on-going masquerade for what it is?

3rd May, 2003

Games ministers play

It is hardly a private spat between two cabinet ministers of the Union government. The minister for communications and the minister for disinvestment may have their subjective reasons to fly at each other's throats. But the issues involved are far-reaching and raise basic questions on the intent behind the headlong rush towards dismantling public assets that were assiduously built in two score years since independence.

A major objection to the presence of the public sector in industry and trade is the stimulus it allegedly provides to crony capitalism. Politicians control the public sector units which produce essential inputs and intermediate goods. These are sold to private parties who happen to be favourites of politicians at subsidized rates. Such transactions include the sale of power, water, ores, fertilizers, pesticides, and so on. The practice, it is argued, allows scope for the proliferation of a select group of capitalists who cannot claim any special entrepreneurial talent, but whose only credentials are their repute as ministerial cronies.

This must end forthwith, thunder the critics; the tradition thus set up not only lacks transparency, but it also makes the system scandalously discriminatory: merit is relegated to an obscure corner and pets of politicians have the decks heavily stacked in their favour. What emerges is a travesty of free competition; darkness at noon even within the precincts of the private sector.

Disinvestment supposedly, once and for all, terminates this ignoble phase of crony capitalism, and activates the animal spirit lying dormant in kindred souls. Let the government sell off all its industrial and commercial outfits, let these be taken over by private enterprises, none of which possesses any differential advantage over others such as are causally related to proximity to government.The upshot is the dawn of quintessential capitalism, leading to all-round economic efficiency and maximization of welfare for each and all.

A lovely theory. The recent privatization of Videsh Sanchar Nigam Limited and its takeover by the Tatas have however demonstrated how hollow the theory is. The Tatas purchased 25 per cent of VSNL's equity through a bidding process. Since it was open bidding, and others too could join in, apart from the shares the VSNL unloaded *via* negotiations, additional share-holding amounting to 20 per cent of total equity was also netted by TTSL, thereby enabling it to acquire 45 per cent of equity and total management control.

Of course the old order changeth yielding place to new. The very first act of the newly constituted board of directors of VSNL was to recommend that a hefty sum of Rs. 1,200 crore be withdrawn from its reserve funds to acquire roughly one quarter of TTSL's equity. It was a marvellous coup. A one sentence resolution led to the diminution of VSNL's assets and a corresponding accretion of TTSL reserves. Should the operation be honoured with an appropriate sobriquet, it can be described as crony capitalism in the service of predatory capitalism. The minister for disinvestment has acted as best man for crony capitalism so that it could transit to predatory capitalism. Or is it the other way round, predatory capitalism gaining new frontiers in the guise of crony capitalism? Definitions will not and do not make any difference to the reality of things, which is as clear as clarity can be: VSNL's loss is TTSL's gain; the magic of inter-corporate investment ensuing in the irresistible advance of a preferred group of capitalists into a luscious segment of the economy without any toil or trouble of financial outlay.

The apologists for the ministry of disinvestment and TTSL—and these include distingushed pseudo-academic journals as well—have ready explanations for the sleight of hand performed. The new management, it is being suggested, did the right thing by buying in TTSL: the link-up will do VSNL a whole lot of good; TTSL owns licences for basic services for six telecommunications circles and will hence be able to pave the way for VSNL's critical access to direct customers; such access will enable it to have a finger in the pie of huge revenues earned from international long distance services. Compared to the potential swelling of VSNL profits, the investment of Rs. 1,200 crore is therefore small beer. But was not an alternative route to El Dorado available to VSNL? It could have created similar access to direct consumers through the intermediary of, for instance, public sector entities like Bharat Sanchar Nigam Limited and Mahanagar Telephone Nigam Limited with zero additional outlay. Was the strategic sale then not disinvestment just for the sake of disinvestment, not just for weakening the assets position of the public sector network, but also for enriching, through an instant painless process, the assets of a favoured private party?

Given the murky nature of goings on both in the corporate world, and the political sphere, it could even be that the ministry of communications too had its own favourite of a private party and it hates to be tripped up by the ministry of disinvestment. Speculations concerning the matter can indeed be endless.

It is conceivable that the minister for disinvestment wanted to kill several birds with one stone: he wanted VSNL to be transferred to the private sector, he wanted to sabotage the expansion of integrated telecommunications services in the public sector; and finally, he wanted a prefered private party to expand its assets at zero cost to itself but at enormous cost to the public. And the minister for communications could perhaps be sore not only on account of the shrinkage of his departmental ambit, but, who knows, also on account of his failure to advance the cause of the private crony he himself favours.

The minister for disinvestment's horizon of expectations need not be unduly constricted either. From crony capitalism to predatory capitalism is only one short step. The next step is the transition of predatory capitalism to monopoly capitalism. Perhaps the minister has a certain perspective plan already worked out. Now that the Reliance group has taken over the Indian Petrochemicals Corporation Limited, and more similar lateral integrations are possible in the course of the next few years, the Ambanis could come to have total monopoly over the petrochemical sector in the country.

The minister might have a similar development in mind for the telecommunications sector, with the Tatas acting as flagship of telecommunications monopoly. In due season the entire spectrum of industry, commerce and other services could be neatly parcelled up among several monopolies. India would then be rendered into a world of monopolies in the truest sense.

A residual question would still be relevant. From the holy beginnings in 1991, we have witnessed a substantial order of disinvestment. The hypothesis that the demolition of the public sector induces foreign invstment to come in has however been belied, thereby also frustrating the hope of fast output growth. Orthodox economics offers few glimmers of growth optimism with respect to the proliferations of monopolies too. Monopoly output, according to theory, is invariably less than output under competition.

The prospect therefore is transparently clear. In the name of competition we will have disinvestment and private monopolies, resulting in thinning national capital stock accompanied by a diminishing rate of output. All this is supposed to be high-grade economics.

Which is why economics is known as the dismal science.

14th June, 2002

Enter the sheriff

Even without the calamity of September 11, 2001, the Indian economy was already in deepest distress. Following liberalization, the pronouncements the Confederation of Indian Industry are as good as official: the private domain has come to reign supreme over the public. For the current fiscal year, the CII has offered some grim predictions. Agricultural growth will dip to as little as 1.25 per cent. The prospect for the industrial sector is much worse. A pall of gloom has descended upon Indian manufacturing. Not only is investment, both domestic and foreign, playing hooky; utilization of existing capacity too is awesomely disappointing. The confederation has stretched itself to the utmost to make the picture as rosy as it is possible to make. No go, the rate of industrial growth in 2001-2002, the CII has concluded, will be barely 0.75 per cent.

Were the projected annual rates of growth for agriculture and industry combined, the aggregate rate of growth for the two sectors will at most be 1 per cent. Even taking into account the famine year of 1966-1967, not once since independence has the rate of growth for agriculture and industry together fallen to such a piteously low level, and this despite the fact that the monsoon has been normal this year.

As mentioned above, industrial growth is being held back so much because of lack of capacity. Even the lack of infrastructure cannot provide an alibi for the quasi-stagnation. In a situation where employment is sluggish and the vast majority of the nation is bereft of the wherewithal to raise the level of its demand, production is bound to be held back. These facets of reality however fail to impress the soulmates of the globalization lobby. They are an undeterred lot. Don't you know, India is as good as an advanced economy, agriculture and industry are no longer as important as they were in the primary stage of the development, more than 50 per cent of our ntional income now originates in the services sector?

True, this sector too has been adversely affected by the slackening industrial and agricultural growth; growth in services in the current year will not be as high as 8 per cent or 10 per cent or 15 per cent as was the case in some of the earlier years. Nonetheless, it will be at least 6.5 per cent so that, what a relief, the overall rate of growth in the Indian economy even in this difficult year is going to be around 5.25 per cent. It is a miracle, the argument will proceed, that the slowdown of the world economy notwithstanding, our growth rate will still exceed 5 per cent. We have therefore nothing to be apologetic about, chime in unison the vanguards of the great economic reforms.

The Indian people have been subjected to a great confidence trick over the past decade. As much as 80 per cent of the nation earns their livelihood from agriculture and industry. Since the rate of population growth during the year will be at least 1.5 per cent, this fourfifths of the community will experience a reduction in their income level, and therefore in their standard of living, in the current year. Given the innate in equality in the distribution of income and assets, overwhelming numbers amongst those who secure their livelihood from agricultural and industrial occupations will actually experience a sharp decline in their income.

Only one-fifth of the nation earn their living from occupations linked to the services sector. Consolation for the hoity-toity ones, their near and dear folks employed in the services sector will on the agerage experience an income growth of 5 per cent or more despite vicissitudes elsewhere. But for the vast multitude engaged in the services sector, the prospects are as grim as for those in agriculture and industry. A seemingly inexorable process is on. In the services segment of the economy, the passwords are efficiency and increase in productivity, such as would enable us to face global competition. Computerization and economizing of labour are accordingly proceeding apace; the number of employees at the lower rungs of the services sector is shrinking every day. The most glaring instance of what is happening is provided by the banking industry: perhaps 250,000 lower grade bank employees are being summarily retrenched each year or given the dubious handshake of illusory retirement benefits; the work they performed will supposedly now be looked after by a couple of hundred computer-savvy young boys and girls from affluent families.

There is a frightening warping of values in establishment circles: newspapers write gloatingly about how five or ten brats, hardly twenty-five years of age, on passing out from the management institutes, land cushy jobs fetching monthly compensations of one or two lack of rupees; the media however have no thought to spare for those thousands who are being served marching orders in firms and factories.

The prime minister is a political animal. He is not yet thinking in terms of discarding the claptrap of parliamentary democracy either. He therefore suggested a measure of "pump-priming" through massive public investment in the different sectors so as to extricate the economy from the morass it finds itself in. The prime mainister obviously spoke out of turn. His *pucca* blue economic advisory council knows better; it has a direct line of communication with the World Bank and the International Monetary Fund. The council has lost no time to rap the prime minister on the knuckle: excessive public investment, it has warned, will disequilibriate the fiscal balance, something the masters in Washington DC will not approve of. The prime minister must have been suitably chastened.

The upshot is a state of cluelessness for those who preside over the economy and the polity. The ultimate destiny in my case now rest with the country sheriff from Texas with a loud-hailer entwined in his hand. Meanwhile, we are being regaled with some wry entertainment. The authorities have asked the nation not to worry, steps are being expeditiously taken to insulate the economy from the ravages wrought by a globalized system.

Besides, growth may be non-existent rise in employment may be zero, the rupee may plummet, the share market may collapse, exports may dip, so what, we have $ 45 billion of foreign balances in the kitty. Once, *inshah* George W. Bush, international ballistic missiles start flying, these foreign balances, for all one knows of can surmise, might well do a Houdini.

There is a soul-filling half-epilogue to the story though. The Indian economy could will soon be reduced to the level of a non-entity. The policy-formulators will be unfazed. The "fundamentals" of the economy, they will confide to countryment, remain strong, and the stock of foreign exchanges assets will perform as a shield. What this stock would dwindle down to should last week's catastrophe in Wall street—acknowledgedly much worse than even the infamous 1929 crash—be followed by further steeply downward slides is not a matter which finds a place on New Delhi's agenda.

28th Septermber 2001

Daylight mayhem

There is one special reason to feel grateful to the Bharatiya Janata Party-led government in New Delhi. It has buried, good and proper, the longstanding hypocrisy of the Indian ruling class of promising to look after the poor and downtrodden. The no-nonsense Union budget is blatantly pro-rich as well as annti-labour and anti-lower middle class. The finance minister has not tried to hide his attitude and bias. He has made it clear that he means business: the poor and the lower classes have no business to aspire to survive in the Indian polity. The rich, he has pronounced without the least hesitation, are going to rule henceforth, and for ever, in this system. So far so good. The budget however has another objective, the manner of implementing which has not been accompanied by a similar transparency.

Allies of the BJP in the coalition include the Telugu Desam Party, which has grown into adulthood sustained by the slogan of a drastic restructuring of Centre-state relations, with an accelerating pace of transfer of administrative, judicial and economic prerogatives from the Centre to the states. True, the thunder of N.T. Rama Rao does not suit N. Chandrababu Naidu's style. That has still not prevented the latter from asserting the rights of states, such as his own, when a specific administrative or economic decision has gone against them. Whenever the Andhra Pradesh chief minister has spoken out on any issue, New Delhi's government has responded speedly to assuage his feelings during the past three years.

But times area-changing, and a process has perhaps begun on the part of the Centre to take Naidu for granted. Anyway, a kind of friction had arisen. Naidu thought the recommendations of the 11th finance commission discriminated against a number of states, including Andhra Pradesh. He insisted on a revision of the recommendations. The Centre was under pressure and in April last year it directed the commision to consider a number of additional terms of reference. The commission duly obliged; the government of India has now accepted in full the second set of its recommendations.

But thereby hangs a major tale. The Union government, in the course of these additional terms of reference for the commission, had asked it to draw up "a monitorable fiscal reform programme aimed at reduction of revenue deficit of the states". The commission was also asked to indicate "the manner in which the grants to the states to cover the assessed deficit in their non-plan revenue account may be linked to progress in the implementation of the reforms programme."

The 11th finance commission has been impeccably his-master's-voice. It has taken the additional terms of reference as an oracular message. It has not bothered to take into account the grave constitutional implications of the government fiat. For the funds a finance commission is asked to devolve every five years under Article 275 of the Constitution belong to the national exchequer; these are not by any stretch resources under the command and control of the Union government. A certain proportion of the funds the commission would allocate to the states, the Constitution categorically enjoins, is for the purpose of covering the deficit in the revenue account of the states. Those states which do not experience a deficit in the revenue account will not come under the purview of the commission in this instance.

That apart, the Constitution nowhere indicates the requirement of considering the opinion of a monitoring agency before funds are to be allocated to cover the aforementioned deficit. The entire procedure suggested by the 11th finance commission, and accepted by the Centre, therefore falls foul of the constitution. And there is more to it. The commission has the temerity to suggest that 15 per cent of the money, which, according to a strict reading of the Constitution, automatically belongs to the states for covering the deficit in the revenue account, should be at first withheld.

The release of the held-back funds will, in each case, depend upon whether the states satisfy the criteria set by the Centre's fiscal reforms measures. The funds withheld, the commission has further suggested, should go to an incentive fund, from out of which awards will be granted to those states which comply with the conditions laid down by the Union government, while disobedient states are to be penalized and cut off from resources the Constitution had arranged for them.

All this is cheeky in the extreme. The device proposed by the finance commission, and accepted with alacrity by the Union government without the leave of the inter-state council, smacks of daylight robbery. The states, which refuse to toe the Centre's line, are to be victimized and those which acquit themselves to be the most faithful servants of the Centre are to be offered additional funds. The Union budget presented on the last day of February has devoted gratuitous space to dwell gloatingly on this piece of constitutional outrage.

It is amazaing that the state governments are yet to rise in unison against this affront. As far as information goes, only one state government, that of Kerala, has reacted sharply and questioned the constitutional propriety of the suggested measures. It has demanded that the issue be reviewed *in extenso* by the inter-state council before the proposal to rob state-right-Peters to pay subservient Pauls is finalized. In case the Centre persists in its intransigence, the priority for the state governments ought to be to submit a writ petition to the Supreme Court and seek an injunction on the Union government's move.

It is yet to be seen whether the Chandrababu Naidus are receptive to this idea, or decide shortsightedly that, never mind the consitutional impropriety, should the Centre consider their states, such as Andhra Pradesh, as exemplary good boys, perhaps they would gain extra goodies in case the proposal goes through. But suppose a less Andhra Pradesh-friendly government comes to power at the Centre, would it not then cook the goose of Naidu and others of his ilk?

Ideas are contaminating, and the pompous set which is described as the prime minister's economic advisory council has drawn inspiration from the 11th finance commission's capriciousness. Taking the cue from the commission, the planning commission too, the council has suggested, should make up its mind to withhold initially a certain part of the plan allocations made for each state; the withheld funds are to be disbursed subsequently only if the states behave properly in the matter of fiscal discipline. The following are the exact words the economic advisory council has used: "from the 10th Plan onwards, i.e., starting from 1.4.2002, half of the normal Central assistance to state plans should be provided on the basis of a quantitatively worked out fiscal reform plan", and "release of Central assistance during the year should be linked to achievement of milestones of policy action agreed by the states as part of the 10th Plan exercise."

Evidently, the economic advisory council is a harder taskmaster than the 11th finance commission. The later has suggested the withholding of only 15 per cent of the grants assessed to cover the revenue account deficit of the states; the council, much blither in spirit, would hold back as much as 50 per cent of the plan assistance already decided for a state in case it fails to meet the stern test of the Centre's fiscal programme.

Again, till now, only the government of Kerala has protested against the economic advisory council's gadflyish recommendation. This time a mere meeting of the inter state council will not satisfy it; it has requested that the national development council be immediately convened to discuss the issue.

The erosion of the fiscal rights of the states is obviously gathering speed. Some months ago, the prerogative of the states granted by the Constitution to decide the rates of sales tax leviable on different commodities—the most important source of revenue for them—was taken away. The prospect of even greater revenue erosion looms large once the value added tax is introduced at the state level within the next few years. The threat at the moment comes from two other directions.

The BJP has a game plan. It wants to swing the country into pre-history. As demonstrated by the budget, it also wants to liquidate the nation's poor and the lower middle classes. But the agenda is not yet complete. Whatever rights the Consitution has enshrined for the states, the BJP wants to obliterate them in order to usher in a unitary, totalitarian Hindu regime. Those politicans, who think to the contrary have had enough prior notice; history will have contempt for them if they fail to take heed of the early as well as late warning signals.

14th March 2001

Afraid to be free

A spectre is haunting Indian officialdom, the spectre of the rupee gaining in strength against the dollar in the international market, thereby raising India's status in the comity of nations.

Pray, what is the ruckus about? Before we delve into its mystery, it may be useful to recount some basic facts. In 1999-2000, our oil imports had amounted to $ 10.5 billion. During the early weeks of the current fiscal year, the international price of petroleum crude had shot up to $35 per barrel;, although there has been an abatement later. Even so, the going price is still $ 30 per barrel. In consequence, in the period April to November this year, oil imports have shot up to $ 11.35 billion as against $ 6.2 billion in the corresponding period of the previous year.

There is a fair possibility that, for the fiscal year 2000-2001 in entirety, the value of aggregate oil imports might reach close to $ 16 billion. This is likely to be so in the context of the proposal being mulled over by the Organization of Petroleum Exporting Countries to cut back the production of petroleum crude and stabilize the price at a level between $ 30 and $ 35 per barrel. As things now stand, roughly 40 per cent of the total value of our imports consists of imports of crude petroleum. Should the OPEC proposal be pushed through, this proportion might rise further.

A new situation, that has arisen of late, deserves to be taken into account against this background. Iraq, the country the United States is trying its hardest to obliterate from the face of the earth, has reportedly floated a suggestion for the consideration of the government of India. Thanks to the American dispensation, Iraqis are being starved of food, medicine and other essential commodities for the past several years. At the same time, they are prevented from earning foreign exchange by selling a part of their huge output of crude petroleum.

In the circumstances, they have made an alluring offer to our government. The ambit of this offer stretches beyond the so-called United Nations food-for-oil programme under which we are to receive an extra quantity of one million tonnes of crude during the current fiscal year. If only we agree to sell them a substantial quantity of our foodgrains, in the production of which we claim to be comfortably surplus, the Iraqis, the special offer suggests, would be willing to send us an unspecified, but negotiable, quantity of petroleum crude at only $ 7 per barrel.

It is a dream offer. Just consider its implications. The price on offer by Iraq would be almost one-fifth of the price at which we have, on the average, bought crude in the current year. If we lean towards Iraq for our entire import of crude next year, the saving in foreign exchange would be to the extent of $ 12 billion, or more. In case we buy half of our requirements from Iraq, the saving in foreign exchange would be at least $ 6 billion. Should we buy even one-fourth of our petroleum crude requirement from that country, even then, the saving would amount to $ 3 billion.

But in this matter we are apparently not our own masters. Since formally Iraq continues to be subject to economic sanctions imposed by the UN—read, instead of the UN, the US—any deal we seek to enter into with the government of Iraq will need the prior approval of the international body. In other words, it will need the prior approval of the US. This is where the snag arises. China cares not one whit for the so-called UN sanctions, nor does France, nor does Venezuela. These countries have negotiated trade and payments agreements with the government of Iraq, and the US has not been able to act as a spoiler. We are, however, different. Our government takes pride in the special relationship it has established with the American administration. We are in fact busy jostling against a handful of other countries for occupying the slot best described as the number one lackey of the US.

Despite the fantastic windfall which the Iraqi offer would allow us to enjoy, our government is still hesitating; it has kept the government of Iraq waiting. The reason is obvious. Unless the Americans give us the green signal, we dare not proceed to complete the Iraqi deal. A certain nervousness is nonetheless abroad in Indian official, and perhaps ministerial, minds.

Were Iraq to succeed in wrapping up the agreement with us, a dramatic improvement could take place in our balance of payments position; we should be able to save, depending upon the quantity we buy from Iraq, anything between $ 3 billion to $ 12 billion in foreign exchange. In case that happens, there will be an immediate easing of the strain we have been experiencing on the foreign exchange front; the rupee will make a spectacular recovery over the dollar; we will have to spend less rupees to buy a given quantity of American goods and the Americans will have to shell out more dollars to buy a given quantity of Indian goods.

This prospect has rendered distraught the Indian bureaucracy, and, conceivably, its masters as well. It has now set up an argument to sabotage the proposed agreement with Iraq. In its view, it would be a great calamity if we import petroleum crude from Iraq at $ 7 per barrel. That would appreciate the value of our rupee in terms of the dollar, thereby, the argument runs, severely inconveniencing our exports; India's exports might actually deteriorate to much that there could even loom a foreign exchange crisis of a dimension as great as the one which visited us in 1991. The nervous Nellys, to stave off such a calamity, would at that point look to intervention by the central bank so that the external value of the rupee could be brought down.

Such is the absurdity of the comprador mindset. If we conclude the deal with Iraq, we might register a saving of foreign exchange to the extent of even $ 12 billion. But, insinuate our officials, this would not be of any good at all, for our exports are bound to decline because of the continuous strengthening of the rupee in the international market. These wise men do not specify though by what amount our exports could fall. Even if the saving of foreign exchange resulting from our signing the agreement with Iraq amounts to $ 12 billion, we must, according to their view, decline to append our signature to it, for our foreign exchange earnings might fall at the other end because of the slide in exports.

This is sheer tomfoolery. For the crucial issue is whether the saving in foreign exchange on account of the deal with Iraq would or would not be more than the possible gain in exports, and therefore in foreign exchange earnings, in case we did not sign the deal. Quite clearly, Indian officials do not consider the matter in this light. Their worry is that a deal of the nature Iraq was proposed would harm global American interest, and what is bad for the US is *ipso facto* bad for India.

The debate therefore boils down to a single issue: are the officials and their superiors ensconced in North Block under commitment to serve the cause of India or that of the bosscountry, the US? The so-called free market hypothesis for international trade postulates a multiplicity of sellers and that of buyers too in order to maximize gain for each county. Here then lies the irony. By tying ourselves to American apron strings, we are not furthering, but hindering, free international trade. In the present circumstances, the mighty US is, really and truly, the arch enemy of freedom. And the local compradors suffer from a genuine fear of freedom.

31st January 2001

Invest in a dream

Beyond a point export pessimism is indistinguishable from growth pessimism. The consequence is more confusion piling upon confusion that was already there.

There is actually a pattern which depicts how pessimism gathers strength. Let it be assumed that the prayer of do-mestic devotees for foreign investment is adequately answered. Foreign investors arrive on the scene with loads and loads of investible capital. They are expected to set up new factories embellished by latest technologies and raise prodigiously the level of production. This process will mean the death of local industries in various sectors. Domestic consumers will cross over from the consumption of locally produced goods in traditional industries to products that are the fruits of foreign investment.

It is however not enough that production by local producers is substituted by production by foreign investors. What the foreigners produce will, it is hoped, prove to be competitive in the international market, thereby raising the country's exports and foreign exchange reserves.

The pessimists will chip in at this point. There is no *a priori* ground, they will argue, for assuming that exports will soar automatically. True, if the foreigners bring in the latest technology, it will be a major gain. On top of that, they will have the advantage of cheap leabour that is locally available. But as realists we have to admit that the imported technology will have a modest labour content; in any event, domestic wages for skilled labour will exhibit an upward trend, so much so that the advantage of engaging local workers will not be as attractive as initially thought.

Even if these apparent trivialities are ignored, one major issue cannot be bypassed. Foreign investors will have to seek working capital from the local banks. The prevailing rate of interest in a poor country such as India is easily double or triple of what the rate is in the United States or any other advanced country. In the circumstances, it is altogether doubtful whether the output generated by foreign investment will be able to compete favourably in the international market with similar or identical goods produced in the advanced industrial countries. The scope of additional exports is therefore likely to be extremely limited despite the generous inflow of foreign capital in the form of direct investment.

Those who persist in dreaming rosy dreams will join issue at this stage. Since so many concessions have already been accorded to foreign investors, why should not the native government decide to subsidize heavily the rate of interest for working capital borrowed by foreign investors? Again, let us hypothesize that this indeed is what is going to happen. But the very moment the decision is taken to subsidize heavily the interest rate for borrowings by foreign parties, there will be a fresh crisis, and not just on account of heartburn among the domestic producers. The banking sector itself will be caught in a jam. If foreigners are to be offered subsidized credit, there is bound to be a sharp drop in the profitability of the banks.

It is even conceivable that, other things remaining the same, the profitability of some of the banks will turn negative. The government of the country will be greatly embarrassed and come under pressure to redress the situation. It might perhaps be compelled to send a directive to the banks that, to compensate for the subsidy to the foreign companies, they should further raise the rate of interest for the local manufacturers.

Can we foresee the outcome in case such a measure is enforced? The unit cost of production of domestic output will increase sharply across the board. Not only will domestic consumers suffer, as a result the rate of inflation in the coutnry will be pushed further up. This will of course act as a damper to exports; that apart, it will have grave social consequences too. With inflation rampant in the economy, conditions of instability and social discontent are likely to spread all over the country. And in case this should be the denouement, foreign investors will take fright and leave the country along with their capital. We will therefore be back to the low level equilibrium form where we started.

But let us be fair. There is no convincing reason why the line of reasoning adopted by the export pessimists will rule the roost. This is largely a matter of specific circumstances prevailing in the country. We have to take into account the hard datum. Take, for instance, the developments in India in the course of the past decade. With all the efforts our government has put in to entice direct foreign investment, the record of achievement is disappointing. Official sources have themselves let out the fact that aggregate foreign investment during the decade was well below the foreign investment that has entered China in a single year in the recent period. Injured innocence will scarcely be of any avail here.

Till as long as the socioeconomic situation in India compares unfavourably with China's in the judgement of Western investors, there will be little prospect of foreign direct invesment entering India attaining the level of foreign direct investment flow into China.

At this point, economists will perhaps be joined by sociologists, anthropologists and others. They will hold intense consultations amongst themselves to ferret out the reasons for the inferior attractiveness of India to foreign investors relative to China, Indonesia and the Philippines. An earnest graduate student from an American university, what do you know, could even rush with a PhD dissertation on the theme and offer umpteen speculations about how the cookie crumbles in different underdeveloped countries. Please do not be unduly concerned if he or she comes up with, for example, what is to him or her a credible explanation for dissimilar magnitudes of capital ingress into India and China.

In China, corruption is not unfamilar as it is not unfamilar in India. However, when a corrupt person is caught redhanded in China, he or she is summarily executed. In our country, the individual will perhaps be chosen to stand for elections, be elected to the Lok Sabha, and sworn in as a minister.

Another plausible explanation is the vastly more efficient administrative set up in China in contrast to the near anarchy prevailing in India. Much worse, there is a tendency to idolize this nearanarchy. Many of these suggestions, some will say, are sanctimonious nonsense. Indians will have an altogether different point of view. Theirs is, they will claim, as much god's own country as the United States is; all it lacks is a quantity of direct foreign investment.

Does it not sound like a parable on viscious circles? Round and round we go, but at the end of our strenuous exertions, we find ourselves exactly at the same spot where we began. This is stagnation par excellecne, did you say? In a free democracy, you are entitled to your own opinion.

5th July 2000

Rupee on the run

Events are unfolding strictly according to the script. The management of the country's external accounts has to all purposes been handed over to foreigners. Institutional investors in the domestic stock exchanges as well as elsewhere have taken charge of the buying and selling of the domestic currency. It is in the interest of foreigners to bring the value of the rupee down, down, down.

Consider this aspect of the matter, along with acknowldegement of the other important factors operating in and around the phenomena of direct investment. Long term external investment in the country has, for whatever reason, lagged woefully behind over the past decade. For instance, notwithstanding the manifold allurements offered by the New Delhi government to external parties, direct foreign investment in the course of the decade has not even approximated the magnitude of long term money that has gone into the People's Republic of China in a single year.

The regime in New Delhi and its agencies are, quite visibly, at the end of their tether. We are the leading votaries of globalization, and, despite vicissitudes, we propose to march ahead in the manner of Christian soldiers. There can be no question of reversing the process merely because political developments have been toward a contrary direction.

There is an impasse though a genuine one, which will not go away on its own. India is infested with website lovers. But the problem of joblessness does not dissolve. Temporary assignments with the information technology sector could take care of a limited number of job seekers from the middle class segments of society. Unless massive investment is on the way—investment involving agriculture and industry—the strain on the system is bound to show soon.

The strain eventuated by the investment lag in the economy is to be reflected in measures which mount further pressure on the country's foreign exchange reserves. We are, as a result, caught in the trap of a vsicious circle. The intensified demand for foreign exchange keeps lowering the external value of the domestic currency, that is, the rupee. Depreciation of the value of the rupee raises the level of demand for foreign exchange. Unless the national government or a major international financial institution intervenes in a big way, the country's reserve of foreign currency is likely to reach the very bottom within a very short period.

Well, it is no longer a hypothesis. A crisis of a sort has in fact begun to afflict the rupee. The foreign exchange markets are full of reports of how pressure mounted by foreign speculators is bound to lead to a run on the rupee, dragging its value down all the way.

The initial reaction of the government has been cautious and on a low key. The authorities know that there is little scope for defending the national currency in case some big external forces are determined to get it depreciated. In any event, it will not be deemed as civilized behaviour if national fiscal and monetary institutions begin to defend the domestic currency against the onslaughts launched by important foreign parties. Foreigners must be shown respect.

The underlying issue calls for some introspection. You are supposed to be a sovereign regime, and nominally in full control of the processes of your economy. The urge is nonetheless irresistible to give in to browbeating by foreigners. These foreigners have made up their mind to do your currency in. Their local cronies have already been informed that it would not be gentlemenly on your part to devise strategies to defend the external value of the currency. Things are so arranged—seek advice from Thailand, or the Philippines or Indonesia—that uninterrupted fall in the external value of the currency becomes the general pattern.

There is no question that such is the fate awaiting the Indian rupee. Irrespective of bunches of foreigners coming with driblets of external funds, the outcome is likely to be stabilization of the rupee's external value at a precariously low level. The sequence of subsequent developments is not difficult to anticipate.

Speculators will move centrestage, the external value of the rupee is likely to decline further, exports consequently will become stickier and imports will go into a spree. It would have been less onerous to mount the plea to suspend the World Trade Organization's provisions till as long as some kind of near normalcy is restored to the system. But we have already slipped into the 19th century colonial mind, royalty is not to be argued with.

Not that the government is unable to see the predicament. The fresh bout of trade liberalization is going to cause the economy to enter into an excruciatingly difficult time. Certain ground realities you cannot run away from.

Do you dare to challenge the imperial order? In case you do, out you go and your assets and properties are to be annexed by imperial order. Should any of the party or parties involved have the temerity to confront the colonial and imperial forces impinging on the country's trade and commerce, the course of events will be exciting as well as unpredictable.

Are we waiting for a re-enactment of that kind of denouement? The external value of the rupee has come down crashing. No reversal of the trend is to be expected. What is additionally noteworthy is that while the government has instructed the Reserve Bank of India to maintain the incentive of exporters, it shows little courage to strike at the root of the problem by adoption of measures slashing the level of import demand for goods and services.

The major breakthroughs the foreigners have achieved through the 2000-2001 budget connotes a triumph for free market activities. Foreign traders and foreign institutions could not care less whether, because of the introduction of unregulated market transactions, there is utmost strain on local activities, including on local employment.

This attitude of mind on the part of the government, including the ministry of finance, supplemented by stances adopted by influential sections of the comfortably placed middle classes, will decide the content of the impending discourse that will shape the fate of the country in the course of the next decade.

Meanwhile, the external value of the rupee will keep falling and some pundits are confident that by Christmas, the dollar-rupee rate will be 50:1. What the implication of such a turn of events is for the Indian producer or worker or trader, nobody is seemingly interested. Under dependent colonialism, the country however learns to survive. There will be no growth and no meaningful redistribution of income and assets. So what; at least some of our countrymen will learn to survive despite the fury of the circumstances.

7th June 2000

Nowhere to go but down

Obviously enough, the season for speculation is still at an incipient stage. The Indian middle class is in a haze. Perhaps as many as a million youngsters are enjoying a gala time because of their association with some aspects of information technology activities. India, it will hardly do to forget, is the largest producer of software after the United States.

This is wonderful tiding; a small footnote nonetheless rears its head, modifying the mystique of the ground reality. The overwhelming part of software production takes place because of the linkage, formal or informal, of branch units with parent units incorporated in the US or some other foreign country. The reason is simple. Technology graduates are available in the Indian market at fantastically low wages, which is a bonanza for North American and European corporate units.

Young graduates from ordinnary Indian middle class homes are experiencing a demand, long distance, for their services from foreign firms specializing in information technology. This will persist till as long as the Indian graduates offer their services at a adequately low wages. But such a situation cannot last indefinitely. The process is predictable. Once the technology graduates from poor countries, such as India, learn global facts, they will venture to hike thir supply price. At some juncture the multinational corporations will do their calculations afresh and go for new collaborative arrangements with young graduates from some other underdeveloped countries lagging behind India.

In case that happens, the general industrial crises in India following globalization is bound to affect in equal measure the software business too. The over all milieu will settle down to a pattern of declining growth rate encompassing both agriculture and industry. The industrial growth rate will decline because public sector units will keep closing one after another, those that somehow survive will be denied both bank and fiscal credit. Unrestricted imports will sound the death knell for other industries as well, including those in the small scale sector. Tariff and nontariff barriers will be off for the farm sector.

But this will be so only in the developing counties. The developed countries in North America and Europe control the International Monetary Fund-World Bank-World Trade Organization trinity, the transnational corporations have their roots there. The cumulative impact of their activities will be the reappearance of the colonial order. But Newtonian physics says every action has an equal and opposite reaction.

Will the colonial renaissance lead to a revival of the anticolonial revolutionary clan as well? One honestly does not know. There will perhaps be some tension within each recolonized country, the middle class will stand divided, a small fraction from among them, those associated with infotch activities, will be happy to stay globalized. The very large majority of the population will however have a different kind of experience. Elimination of tariff where there were barriers previously will emerge as an outstanding phenomenon. The threat will loom ever lowering tariffs all the way to zero per cent across the board. These are all part of the commitments, the nation will be told, following the signing of the Marrakesh treaty and the establishment of the WTO.

The general attitude of the authorities in New Delhi—cynical, with a hint of the comprador ethos—is easily summarized. True, the rate of unemployment is steadily increasing in the system. Everyday, some more industrial units are going to the wall, which is all a great pity. Nothing however can be done about it, we have made our pledges to the WTO, and that is the last word in the matter: it is not the national interest, but the interest of foreigners that is to prevail in every instance.

Do the official spokesmen who dish out such garbage realize the meaning of meaning? What they are stating amounts to an open declaration of a return to the 18th century. The overall picture could not be any gloomier. The banks and insurance companies are in the process of being handed over to foreigners. Public undertakings, responsible in a major way for the aggregate economic growth that has taken place over the past half a century, are being sent to the gallows. As stated above, they are being starved of funds, both budgetary funds and liquidity from the financial sector. Banks and financial institutions are under instruction to concentrate on speculation and dubious transactions in the stock exchanges. Advisors from distinguished finacial institutions have kept drilling the lesson that speculation is the central source of national welfare.

The other underlying assumption is that the economy will take off consequently to the inflow of investment funds from overseas, the local tribes who have money to spend should therefore focus on consumption and not savings. The hard data now available indicates that the assumption should not be taken seriously, long term investment in the system has struck a sluggish patch since the initiation of "reforms". It is as if the colonial comparador arrangement is back with a bang: comfortably placed among the local populace should use their funds exclusively for high consumption.

Investment in the system, this model says, is to be left to the exclusive care of foreign parties. That the foreign parties are not performing the job expected of them is seemingly nobody's affair to keep track of. The fact the rate of foodgrain output has again fallen below the rate of population growth in the course of the past decade does not cause any concern to those in charge nor does the prospect of massive unemployment in the cottage and farm sectors in the wake of compliance with the WTO's directives on the withdrawal of trade barriers.

This lassitude of the mind is, in fact the hallmark of the colonial epoch. Our fate is being datermined by decision taken elsewhere. The Europeans and the North Americans know how to take care of themselves. Or rather, since they themselves have written the WTO's documents, the world trade body's long arm does not reach them. The developing countries in contrast continue to be in the soup. The proceedings have been planned that way. India is, at the moment, being compelled to give up nontariff barriers of all descriptions on a whole range of commodities. Article XVIII of the Marrakesh treaty, allowing special dispensations for balance of payments reasons for the poor countries, has been divested of all its relevance.

Both Europeans and North Americans can get around the proscriptive clause concerning farm subsidies even when such subsidies are close to 100 per cent of the total cost. In contrast, the swords and choppers are out the moment a poor country like India suggests even a 10 per cent subsidy for its farm products or for publicty distributed foodgrains with the object of protecting the level of the poorest segments of its population.

This is an absurd, unfair regime the WTO is determined to impose on the global system. It may be the century of infotech. It may be claimed to be, thanks to the website, the freest of the free market ambience. None of this can however obliterate the harsher facts of life. India's rate of economic growth is declining. The distribution of income and assets is getting further tilted away against the poor. But as long as members of the comfortably placed middle class who have implanted themselves next to the website, are disinterested to listen to the roster of travail experienced by the numerically dominant population groups inconvenienced by the challenge of technological advances, it will be a toss up of the severest kind.

A dicey circumstance all told, with the realization by some of us that we live another day because we have been allowed to do so. This further extension of longevity, there should be no illusion, is something for which we cannot post any claim. We survive. That is all. We survive for today, the agenda could well be different tomorrow.

24th May 2000

Closing the gate

The up and coming generation has reasons to feel flabber gasted. Bill Gates has been to them the next thing to god. Now an archaic piece of American legislation, the so called antitrust law, is being applied to cut up his Microsoft empire.

This is bizarre, for it send across the message that free market transactions are not the *summum bonum* of human civilization; limits exist to what a private industrial or commercial entity might aspire for; these limits are set and enforced by the government of the country. Which is another way of stating that restrictions operate on the supposedly free functioning of market forces. Even Gates, his divine circumstances notwithstanding, has to come under the social discipline enforced by the government. The government acts as agent of the state.

The up and coming generation is bound to be beffelled. This is outrageous they will argue among themselves, and keep shooting questions at society's decisionmarkers. One cannot blame them too much. They have been reared in an environment where the untrammelled functioning of the free market has been taken tq be sacrosanct. No exceptions to the competitive roles have till now been communicated to them.

The information technology has had an uninterrupted run in the United States and the rest of the Western world for almost a quarter of a century. Discovery of fresh arenas of deployment of capital was taken for granted, and the demand for investment funds in an industry by nature acutely capital intensive was seemingly without end.

The entire community was exposed to the spectre of monopolization of the market by the market leader. Bill Gates proliferated all over in activity after activity. That was assumed to be quintessential capitalism. But now both the executive and the judical wings of the government have stepped in, in the US itself. The likes of Bill Gates, they have decided, are infringing on the grammar of free market operations.

Part of the problem has arisen because the standard literature describing the emergence of a monopolized market has long been thrown out of the window—or allowed to go into disuse. Monopoly equilibrium is a concept from another era. The world was then marketed by lack of demand, for goods and services, leading to large scale unemployment in one capitalist country after another.

Textbooks on market imperfection, such as the volumes written by Joan Robinson in the United Kingdom and Edwin Chamberlain in the US, came into circulation. Terms like monopoly, duopoly, oligopoly, *et cetera,* entered common usage. Clever geometrical diagrams were drawn, supplementing derivations from differential calculus, to convey the harsh fact of life in a way that monopoly equilibrium was always to the left of competitive equilibrium. Which was another way of stating that, other things remaining the same, monopoly output lags behind output under conditions of free competition. Unemployment, it followed, would be less in a monopoly situation compared to what perfect competition would yield.

This phase of economics the up and coming generation has not generally been acquainted with. Nurtured in a milieu of relative naivete, the market forces, they have summed up, are a magnificent phenomenon, if only the wretched state could be stopped from interfering. Once such interference stopped, that would lay the foundation of all round economic efficiency with optimumm utilization of the factors of production involved.

The economic depression of the late Twenties and the Thirties gave the lie to assumptions of this nature. A grim chapter of history ensued. The free market was a non-starter. It was considered essential that the state intervene massively so that public works could come up here, there, everywhere in the economy raising national output and the quantum of national output and the quantum of national employment. Textbooks get written to explain how the process of state intervention worked like magic, with supply creating its own demand.

Those textbooks are now by and large extinct. They have been withdrawn from the market since they contain arcane, often dangerous, thoughts. The hangover of that genre of economics has stretched for a long while.

Thank goodness, once the Cold War ended in the manner that it did, it was victory time for the free market. The new economics that has accompanied globalization is replete with commonplace, straightforward notions stressing the suzerainty of the market and knocking off the pedestal the role of the state as the saviour of the economic system.

Several developments have followed. The US has been an active patron of the free market philosophy. It has its clout as the world's only superpower. A pattern of a new international culture is in the pipeline. The vassal states, for dear life, have rushed to sing the praise of the free market philosophy. Whatever his majesty the king might think, the subjects too must think in the same way and with alacrity. The onrush of legislation choking the Indian

Parliament, slashing subsidies and closing down public undertakings of all descriptions, are illustrative of the sycophancy that is at work.

Life is not worth living unless we do the bidding of the world's only superpower. Come hell or high water, we, the subalterns, will obey the wishes of the master. The blind adherence to the goal of maximizing the takings of the boss's interests even if in the process our own interests suffer irreparable danger, is one issue the country's formal leaders are most reluctant to discuss in public forums.

The Microsoft story is a bit of a setback for those who have strongly invested in the new horizon. For resons of state, the likes of Gates, it is being understood, will not be allowed to exploit the possibilities of the free market to the hilt. The US administration, than whom there can be no greater admirer of the practice of globalization, has inserted a spoke in its standing legislation. Untrammelled human endeavour in any particular direction, howsoever brilliant and innovative, is out, the freedom of one cannot impede the freedom of the multitude.

The nonresident Indians, with universal admiration for all things American, will have reasons to experience disappointment. They were, they thought, in the early blooming stages of capitalism in India, why frighten them with the Microsoft story?

And yet it is not that simple, accepting the reality of the US itself agreeing to the imposition of restriction on the functioning of the free market mechanism. The mind wavers. Should not the concept of clamping restrictions on the activities of a monopoly power be extended in other spheres as well? Whould there not be at least some informal legislation to prohibit the global superpower from monopolizing the wealth and resources of the earth?

Once upon a time the United Nations was thought to be the iedal agency to keep in check superpower overbearingness. That organization has, however, been comprehensively destroyed by the US and its agents. The felt need is nonetheless there for a keeper of morality in this world, often the victim of vulgar emotions and whimsical programmes taking precedence over decency and a humane order.

Much more than the superpower itself, its sycophants will be scandalized by proposals to impose restrictions on the exercise of power by the big boss. It is difficult to believe, on current data, that this country had wrested its freedom from foreigners hardly half a century ago.

26th April, 2000

Survival of the Freest

Naivety, or knavery, or a mixture of both? The free-market cavaliers are unconcerned; what is euphemistically known as ground reality is no part of their paraphernalia. The procedure they recommend, they are dead certain, leads to the optimum use of inputs and therefore epitomizes economic efficiency. The word's underdeveloped nations have remained underdeveloped, they do not have the least doubt, becuase of the failure to ensure the most efficient use of the resources given to the system; remove impediments to optimum factor utilization, such as trade union intransigence, the economy will take off along the optimum path of growth.

As if the workers are not a constituent factor of production and Adam Smith himself had not some biting comments to offer on the waywardness of private employers. The propensity of the latter to deal unfairly with the working class, Smith had hinted, threatens to destabilize the economy. The first half of the 20th century coincided with the realization that the idealized free market is a fiction. The analysis of the morphology of imperfect markets, by Edwin Chambarlin and Joan Robinson, was an admission of the ground reality. If John Maynard Keynes had not intervened with his general prescription for large scale state intervention, it would have been curtain call for Western capitalism, on the eve of World War I itself.

Two generations later, it is a totally transformed picture. Developments, particularly over the past decade have spawned euphoria of a sort among free market lovers. Since the other side is vanquished and the Cold War has been decisively won, it would be puerile, it is stated, not to admit that there is no visible alternative to the capitalist order. Give up all regulatory controls, let the factors of production be free to move in and out of different markets, let demand be similarly liberalized, let government activism be cut down to such minimum hores as maintenance of law and order and defence, an economic miracle will visit country after underdeveloped country. Untrammelled activities on the art of the private sector will be progenors of efficiency and growth; therefore have the good sense to hand over the harge of economic management to private parties; you could then sit back and enjoy high living.

A lovely formulation, but it is disdainful of history. The purveyors of the capitalist dream do not naturally like to be reminded for instance, the predatory state of affairs in the sphere of banking and insurance prevailing in this country before these were taken over by the state in the Fifties and the Sixties. Market lovers hate to be reminded of these rude facts, and are taken aback at the massive resistance put up by the employees against official proposals to surrender public undertakings one after another to private parties. The urge to sell out public property at throwaway prices seems to be overwhelming among the liberation leaders: telecommunications, followed by petroleum and natural gas extration, followed by surface transport and port, followed by land belonging to the railway system, followed by broadcast and telecast channels, followed by the Indian Airlines, no less.

The simplicity, feigned or otherwise, of the underlying assumption is devastating: the public sector means blackmail by trade unions and their lazy membership, the sale of such public undertakings, to private parties would herald the prospect of more competent use of factor endowments, thereby promoting efficiency and growth.

In the calculation of efficiency, the point of view of the working class is of course not taken into consideration. Additionally not taken into account is the consequence of allowing the nation's limited investible resources drift into areas and sectors which contribute little or nothing to the wealth and welfare of the majority of the national population.

At this juncture, Adam Smith and David Hume are actually overshadowed by Charles Darwin. Survival of the fittest is the mantra and emphasis is on the adage that those who cannot stand the heat should exit from the kitchen. It is a polite way of indicating that the vulnerable sections have no right of survival and, moreover, it will be a flrist-rate scandal if the state activizes itlelf so as to further the interest of the poor.

As the debate lingers, curious axioms are slipped in: whatever is private is noble, uplifiting and supra-efficient: whatever is public, vile. Take the recent case of cease-work by the state electricity board employees in Uttar Pradesh. It demonstrated class solidarity of a remarkable kind. Dismissals and arrests failed to break the spirit of the striking employees; the authorities had finally yield to ground.

Capitulation in this manner by those whom they consider their servitors in government has greatly distressed the lovers of the free market. Don't you know the state electricity boards are the other name of gross inefficiency? They generate power at plant load factors that are as low as 30 or 40 per cent or even less. It is as if in case the SEBs were sold off to private parties, the plant load factor will automatically soar.

This is one of the principal myths nurtured by the narrative of post-independence Indian economic discourse. The private sector spells efficiency, the public sector is ipso facto inefficient. Some crucial facts are carefully ignored here. Public enterprises are subject to annual audit by the controller and auditor general of India; they also come under the scrutiny of parliamentary committees including the committee on estimates and the committee of public undertakings. Reports submitted by the CAG and the parlimentary committees are open for discussion by the general public. They are also debated in Parliament; editorial writers have a whale of a time commenting upon the supposedly huge waste of national resources the public undertakings indulge in. In contrast, whatever is managed by the private sector is supposed immediately to turn into gold.

The accounts of corporate units in the private sector do not have to go through the toothcomb of official audit. Corporate firms submit reports by complaisant licensed auditors on their performance. These reports conceal much more than they reveal, the newspapers and other media, driven by the urge of advancing class interest, faithfully reproduce the words of self-praise private entities specialize in.

As if efficiency and the private sector are coterminous. Forget for a moment the instance of the miserable state electricity boards and instead focus attention on the plight of the private automobile units operating in the country. If reports are to be believed, barring Maruti Suzuki, all the other automobile manufacturing units, including those set up with pomp and fanfare in the course of the past decade, are currently running at 20 or 25 per cent, or even less, of their rated capacity. Should not such inability to make full uses of invested capital be as deserving of condemnation as the incompetantly running state electricity boards?

The ambience is however the ambience. It is accordingly easy to pitch higher and higher the shrill demand from privatization of the SEBs. A familiar opening gambit is to hand over to private units the distribution network belonging to the SEBs. This plea is understandable since the margin of profit for power undertakings is the highest in the sphere of distribution, particularly where the distribution network has already been set up with public funds.

What is bound to happen will nonetheless happen. The authorities want to dismantle wholesale, the great Indian public sector, built brick by brick over a span of three and half decades following independence. The post-1990 Russian model has evidently set a dazzling example. Mafia groups are already around, some of them have leased in expertise, such as young management geniuses from this or that American university. The object is to establish intermediate chains which will buy cheap public sector units, cannibalize them and dispose them off at a price as high as the market will be able to bear.

The upshot of the post-1990 Russian experiment is by now well known National output is down to one half of that what it was in the Eighties, employment has shrivelled to one third of the level obtained in the preceding decade, aggregate capital formation is barely 20 per cent of the achievement in the Nineties, the education and social service system have all but collapsed, the great Russian people have transformed themselves into a nation of blackmarketeers and pimps.

If the apprehension expressed by the nation's president has any basis, the privatization process in India could have even worse consequences and the country's survival may itself turn into a question mark. So what? Indians ought to be thankful that they have been chosen as victims in the great cause of underwriting one hundred per cent perfection in the mobility of international capital.

If Aldous Huxely were around, he would conceivably write a fresh version of *Brave New World.* Besides, there will still be need for a ministry of public undertakings to buy up loss-making private units, such as those in the automobile industry.

16th February, 2000

Play of passions

The carnival planned by the World Trade Organization at Seattle ended in a grand fiasco. The authorship of the flasco will nonetheless continue to be a matter of dispute. The nongovernmental organisations, who spoiled the broth, were a mixed lot. Several amongest them were idealists and do-gooders par excellence,de-termined to prevent the bloody-minded monopolists who were bent on maximizing their rate of return by exploiting men, women and children working in fields and factories in the developing countries, offering them starvation wages, or not even that. These helpless people were also made to work in indescribably unhygienic conditions.

The NGOs flocked to Seattle from different countries, rich and poor. They knew their mind. The monopolists must not be permitted to further extend their empire, no pasaran. Alongside these ideologues, there were however other NGOs basically indistinguishable from pure mercenaries.

The United States administration, hand in glove with leading multinational companies, spent money like water to set up sham outfits who took over Seattle's boulevards and waterfront, vociferously demanding that the WTO immediately enforce labour standards and environmental restrictions for internationally traded goods.

The avowed purpose of all this was to install fear of god in the block of official representative from the poorer coutries: how dare you not agree to the incorporation of clauses relating to labour standards and environment in the WTO agenda when there is such intense support for their enforcement all over the world?

A third group too was active though. Trade unions in Western nations have long dispensed with the credo of the international brotherhood of the working class. They are genuinely afraid at the prospect of cheap consumer goods of all varieties and not just textiles, produced by transcontinental firms with the help of low cost labour in, for example, South Asian countries flooding their domestic markets and thereby threatening their employment and livelihood. Mercenaries, ideologues and pragmatists had different, distinct points of view, but WTO provided them with a common cause.

This, then, was the irony of the situation: the NGOs, the overwhelming majority of them, where for discussion and incorporation of labour standards and environmental restrictions in the WTO's future programme of work. In ordinary times, they are sworn enemies of the rampaging multinational corporations spearheading the global conspiracy of monopoly capital. But on this particular occasion, the difference between their approach and that of Levers and Monsantos was obliterated. Death to monopoly capital was okay. Coincidence being concidence, in the Seattle battlefied the NGO's found themselves on the same side as monopoly capitalists: the developing countries were totally isolated.

The well laid out plans of the US administration to use the NGOs for its selfish purpose however came a cropper. For there was also a fourth force which unleashed itself in Seattle with passion and furty. It was made up by thousands and thousands of radicalized American youth. While the latter were by and large on the same wavelength as the anti-monopoly capital ideologues, the primal thrust they injected in their anti-WTO slogans had a purity and an earnestness which set them apart. They had a cause, but no programme as such. They were disenchanted with the system. They hated the materialism which is conspiring to make everyone slaves of a website non-civilization. Those assembled at Seattle inducted a sizeable number of such desperate souls, crying out for liberation.

What was enacted by them was a passion play packed with extraordinary power. These zealots did not mind the introduction of violence in their schedule of activities. Nothing was lovelier to them than chaos. For chaos set at disarray the grammar and accountancy of the monopolists and of the country governments which operate as their servitors.

They did not have the least doubt that the ministerial conference organized by the WTO was at the centre of the evil design of international finance capital to dominate the markets of the poorer countries in the name of free international trade. Death to monopoly capital; death to the WTO.

These four different forces took charge of Seattle's streets and ramparts, broke glass panes, upturned cars, and challenged into a direct confrontation the conspirators plotting to enslave the world. Gunfire, smoke from exploding tear gas shells and torrents of water unleashed by the water bombs transformed the ambience. Law and order as defined by the US administration broke down. Soon it was curtain time, and nothing worthwhile could be salvaged by the capitalist mafia from the debris.

True, a fifth influence too was at work hastening the final collapse of the WTO farce. The European Union and Japan found themselves in total opposition to the US resolve to banish all subsidies for farm products. Over our dead bodies, said the Europeans and the Japanese, who were hardly in a position to ignore the strong agricultural lobby in their backyard. They would not yield, the Americans would not yield either, it was, in consequence, a magnificent impasse.

Confusion crowded upon confusion, and soon the hour of adjournment arrived. No firm agenda could be agreed to for WTO's activities in the new millennium, thereby providing a respite, even if it be temporary, for the poorer countries.

International monopoly capital has received a setback. But there should be no illusion, this is only an interrupted chapter. The multinational corporations and the governments they support will regroup themselves; it is a matter of only a few months. Attempts will be made to thrash out a reconciliation on the issue of agricultural subsidies between the Americans on one side, and Japan and the EU on the other.

It is a mixed-up situation from all accounts, whether in the advanced economies or elsewhere. Agricultural workers and non-surplus raising small farmers have not received any worthwhile benefit from the ongoing farm subsidy schemes.

The termination of the subsidies will perhaps not cause them irreparable harm in the long run. But if export trade of farm products shrinks because of the withdrawal of subsidies, rich peasants and big farmers may try to protect themselves by coming down hard on farm wages and by selective layoff of workers. Tension will then grow in the rich and poor economies alike. Whether or not such tension is welcome will depend entirely on one's class point of view.

The temporary respite the Seattle fiasco has brought about will prove to be a mirage unless the developing countries give themselves a second chance. The tidal wave of emotion on the part of the American youth was a chance occurrence at Seattle.

Whether it will sustain itself remains uncertain. It is also altogether possible that idealist youths and NGOs will actually team up in support of speedy enforcement of labour standards and environmental preconditions in international trade. Developing countries will be left in the lurch should such a thing happen.

There is not much time left, the so-called third world countries must learn once more to come together. The hangover of the 19th century adage insists on the non-existence of permanent enemies or permanent friends in the sphere of international politics. The adage certainly does not hold for international economics; there can be no question of monopoly capital experiencing a change of heart and defending the interests of the poor, developing nations; that kind of denouement will erode global profitability.

The confrontation between the expolitiers and the exploited will therefore continue. The rules of the WTO will, sooner or later, be drastically rewritten to promote further the common interests of the industrialized Western nations and monopoly capital; the poor countries will be advised that in case they are unable to stand the heat, they should rather not enter the kitchen—which is another way of telling them that, taking all factors into consideration, they have no business to survive, their historical role is to serve the imperial-colonial order in its new incarnation—and then to fade away.

The story will still not end though. China is on the threshold of entering the WTO. Unlike the governments of countries in the rest of the world. China is in no dread of the United States, it is in fact the other way round. For coping with the assaults the US administration will soon launch to bully them into submission to the tyranny of the WTO's unfair rules, the poor countries, including India, need a ballast. China—with a rate of economic growth exceeding 10 per cent per annum and a population approaching 130 billion—will be a mighty ballast. But she has to be approached, and in a proper manner.

Our ruling politicians and their mandarins still exist in a time warp. They need to appreciate the fact that there are more things in heaven and earth than are written in the motheaten manual for international governance authored by the United States of America.

22nd December, 1999

Forget 1962

In harsh summertime, the instinct is to seek cloud cover. The regime has made use of the cover provided by the distraction of the announcement of the Lok Sabha poll results so as to escape the embarassment of across the board increase in diesel prices as well as of signing the comprehensive test ban treaty. Pressure from the American administration as well as the World Bank-International Monetary Fund bosses was obviously intense.

The wages of both Pokhran and Kargil had to be paid. The additional budgetary deficit expenditure necessitated by the line of control clashes must be narrowed, say the wisdom dispensers from Washington, DC.

In any event, the fund-bank entitties follow the signals set by the United States administration, which wanted to even scores and snub New Delhi because of its intransigence demonstrated by the implosion at Pokhran. The Americans now know they have got India comprehensively entrapped. The CTBT must be signed, or else the Indians will be cut off from all victuals.

Forget the American pressure. It is legitimate for anybody to raise questions on the issue of the waste of public money, of the tens and tens of billions Pokhran had called for. Within a week of Pokhran, the Pakistanis responded in kind; the supposed additional superiority in military prowess accomplished *vis a vis* Pakistan immediately proved to be a myth. This was on top of the opprobrium attracted by the obstinacy of our government in not signing the CTBT. The pretension of being a big power when the back up clout is missing is easily exposed.

It has therefore been a harrowing time for the government in New Delhi in recent months. A globalized economy has its own compulsions. Imports are up, exports are down, foreign institutional investors and non-resident Indians are proving to be exceptionally volatile in their mood. The US administration is in a position to choke the inflow of funds from these external sources. That is a terible thought; the surrender to the Americans has accordingly to be most thoroughgoing. On top of all this, the consequences of the World Trade Organization's tough regulations have to be coped with.

Pokhran and Kargil have set in train logistical requirements, the purchase of arms and material must have soared. Only the Americans have the capability to bail us out in these circumstances. There have been no screaming headlines, but the superpower, it can be taken for granted, is fulfilling the role history has assigned for it. The price it is extracting from India is extraordinarily harsh. But it could hardly be otherwise.

India, the Americans have judged with precision, have no where to go. The government of India will now sign the CTBT, with not a squeak of protest. It will also have to be on its best behaviour while expressing views on the WTO's Seattle agenda. It is in fact the beginning of the season for signing on the dotted line as behaves a subordinate power.

John Foster Dulles's dream of a pan-American universe has finally come true. Were he around, he would have been happy beyond measure at the turn of events. India is now no different from a teeny-weeny country such as Thailand or the Philippines, meek as sheep, doing the bidding of the master.

Even so, it continues to be an unstable state of affairs. The Americans are more than likely to discover to their cost that, whatever the superficial resemblance between emerging situations, India cannot be treated in the same manner as Thailand and the Philippines had been during the Cold War. It is much too big an entity. It also retains the memory of a not too distant past when it indulged in the luxury of a delusion of grandeur. It was, the records would show, the leader of the Afro-Asian movement and of the movement of the non-aligned nations which culminated in the Group of 77 in United Nations forums.

Its government has since fallen on bad times. Adverse consequences have followed. It made a hash of the model of independent economic development. The experience of globalization the economy is currently going through has no central focus. The economy cannot sustain itself at practically any level without huge external accommodation.

The country's political leadership, given its class roots, is quite prepared to yield all the way to the Americans. At least these leader know how hollow the recent claim of a famous victory at Kargil is India and Pakistan have been shown their place by the superpower, both countries better agree to play lapdog to the good Americans, thereby entering the zone of tranquillity.

Can this be a stable arrangement though? Memory will rankle the leaders of the subcontinent, the memory of times when they were the cock of the show. Ideological chasms have perhaps long ceased to be an issue, but the pride the nonaligned movement had bequeathed does not wither away. The pride, alas, has no longer any rational basis, Indians as a nation are alas, yet to appreciate that fact. Chafing at American superbossism, they seek a credible way out. For a while the hope is cherished that the European Union could offer a conceivably appropriate challenge to the US. That hope has since dimmed. The Europeans, it seems, have little interest in the pastime of placing roadblocks to colonial-imperial pursuits by any neighbour, big or small.

Look around, look around, there may still be someone else willing to protect India from superpower overbearingness. Despite its immense wealth and resources, Japan though has not the least intention to assume any such role. It is well satisfied with its status as a sleeping partner of the Group of 15 community; if the Americans say it is high tide, so says the government of Japan; if the Americans say it is low tide, ditto say the Japanese. Against this background, it will be altogether absurd to appeal to the Japanese to rescue us from the clutches of the superpower.

Quite candidly, just one country is in a position to help India escape the claustrophobia born out of American hauteur. The regard and deference China commands these days is without parallel in global history. The Soviet Union even in its heydays evoked widespread derision. No country, in contrast,dares to hate China.

China has maintained a rate of economic growth averageing more than 10 per cent per annum during the last decade, Western powers keep vying with one another to have a share of the huge market the world's most populous nation is able to offer. China is no part of the WTO, and yet the Western countries lean backwards as much as they can to offer most favoured nation treatment to the Middle Kingdom. The prayer on every lip is to stay on the right side of China.

The noise Chinese leaders made on the occasion of the 50th anniversary of the People's Republic indicate that they are now willing to consider donning a more expansive role, in world affairs. They have the werewithal to offer challenge to the Americans and other Western powers. If Indians are in desperate search of a senior patron to speak on their behalf and rattle the American establishment, China can fit that bill. And perhaps the Chinese, pragmatic to the core, will be willing to let bygones be bygones and agree to protect a distinguished fellow member of the ancient NAM from economic exploitation by the west.

It is the Indian administration which will be in a jam here. The Chinese can save us from American boorishness. *Realpolitik* would therefore suggest the wisdom of opening a line of communication with China. But, wait a minute, is this not the same China which, "invaded" our territory in 1962? How can we then accept the protective cover offered by it? To do so will be an affront to our national dignity!

These issues will crowd the arena now that the counting is over and the Lok Sabha is about to be called to order.

13th October 1999

Colonialism with a new face

Indians, along with the rest of the lot, should feel proud. Bossmen from Washington DC have decided to call countries such as ours by a new name. We are henceforth to be known as "Transition Countries". Better be careful not to press the bossmen too hard to explain the transition aluded to is from what level of existence to what other. Is it a transition from a kind of social stability to near chaos? Or transition from a reasonably tolerable economic circumstance to one where all indicators are down, including those connoting growth of income or of employment, levels of savings and capital formation, the rate of expansion of basic infrastructures, apart from a precipitate fall in exports and a corresponding rise in imports, resulting in an acute crisis in the balance of payments?

The symptoms just described ought to have a familiar ring; these have afflicted the Indian economy since 1991. We are not of course the only country heading for disaster on account of the adoption of the policy of liberalization at the command of patriarchs from overseas. For nations ensnared by bossmen ahead of us, for example, South Korea, Thailand, Malaysia and the Philoppines, the experience was almost identical. Or perhaps not, since in their case the economic situation had in fact initially imporved before taking a turn for the worse. With us, it has been, right from the beginning, a rapid downward slide. A great conspiracy of silence is on to snuff out this particular truth. If you would watch the media or listen to politicians of almost all hues, the impression is unavoidable that, following liberalization, it is pardise for this country.

No point in blinking, the class bias intrudes here in an unabashed manner. For the nation's top 10 per cent, the takeover of the system by so called free market forces has been quite a boon. Linkages have been established by this top decile with foreign parties for whose benefit the ritual of reforms is primarily intended. You can pick any criterion by which to judge the merit or demerit of an activity or measure that has been initiated in the wake of globalization and liberalization. Each such activity has, unfailingly, helped the interests of foreigners, a foreign bank, a foreign commercial outfit, a foreigner owned industrial form picking on India for a limited investment experiment, a stock market whose rules have been reframed to facilitate easy come easy go capital movements by foreign institutional investors.

After a gap of half a century or thereabouts, colonialism is back, with strong support from the nation's rich, who are happy to greet the return of forein rule, at least foreign economic rule, as long as their interests are taken care of.

Even so, the possibility of hiccups cannot be excluded. All of a sudden, bossmen in Washington, DC, occupying cosy offices in the World Bank and the International Monetary Fund, have started to sound contrite. It is time, in their view, to rethink the tempo of privatization in the "Transition Economies". In some of these countries, successful transition from a milieu dominated by state owned public enterpirses to full blown capitalism has been hampered because of a lack of basic infrastructures.

This has resulted in the appropriation, at dirt cheap prices, of major public sector undertakings, by groups of mafias. The latter have ransacked the units in quest of ready cash, sound economic management be damned. In a number of other instances, public banks have been unceremoniously handed over to private parties who have again assumed their kingdom to have come; the resources of the banks have been blown away in wild sprees.

Episodes of this nature have been common in the counries which once constituted the Soviet Union. By its wild experiments with liberalization, the IMF-World Bank fraternity has brought these countries to the brink of economic ruination. Great news; the two financial agencies are now in a *mea culpa* mood. They want to review their policies and introduce changes.

For countries which have already been led to irretrievable disaster, it is little consolation that bossmen are going through a revisionist phase. What has been done to these countries cannot be undone. One cynical view can be that, in the given circumstances, the best thing for international institutions such as the IMF and the World Bank would be to forget for some time that these "Transition Countries" existed on the map of the world. Let the TCs be on their own for a certain stretch of time; they will then learn the hard way about where they have gone wrong largely because of unwise advice transmitted from overseas. In the process, they will reassimilate the virtues of savings and capital formation, as well as reappreciate the worthwhileness of a matrix of priorities formulated under the guidance of a central planning authority.

There should be no illusion on this score. The bossmen are unlikely to allow the TCs a tenure of freedom for along. They will follow the pattern of the accounting methodology of yore, "First in first go, last in last go". India is a late entry in the liberalized world, the bossmen might prefer to play around with this country for some more before striking the repentant mood. Given the concatenation of political and military power across the globe, this country will have no alternative but to yield.

We can hope for little mercies though. The IMF-World Bank duo has a stablemate, the World Trade Organization. The WTO nurtures the same world view as the IMF and the World Bank do; the bossmen are in total control of this agency too. The WTO's objective is to use the mechanism of trade liberalization to ensure that the former colonial powers garner the same benefits from international commerce as they enjoyed throughout the 19th and the first half of the 20th century buy the deployment of naked imperial might.

Its charter has been drafted exclusively with the objective in mind. Western manufacturing units must have uninhibited patent rights, no allowance is to be made to special circumstances afflicting this or that poor country; all tariff and non-tariff restrictions must be off for imports into the developing countries while their exports will be subject to the regimen of "social factors' cooked by Western governments. Rigid and uniform trade related investment rules are proposed to be set up, even the structure of taxation on foreign investments in developing countries is to be determined by the world trade body, forget the notion that it, the WTO, is dealing with formally sovereign national entities. A test of the extent of contrition the IMF-World Bank bosses are suffering from will be their eillingness to advise the WTO to go slow. What they have done cannot be undone, but that the WTO is about to do can still be averted.

The balance of probability however indicates that no such suggestion will be entertained. The IMF and the World Bank have grown into huge employment offering agencies. Young Ph Ds from this or that Western university are recruited by the two institutions as a matter of course. These youngsters are free to roam about in their imagination and even free to suggest a few heresies, such as the the IMF and the World Bank had committed a few operational mistakes in the not too distant past which need immediate correction.

The heresies formulated by the young brats will receive some publicity. A leopard does not, however, change its spots. The imperial powers have won decisively the Cold War, the 19th century model of colonial rule is crying out for full fledged readaptation. The young graduates recruited by the IMF and the World Bank, rest assured, will be put to graze in the due season.

For instance, consider the latest developments within the WTO. An impasse was reached over the appointment of its next director general. Western governments had lobbied hard for a New Zeland politician to occupy the slot. But the poorer countries were determined not to let go of this opportunity to gain direct control over the management of a major international institution. They handed together and named a former finance minister of Thailand as their candidate for the office. For nearly six months, activities in the WTO screeched to a halt; neither side was prepared to give in. But as is the wont in an iniquitous world, pressure mounted, pressure of diverse kinds, and the colonial powers managed to squeeze a victory in the final round. A compromise was mediated upon; the six year term of the director general was to be divided into two three year tenures so as to accommodate both the New Zealander and the Thailander.

A livable arrangement, did you say? No, the Western powers saw to it that there was "frontloading" of their candidate, while the aspirant from the third world was "backloaded". That is to say, for the first three years, the Western governments would be in command, enabling them to rush through the WTO statutes concerning patents and global investment rules they have set their hearts upon. The "Transition Countries", demoralized, would give up their cohesion and render themselves putty in the hands of the rebuilders of pristine colonialism.

Read the electoral manifestos of this country's two main political parties. The issues of growing foreign dependence from no part of the agenda of either: This chould hardly cause any surprise. Did not the two of them, comrades in thought and deed, vote together to scuttle the Patents Act of 1970? They will now march together, joyfully, into the fading sunset.

1st September 1999

Circular argument

Ripley's wonders are not yet quite defunct. That moribund body, the Indian planing commission, has suddenly sprung into news. Liberalizatrion has made an ass of the concept of economic coordination under the stewardship of a Central authority. Forget the halcyon days of P.C. Mahalanobis, whatever limited initiatives the planning commission was allowed in the decades immediately following independence have now been snuffed out by the ministry of finance.

The commission was in fact an oddity from its very beginning. It was charged with the responsibility of reaching an objective judgment on processes to optimize the country's economic and social development and assign priorities for observation by both the Centre and the states.

This theoretical framework was a non-starter, since the commission got constituted as a regular department of the Union government. The commission's working head, the deputy chairman, was, more often than not, a member of the Union cabinet of ministers. Even otherwise, things were so arranged that he was a permanent invitee to meetings of the Union cabinet. The notion of a planning commission, equidistant from the Centre and the states and reaching independent decisions on the contents and contours of five year plans, was unceremoniously buried.

Things have worsened with the onset of liberalization. In the more recent years, the commission has functioned as a lugubrious *sarkari* agency, doing minor routine chores. Its major residual activity has been to decide the size of the state annual plans and the magnitude of plan assistance to be advanced to each state, 70 per cent as loan and 30 per cent as grants. The *inter se* allocation of plan assistance was in terms of a formula enunciated way back in 1968 when D.R. Gadgil was the deputy chairman of the commission. The formula has been revised a number of times but the primary stress has been to earmark funds after taking into account the level of underdevelopment at one end and capacity to raise resources and execute projects at the other.

Few took the planning commission seriously. In any case, plan allocations were a mere ritual, for overall resources available to the states have tended invariably to fall short of what was needed to reach the assigned plan targets. The principal reason for disparate development among the states has actually been the inability of the poorer states to garner adequate resources while the better off states enjoyed the advantage of a strong resource base; the retrograde decision to channel proportionately larger funds from Central sources, such as the public financial institutions, to the better performing states has rendered the situation worse.

For a majority of the states the shortage of resources has led to largescale diversion by state governments of plan funds for non-plan purposes. Pundits occupying planning commission cubicles in New Delhi, having little touch with the country's ground reality, have written long notes deploring such conduct on the part of the states. Their pedantry has been laughed away.

Every dog, however, will have its day, or thinks it will have. A caretaker government is having an unusually long tenure because of the Election Commission's reluctance to hold the Lok Sabha polls during the rainy season. The Pakistan administration has been most cooperative and its probings in Kargil have enabled the caretaker regime to create the verisimilitude of a warlike ambience. Each of a the established political parties, fearful of losing votes in case there is the faintest suspicion that it is a shade less patriotic than the rest, has joined the orgy of war hysteria. Life is seemingly no longer worth living for any political party unless the neighbouring country is given a bloody nose.

Meanwhile, taking advantage of the prevailing confusion, the authorities temporarily ensconced in power in New Delhi are playing an altogether mischievous role. Even the half dead planning commission is back in harness. In a circular to all state governments under the dateline of May 26 last, the commission has chosen to imagine itself as the *czar* imperial extraordinary. Block plan assistance as per the Gadgil formula—this circular has informed the states—is being suspended; instead, from now on, the planning commission will recommend plan assistance on project to project basis.

This will be a throwback to the pre 1968 format, which the states disliked immensely since it reduced flexibility of state plans and led to increasing centralization of development programmes. The states had fought tooth and nail against such overcentralization. As a result, a more relaxed framework of Centre-state economic relations had emerged in the more recent period.

Every dog, however, suffers from the illusion that its day has arrived. The planning commission perhaps surmised that each and everybody is apparently agog over Kargil, this was the time to turn the tables on the states and bring back the climate of economic authoritarianism that was the hallmark of the Indira Gandhi days.

The Gadgil formula, the commission says, is off. It proposes to set up in its place a fund for Central assistance "linked to specific projects" and "on the bais of certain laid down criteria and performance parameters". Mind you, this *diktat* has been issued *suo moto* without even perfunctory consultations with the state governments. It has not been placed before the national development council for its concurrence either.

The motivation behind such a major change in the modality of Central plan assistance is a couple of complaints alleging diversion of funds for other purposes by some states and "non-performance" by some states. These are agiain suo moto judgements reached by the commission. Going by the contents of the circular, it does not show the least interest in delving into the causes which contribute to aggravated financial difficulties experienced by the states, forcing them to divert funds from one head to another. The advisers in the planning commission in charge of the different states will supposedly act commissars from now on. They, the circular says, will decide whether monthly releases of Central plan assistance have been properly utilized by the respective states. If these civil servants think otherwise, assistance to the states will be summarily cut off.

The effrontery of a caretaker regime has without question crossed the accepted bounds of decency. For fun's sake, one could raise one query: whether the planning commission would dare to enforce a similar regimen of fiscal discipline for plan projects sponsored by the Central ministeries?

Never mind, there is no dearth of black humour though. The planning commission has ventured to remind the states in the aforementioned circular that additional resources provided to them as plan assistance till now where akin to an act of charity on the part of the Centre, for such assistance is not "constitutionally mandated". It itself, someone might point out to the commission, has no constitutional mandate either: it was set up by a government resolution and it can be packed off into oblivion any time, any day.

The Union government, as it exists at present, has a caretaker existence; its planning commission is equally of a caretaker nature. If these entities do not respect the boundary conditions they are expected to follow, an appropriate constitutional authority has to tell them, please, this far and no further. The president, it is to be hoped, will take note of the mischief that is afoot and will order the annulment of the commission's circular.

23rd June, 1999

Rich man, poor man

Spokesmen of the Indian Institutes of Management strewn across the country—Ahmedabad, Calcutta, Bangalore, Lucknow, *et al* have gone to own, and for reasons to be presently dislosed. These institutes were set up over the past four decades with the objective of lifting the level of efficiency of Indian managers. Whether the efficiency of the executive cadres has in fact gone up as a consequence of superior managerial education is a matter of debate, the criteria by which to assess the secular trend of efficiency are not at all clear cut.

That does not however hinder discussion on the allegedly poor performance in the part of inferior level employees. superior grade managers are, by definition, taken to be impeccable geniuses. Others may abide the question, senior managers, such as those groomed by the institutes of management, are free. For poor wage earners, on the other hand, the rigimen is overly strict.

Globalization has also wrought one wonderous transformation. Efficiency has nothing to do with it, it is exclusively on account of wholesale deregulation of corporate emoluments that the level of earnings of the senior managerial staff has juamped 15, 20, 30, in some instances even a hundred times compared to what it was a decade ago. The statutory celling on salaries prevalent in the country during the post-independence years has been given the go by. Foreign forms are briskly sicking recruits to man their freshly opened outposts in the country. Given the huge profits they are squeezing out of the Indian economy, payment of emoluments to the selected staff on a global scale hardly causes them problems.

Spokesmen of the institutes of management are therefore having a field day of late: what a grand phenomenon, the labour market could not be more generous; some of their graduates, barely 24 or 25 years of age, have landed jobs fetching salary of close to rupees five million annually, or more than Rs. 4,50,000 per month. Five to 10 thousand individuals in the country, a quick count suggests, are receiving emoluments in this range. Please do not be shocked. Compared to American salary levels, what these Indian executives are being paid is not at all ourageous. Globalization is as globalization does.

These would appear to be scandalous only if average payments to the overwhelming sections of the Indian working class are taken into consideration.

The latest pay commission is recommended an increase of roughly 20 per cent across the board in government salaries. That official body, the Central Statistical Organization, has these days chosen to cross over from pure data gathering to social preaching as well.

One part of the reason for the hefty increase in the relative proportion of income from the service sector in gross domestic product in the course of the past decade, it has commented, is the scale of improvement in government emoluments. The CSO has scrupulously stayed away from mentioning though that the rate of increase in earnings from service activities in the private sector has been several times higher. The idea of the ruling classes becomes the ruling idea of the epoch; it has certainly turned out to be so for our official statistical agency.

The written media and those others who matter in the world of communications are equally partisan, and equally reticant. There is at least no evidence of surprise or consternation in the pages of newspapers or in discussions in political circles, including in Parliament, over the datum that, in this poor country where nearly 30 per cent of the population cannot even afford the calorie intake needed for bare subsistence, some organizations have the temerity to offer their fresh recruits as much as Rs 4.5 million as annual salary.

Replying to the debate on the president's address in Parliament, the prime minister went into raptures over the supposedly magnificent achievements in the country's agricultural front in recent times. The granaries, he was ecstatic, are overfull and the government is in a predicament over the rising level of foodstocks lying with the Food Corporation of India. Should not the prime minister be a shade better informed? Stocks of foodgrains are not being offloaded from the public distribution system because the prices at which these grains are offered for sale to the nation's poor are much too high at the given level of their earnings.

The majority of the Indian consumers, who mostly comprise small peasants and landless workers, are, let us have the honesty to admit, being priced out of the foodgrains market. The enactment of this great human tragedy misses the satellite channels just as it misses the hi-tech daily newspapers. At one end, immense pressure emanates from the World Trade Organization and other lobbies, foreign and domestic, to globalize farm prices, including grain prices; these prices accordingly zoom. At the other end though, for the overwhelming majority of the nation, income is pegged at where it was a decade ago.

There is officially sanctified statistics to back up the point just made. The crucial information the latest *Economic Survey* has let us on, however elliptically, is with respect to the overall rate of growth of farm output in the country. This growth rate has, in the course of the Nineties, just kept pace with the rate of growth of population. Which is another way of saying that the per capita availability of agricultural output, including that of foodgrains, has remined stagnant since the initiation of the great economic reforms.

That respectable Mumbai research body, the Centre for Monitoring the Indian Economy, has gone on record expressing some scepticism about the official data on growth rates. According to it, government agencies have overestimated growth in the farm sector that has taken place between the early Nineties and now. Should the CMIE presumption be correct, per capita growth in farm—and foodgrain—output must have actually lagged behind the rate of growth in population since 1991. Per capita availability of foodgrains in other words, has shrunk since the begining of the liberalization spree.

Another conclusion is also derivable from the same data. Roughly two-thirds of the Indian population continue to draw their livelihood from the farm sector. This was the situation five decades ago; it remains so even today. As vouchsafed again by official statistics, there has been no relative displacement of workers away from agriculture in the course of the past decade. With per capita income in agriculture at best remaining stagnant, two thirds of the Indian population have experienced no increase in real earnings since reforms began.

However, over the same period the level of service incomes has jumped 15, 20, or a hundred times; young graduates from the IIMs have come to enjoy a salary level of roughly rupees five million a year as against the per capita income level of barely Rs. 5,000 or thereabouts for 60 percent of the coutnry's population. If the arithmetic is right, the income differential works out to 1:1,000.

We can allow ourselves to proceed a bit further. It would be altogether surprising if, in the course of this past decade, income distribution within agriculture has not got further tilted in favour of the top 10 to 15 per cent of the agrarian community. After all, no worthwhile land reforms have taken place in this period and most of the advantages accruing from the availability of water, fertilizer and high yielding varieties of seeds has gone to the rich peasantry and landlord classes. Such being the case, the smallholders, share corppers and landless workers who make up the preponderant sections of the Indian population must have experienced a decline in their per capita real income in the course of the Ninetes while those in the upper income brackets, particularly those in the services sector, have enjoyed real income growth of an astronomical order.

Such facts are not supposed to be mentioned in the etherized, culturally refined, globalized ambience of post reforms society. The pigheaded ones who nonetheless venture to raise these issues are ostracized and their voices stilled. But a doubt persists. Can the upper classes who are ruling the roost be at all confldent that despite the system they have ushered in being against nature and against rationality, it would be sustainable for any length of time?

It is a bizarre situation. The landless cultivator earns at most Rs. 5,000 annually, while the young IIM graduate is paid ruppees five million. Does it mean that the latter is one thousand times more efficient than the poor Indian peasant? Suppose the multinational company which employs the IIM graduate decides to raise his annual emoluments overnight from rupees five million to rupees 10 million, does it then mean that, instead of being a thousand times more efficient than the wretched peasant, he has become, overnight, two thousnd times more efficient than the rustic fellow?

14th April 1999

Paid the pipers

An official status report was being presentated in the house on the progress of the ongoing discussion between this country's minister for external affairs and the deputy secretary of state in the United States administration over such issues as India's non-signing of the comprehensive test ban treaty and the sanctions imposed by the Western powers in the wake of Pokhran. A member of parliament was obviously lacking in manners. He rose to enquire of the prime minister whether it was right that while we were represented in the discussions by our minister for external affairs, no less, the US administration had condescended to send only a junior level functionary, a deputy secretary; this was no way, he felt, to treat a sovereign nation; should not we protest?

The prime minister promptly rose in his seat: in this very sensitive matter we should not insist on protocol; after all, when the talks with the US started, our external affairs minister had no official status and was only deputy chairman of the planning commission; the US authorities did not however, the prime minister said, stand on ceremony and readily agreed to enter into formal negotiations with us; we should have the generosity to reciprocate the gesture, and desist from raising a furore over the fact that our minister for external affairs had to sit down for talks with a mere deputy secretary from the dumps of Foggy Bottom.

The prime minister was wrong in a matter of important detail. The deputy chairman of our planning commission, he forgot—or chose to forget—has the official status of a cabinet minister. He has the right to attend all cabinet meetings. So, even in the early stages of the India-US talks, the country representations were asymmetrical: the US administration had rubbed it in that we were little more than a vassal state which had deviated from discipline, a deputy secretary despatched from Washington DC should be enough to straighten us out.

It is this deputy secretary who has now announced to the world that the phase of insubordination is over, India is soon going to sign the CTBT, but that sanctions will for the present continue. Our Parliament is yet to be consulted over this major switch of policy on the part of our government. But leave that out. There was not even a joint communique on behalf of the two governments.

A vassal state should know its place. The government installed in New Delhi does.

It took a bare half year for the bravado of May to be buried in the hailstorms of January. We need not ourselves inform the neighbourhood that we have ceased to be a sovereign and independent nation and been reduced to the status of a banana republic; a serf gets known as a serf because he conducts himself as one. Decisions reached by the US administration are henceforth to be regarded as our decisions. That is the essence of servitude, notwithstanding the mild apologia voiced by the ex-socialist who takes pride in describing himself as the country's defence minister.

In this situation it is pointless to raise epistemological queries concerning sense and sensibility. The government in New Delhi does not know how long it is going to survive. Internal dissensions are tearing apart the major party in the ruling coalition. The economy is in deep recession and a serious balance of payment problem is threatening to re-emerge. Signs of anarchy and disorderliness are rampant all over the country. India's name is mud in international concourse following the grisly happenings in Gujrat and Orissa. The Shiv Sena's antics over the visit of the Pakistani cricket team have contributed another black mark to the reputation of the nation.

Hope nonetheless springs eternal in the human breast, hope that a saviour, you know who, is round the corner. The message must have been transmitted along the shivering corridors of North and South Blocks; since our very existence is in peril, do not ask any questions, just surrender to the superpower. Just five decades and a couple of odd years, the *maa-baap* ethos is back with vengeance.

What else too can be inferred from the extaordinary manner the finance minister is going about to budget eve. His perambulations strongly resemble the calisthenics indulged in by a jumping Jack. He claims he does not mind spilling the beans: it is going to be a stern, hard budget. By which he means that the financial side in the budgetary presentation will be of little cheer. But do we not already know that?

We also know a bit more. Formulating the contours of the government of India's budget is no longer the prerogative of the country's finance minister and his associates and advisers. It is not subject to the wishes and predilections of the Union cabinet either. Let there be no mincing of words, the budget is a prepackaged material despatched from Washington DC. This country owes to the various entities headquartered in the US capital roughly one hundred billion dollars. He who pays the piper calls the tune. None can therefore question the right of Foggy Bottom to announce India's defence policy in the future. The terrain ought to seem to be familiar; for in the not very distant past, the secretary of state for India was wont to declare war on sundry foreign powers on behalf of the subject country, India. In any event a nation's defence, foreign and economic policies are intertwined.

It is a well publicized fact—South Block dare not contradict—that the US authorities insisted, as precondition to the lifting of the post-Pokhran sanctions, a pledge from the Atal Behari Vajpayee regime to ram through Parliament the insurance and patents legislations. That the principal opposition, the Congress, was also a party to the arrangement does not detract from the substance of the story.

The finance minister's pre-budget barkings are hence not to be taken as any major departure. He is barking because quarters in Washington DC want him to bark, and bark according to a particular cadence. The American mindset—with additional inspiration bequeathed by Margaret Thatcher's writtings—has come to shape the views of India's finance minister. His focus is narrow, inordinately so. As if the nation's existence depends on trimming the size of the fiscal deficit alone, the rest of the considerations—including those related to the problems of poverty, malnutrition, educational backwardness and unemployment—could be relegated to the back corner. It is a no nonsense message Washington DC has transmited to India's budget framers: the deficit must be scaled down, but raising direct imposts is out, hiking import duties is equally anathema, therefore concentrate on steep increases in the levels of administered prices.

This, it goes without saying, has to be accompanied by, as the quaint expression goes, "downsizing" government outlays, including on subsidies and the public distribution system. Some window dressing is of course called for allocations of a few social sectors because of the exigencies of domestic politics, otherwise the command is to cut back public expenditure here, there, everywhere.

It is necessary to be candid though. Why venture to put only this finance minister on the dock, the shift in India's fiscal circumstances really got going in June 1991. As to foreign policy, especially foreign economic policy, the concordat between India's ruling classes, irrespective of the different political parties they usually belong to, remains strong and firm despite the visible outward signs of dissonance: the economy has to be opened up, our dependence on external resources in order to accelerate the pace of economic growth must be total, all that is required to bring about that denouement should be pursued singlemindedly.

This, then, is the *curiosus*. The principal political formations will swear their faith in the concept of national unity, they will still not be averse to set in motion centrifugal forces that spell disintegration of the polity. They cannot tolerate one other and ceaselessly plot the downfall of the adversaries on the domestic front. And yet, a common thread of understanding binds these sworn enemies on one particular issue: come what may, foreign investors must be accorded the red carpet treatment in all seasons, the age of imperialism, know ye all, belongs to the dump heap of history and exploitation as a philosophical concept has lost its relevance.

Perhaps it is such fullscale globalization of finance capital this country's finance minister is working for. His prebudget perorations are a curtain raiser.

17th February, 1999

Unrevealed text

Developments in the course of the past month appear to have rought into the open a dilemma entrapping the Bharatiya Janata Party regime in New Delhi: it is as if cannot quite decide whether it wants to stay or get out. If market gossip is to be lent any credence, a kind of working arrangement has been worked out with the Congress—or at least the occupant of 10 Janpath: as long as the Atal Behari Vajpayee government does not make too much of a fuss over Bofors, it would be allowed to survive.

There is an important pragmatic reason, it will be said, for this decision on the part of the Congress: the party is not at all sure whether in case the BJP led coalition is voted out and a general election follows. it will succeed in improving its position in Bihar and Uttar Pradesh. Without significant strides by the Congress in these two states, the BJP and its quarrelsome partners have a fair chance of holding on to power.

The predicament the BJP is facing has no doubt other sources as well. With an ally like the Shiv Sena in tow, the country's international rating, both political and financial, is bound to plummet continuously under Vajpayee-L. K. Advani helmsmanship. There should be, BJP acolytes may argue, some objectivity in assessing the relative performance of the various national political parties, and to single their favourite party out for condemnation on account of the wayward behaviour of a coalition partner is in-fairness unbound.

True, the BJP is in no position to rein in Bal Thackeray and his wild ones. But then, the BJP apologists could chip in, the Congress's record in this respect is no better. Not only did the P.V. Narashimha Rao government watch philosophically as the Babri Masjid was pulled down on that grim December day in 1992; it was equally otherwordly when the Shiv *sainiks* went on the rampage later that month and during the most part of the following month, Mumbai and Maharashtra were held in ransom, and Thackeray gave a throaty call for the extermination of Muslims. The agenda included killing and arson and appropriation wholesale of the assets and properties of the infidels.

The scope of the holy war against Muslims was soon extended to cover the non-Maharashtrians settled in the state as well. It was total non-rule of law and order. The Congress regimes both at the Centre and in Maharashtra however dared not, or wanted not to, step in. Thackeray was left undisturbed, no prosecution was launched against him, and there has been not a single occasion in the last six years when he was made to spend a night in a cold cell for his misdoings. If offering a *carte blanche* to the Shiv Sena for indulging in murder and mayhem is the core of the issue, obviously the Congress cannot flaunt a clean record.

In sizing up their judgment on the evolving political situation in India, foreigners may or may not agree with each of the sentiments reflected in the preceding paragraphs. What conclusions nonetheless would you expect them to reach? This is precisely where the irony latent in the circumstances strains to reveal itself. One outstanding feature in recent developments is the increasing convergence of views between the two major political parties in the country on the entire gamut of economic policy, both domestic and foreign.

A glaring illustration of this was the closing of ranks over the patents bill. The Congress went to the length of issuing a whip to its memebers in the Rajya Sabha to support this particular piece of legislation. The concordat over economic policy is even more strongly mirrored in the attitude towards foreign investment. Neither party has failed to try to satisfy, to the extent of one hundred per cent, any wish or predilection of foreign investors, however otiose.

Concessions have been piled up on concessions. The declining trend in actual long term foreign investment has not led to any critical ressessment of the open door policy by either political party; on the contrary, disappointments of this nature have been the precursor of further and yet further acts of liberalization. Countrymen have been assured by both parties that, if not in this round, certainly in the next round, the concessions accorded to foreigners would be reciprocated by a gushing flow of foreign capital into the country. But no such thing has happened till now. Prospects of increased foreign investments have dimmed even as prospects of export growth have shrivelled over the past couple of years. Negative ratings by foreign investibility rating agencies have moved in tandem. The post-Pokhran sanctions have very little to do with this course of events.

Here, then, is the dilemma. Both the Congress and the BJP are pinning their hopes on unlimited supplies of foreign capital. The common expectation of the two parties is that as long as national policy, including national economic policy, is patterned to placate the foreigners, the good Samaritans from Western lands would bail out India.

Things however are not turning out that way; the practice of not speaking out against the United States—exemplified once more by the failure of both the Congress and the BJP to take a principled stand over Bill Clinton's barbaric maraudings in Iraq—is proving to be of little avail, foreign capital continues to be scarce and scarcer with every day. The reason, at least one part of the reason, is without question the image of the Indian polity that is crystallizing in foreign minds ever since those gory final weeks of 1992. Fundamentalism of the species demonstrated by the Shiv Sena and its cohorts such as the Bajrang Dal has a lethal quality which has put paid to the hope of ruling politicians to extract kudos from foreigners.

A race has seemingly ensued between two separate strands in the consensus politics structured by the two leading political parties: they are determined to follow economic policies which will gladden the heart of foreigners; at the same time, the ballistic support they are providing to rebuild medievalism of the vilest kind, even as the nation, along with the rest of humanity, approaches the 21st century, cannot but alienate foreigners even as it does millions and millions of countrymen too.

The Congress may protest that no such consensus exists between it and the BJP. The proof of the pudding is in the eating though. If it were worried in any measure over the consequences of permitting fundamentalism to be on the rampage in the country, the Congress should have felt no hesitation to straightaway pull down the BJP government in the aftermath of Manoharpur.

What after all, are the likely spinoffs in case the present government is brought to an end? Possibility number one: its substitution by a Congress regime backed by the left and an assortment of state level parties. Possibility number two: fresh elections which, again, could imply either of two alternatives—the Congress, with outside support from the left and the state level parties, performs well in the polls and forms the government at the Centre, or a return of the fundamentalists and quasi-fundamentalists to power. The nation deserves to be given a chance to choose between these alternatives by the Congress. Should that chance be deferred, the danger of the nation coming apart would multiply even as its economic development remains stifled.

It is however conceivable that the matter of Bofor apart, the Congress has another hidden agenda. Some elements within the party may be anxious to see foreigners return to political and economic dominance in this country as that would hopefully herald a return of efficiency and competence. But they cannot say so openly, and would not for the present stand in the way of a regime which is anathema to foreigners but which is supportive of the Congress policy of all out economic liberalization.

As long as foreign direct investment does not zoom, these manoeuveres and counter-manoeuvres will constitute the staple for old wives' tales, and India will countinue to be in the jam it is in doday. If the rate of exports falls further and imports remain unbridled, while short term external capital movements too are rendered volatile by the Shiv Sena doings, the crisis for the country could actually be brought forward.

Which leads one to mull over a final puzzle. Has the BJP too a hidden agenda, its acceptable Vajpayee-esque face notwithstanding, and is the Shiv Sena its revolutionary vanguard, with a "Compleat Strategyst" lurking some where behind the screen? And what if the so called "strategyst" is a marionette whose strings are pulled by an invisible hand operating from alien shores?

3rd February, 1999

Great leveller

The truth is finally out. The United States administration has stated in quite explicity—the so called United Nations sanctions against Iraq can be lifted on fulfilment of only one condition: Saddam Hussein, the president of Iraq, must stand down from his office. A peremptory decision, and no prior approval of the UN security council or the general assembly was taken before the state department spokesman made it public. It is in the name of the "international community" that till now the US and some of its luckeys had been pursuing their brigandage all over the world, and not just in Iraq.

There was indeed no limit to the presumptuousness. The last round of raining of missiles on Baghdad and its out skirts has made it plain that the fiction of "the international community" has zero credibility. Even within the Western powers, the divergence of views in the wake of these attacks could not be sharper. Germany and France have openly disapproved of the outrage perpetrated against Iraq, Germany even more stridently than France.

The US in a sense stands totally isolated, the decisions the US president has taken, and is taking, reflect the rantings of a depraved man. It is as if he has a personal vendetta against Hussein and, come what may, he would go ahead with this subjective agenda notwithstanding the shock and disgust it has evoked across the continents: what does he care, he is the supreme leader of the world's only superpower.

This international bully has continued to proceed on the assumption that his word is law. The rest of the world has an obligation, for the sake of humanity, to solence this bully. The irony in the situation can hardly be missed. The president of the US is the subject of impeachment proceedings before the senate; the formal prosecution is likely to begin this week. The formidable set of allegations against him, supported by data of various descripitons, cannot be easily brushed aside.

And yet, if opinion polls are any guide, the American public could not be overly concerned whether their president is a scoundrel and a debauch as long as he is reasonably successful in ensuring income and employment at home. His sexual deviance they tend to ignore; his misdoings in Iraq or elsewhere do not bother them either; even the speculation whether his latest acts and activities were not intended to divert attention from his domestic difficulties, leaves them indiferent. This is what liberalization has done to the psyche of men and women in country after country, they themselves are all right Jack, let Bill Clinton do whatever he likes.

There is nonetheless a wrench in the heart, more particularly because overwhelming sections of the black voters in the US have, for their own reasons, emerged as strong supporters of the Clinton regime. He has initiated a number of measures in the arena of civil rights which have eased somewhat the conditions of living for the black community; they deem it their moral obligation to be grateful to the president on that score.

This too is the bequest of liberalization. The argument is simple and straightforward: since this man has proved to be good for them, they would support him through thick and thin despite his lurid record both in the conduct of his personal affairs and in the conduct of the nation's foreign policy. It would be an arduous exercise to convince them that it is sinful to support a president who is little more than an international ganster and has designs of weak and helpless countries in Asia, Africa and Latin America.

This process of changing the mindset of large sections of the American electorate will take time. Conceivably, the impeachment proceedings too will drag along for weeks and months. Meanwhile, there is altogether no certainty that a desperate Clinton would not, once the vote on impeachment becomes imminent, launch another barbarous attack on Iraq or discover a pretext for lashing out against another country. He might well nurture some leftover hope that another round of jingoist adventure could still save the presidency for him.

Which is precisely where the role of countries such as India suddenly looms larger. That wily fox, Yevgeny Primakov, has dropped the hint, during his recent visit to New Delhi, of the positive aspects of a network of alliances among Russia, China and India from which the world could gain much. Around this triumvirate, new forces could also foregather and tilt decisively the balance of international rèlations away from the current uncomfortable phenomenon of single power domination.

Irrespective of the course the impeachment proceedings take, the focus of the new international concordat could be on containing the excesses of the megalomaniac at present in control of the US administration and who could, till the other day, browbeat the UN security council into doing his bidding. Should Russia and China be able to swing germany and France to their side, the picture within the security council is bound to change qualitatively.

Primakov however received little response to his suggestion. A sorry pack of ministers and civil servants happen to be in charge in New Delhi. A profoundly conservative lot, they continue to believe that the post-Cold War non-equation of powers is for ever. It is not; it is already a changing landscape in the UN. Furtheremore, the developing economic uncertainties in the world have eroded the sense of smugness in some entrenched quarters.

The multinational corporations based in the US have nonetheless a stake in the existing arrangements. They are doubtful of the degree of penetration they could achieve in the Chinese market, given the fact that China is maintaining an annual rate of industrial growth touching 10 per cent, which cannot but hasten the pace of the country's import substitution. Once the Chinese authorities reach a kind of entente with Japan, the potential market dreamt of by the multinational corporations is likely to shrink further.

The later are, in the circumstances, anxious to maintain a toehold on the Indian economy. The designing foreigners draw sustenance from the datum that India's politicians and civil servants have developed a taste for venality. Some of the multinational companies are certainly hoping to bribe their way into India. After all, going by his reputation the upper class Indian is not only generally venal, but is also the greediest of the human species, who will not mind selling the country short if the price is right. It is not for nothing that young Ph.D. aspirants in American universities are encouraged to do extensive fieldwork before they sit down to spell out on the computer their lush ideas on the role of corruption in economic development in poorer countries.

The insurance and patents bills are therefore not the central issue. The issue is repairing the moral fibre of which that modest Gujarati, Mohandas Karamchand Gandhi, had once talked about. Come to think of it, what he said is not qualitatively much different from the lesson derivable from the magnificent social dynamics Karl Marx had expatiated upon: a revolution succeeds because it is built on morality. Who knows, once liberalization reaches an impasse, it would be the season for a moral comeback, even for the cash counting Indians.

6th January, 1999

The cheek of it

Is not the show of anger organised by the Opposition parties, both inside Parliament and outside, somewhat beside the point? They have gone to great lengths to establish a specific nexus between the commitments made in the finance minister, Mr. Manmohan Singh's memorandum to the International Monetary Fund last August and in his subsequent letter to the World Bank president in November and certain decisions now up for implementation through the Budget.

Nitpickings of this nature are indeed fatuous. For the sake of maintaining nominal parliamentary propriety, the finance minister and the rest of the government would keep denying that the contents of the Budget were discussed a *priori* with Fund-Bank representatives; the finance minister might even be formally right in claiming that the text of the Budget speech had not been shown to the minions of the Fund and the Bank before it was read out by him in the Lok Sabha.

None of this however contradicts what has been accepted as basic reality in the market place as well as in hearths and homes: each and every aspect of the Budget has been discussed threadbare, at the stage of both its conception and its incubation, with the Fund and the Bank, and matters over which difficulties arose were sorted out by exchange of communications between downtown Washington and the North Block. It was in essence a multi-stage operation. A number of measures the international financial institutions insisted that India must pursue and put into shape through the Budget were vetted by dummy committees set up under the auspices of the government of India; the recommendations these committees made were in closest conformity to advice rendered, and sometimes, even drafted to the minutest detail, by Fund-Bank staff.

Several such recommendations have been incorporated in the Budget the government is under pledge, as per the finance minister's deeds of surrender forwarded to the Fund managing director and the Bank president, to implement a few other decisions as well in the course of the year through assorted monetary, fiscal, legal and administrative measures. Were they sharp-witted enough, members of Parliament belonging to the Opposition could have turned the table on the finance minister the moment he bragged that the fiscal deficit in the current year was being contained to within 6.5 per cent of the gross domestic product. Whether the actual deficit would turn out to be as low as this, or some fudging of accounts is involved, is a tale which will be revealed only subsequently. But it has been a widely known fact for the past several months that the Fund-Bank had been insisting that the deficit must not, come hell or high water, exceed this proportion of the GDP, and the finance minister jolly well had to conform to the directive from Washington DC.

The Opposition has failed to avail of the opportunity to make the government cower for cover.

Consider some of the nuggets the Budget speech contains. In the opening paragraph itself, there is a reference to the grave economic crisis the finance minister and his government had 'inherited' even as they entered office. An inheritance is an external bequest, for which one does not, and need not, have to own up any responsibility. This was hardly the case with the exchange crisis which confronted Mr. P.V. Narasimha Rao's government.

The exchange crisis and the nation being on the verge of defaulting on its external debt-servicing obligations were not phenomena which could, by any stretch, be attributed to outside malefactors. It was the Congress party and its high-flying regime, crossing over to the philosophy of unbridled capitalism, which created the crisis and ensured that, in the five years between 1984 and 1989, the country's total foreign debt soared from less than $15 billion to as much as $70 billion. There is little purpose in hiding the point that the regime, bitten by the bug of globalisation and consumerism, pushed the country into a permanent irretrievable external debt trap. Given the structure of our production and income distribution, we did not possess the capability to service such a huge debt; this was possible only by incurring, continously and indefinitely, further and further loans.

The present finance minister's exclusive claim to glory is that he has succeeded in presuading his colleagues, including his prime minister, to agree that the only way out of the dilemma is to convert this country of close to 900 million people into a docile banana republic of the Latin American species, and thereby escape the ignominy of defaulting on debt servicing. At the time the finance minister took over last year, the country's aggregate foreign balances had been run down to as low as the equivalent of Rs. 1,500 crores. Because of the dexterous servility he has displayed, he has since received substantial additional lines of credit from the Fund, the World Bank, the Asian Development Bank and one or two other international financial institutions. What he has done is in strict accordance with the classical pattern follwoed by all countries caught in the mire of an external debt trap: you borrow more in order to meet your past obligations, and thereby sink even deeper into debt.

The hoopla in the media reflects either the level of illiteracy of our so-called literati—or perhaps their genuine desire to surrender the prerogative of independent decision making if in the bargain they could ensure enough short-term goodies for their own narrow set. As a consequence of the government's—and the finance minister's—exertions, we are now amongst the Third World's leading debtors, coming immediately behind Mexico and Brazil.

There are some concomitants attached to occupying such an exalted position: not only do one's economic policies become subject to the dictates of foreigners, one's foreign policy too is made to turn a full circle. Leave aside other aspects, we are now on the point of accepting Israel's Mossad as principal advisers on how to contain insurrectionary activities.

The gloating headlines in the newspapers are artfully contrived; they make it difficult to separate the wheat of concrete achievements of the government from the chaff of public relations exercises. On the supposedly "positive" side, the finance minister can lay claim to having raised eight to ten thousand crores of additional medium and long-term credits from overseas and to having enticed the entry of a couple of thousand crores of hot money, mostly belonging to smugglers and other who have been promised that no legal discrimination is to be made between them and otherwise slightly more honourable citizens.

Ten thousand crores of extra foreign exchange are certainly not to be scoffed at by such a spirituallyminded nation as ours, but let us tot up the negative side of the balance too: two devaluations, and subsequent further depreciations of the rupee, which have offered no boost to exports but have further strengthened the forces of inflation rendering exports even more difficult; the scuttling of economic planning, the Planning commission now exists only in name; a severe cut-back in rural employment programmes and antipoverty projects; a Fund-Bank directed fiscal and monetary policy which places premium on credit squeeze and high interest rates, thus further invigorating the trends of industrial recession; the purposive draining of public savings and state-assisted diversion of savings to private mutual funds so that resources are freely available for stock exchange speculations; and similar other indulgences on the part of the nation's affluent; the aggravated squeeze on public expenditure which threatens the jobs of millions as well as erodes the basic social services, including public distribution and education.

Scan the nation's newspapers, these are minor footnotes to be ignored: the country is globalised, income and corporate tax rates are lowered, imposts on air-conditioned restaurants are off, corporate shares have reached dizzy heights, there is pormise of both full liberalisation of imports and partial convertibility of the rupee, so that the Naipaulian craze for *phoren* could be fully satiated. All impediments on big monopoly houses and foreign investors are off; small enterpirses will go to the wall; local scientists and technologists are likely to be left with no opportunity to devote their talent to serve the nation's cause; the kneejerk approach to the Dunkel proposals and the glee with which collaboration agreements are being signed with foreign parties would see to that.

The crucial facts pertianing to the economy are meanwhile to be pushed under the carpet. Per capita output of farm produce has dipped in the past decade. And irony of ironies, only public sector industrial units, including power-producing units, have maintained the modicum of a respectable rate of growth in recent years, otherwise the index of industrial output is comprehensively down. The service sector is however booming. The rich and the affluent *a la* the banana republies, never had it so good. And don't you know, gold can now be freely brought in: stagflation affects only the nation's majority, but do they matter?

The pressure is now likely to develop ot make the rupee fully convertible and let go of all import restrictions. The Rs. 10,000 crores of extra foreign exchange borrowed over the past nine months might then disappear overnight. But the finance minister conceivably would not mind being out with a begging bowl once more.

As a self-respecting nation, we cannot affored to default on our external debt servicing, we must therefore borrow further in order to meet our obligations to foreigners. Our self-respect is however of a very selective kind: it is not hurt if the nation's major economic decisions are abdicated to foreigners. With no economic planning, we have not the foggiest notion about which direction we are heading. All we know is that the poor and the middle classes are going to face hard times. That, in any case, is the role assigned to them by destiny—they should therefore lump it.

Two additional comments are still worth making. Suppose we defaulted on our debt servicing, would the heavens have collapsed over us? Brazil, for example, defaulted during the last decade, faring no worse as a consequence. They simply had to get the bulk of their money back; so the Fund, the Bank and the private American bankers made special arrangements to keep Brasil afloat and even scaled down some of its outstanding debts. Even if we, because of religious reasons, abjured the path of self-reliance could, we not at least have emulated some of these Latin Americans, which would have entialed a lesser order of abrogation of our sovereignty?

Finally, one wishes that the finance minister, in his quieter moments, would seek some forgiveness for the ultimate sacrilege he committed in his Budget speech. He quoted Sardar Bhagat Singh to justify what he was doing.

Bhagat Singh sacrified his life in order that the imperialists could be evicted from his country; the entire thrust of the present finance minister's act is to invite the imperialists and colonialists back. If the effrontery would have no surcease, there should at least be some leftover decency. Or is it already too late for even that?

11th March, 1997

Patent noster

It happened just before the United States congress recessed in September for the elections. By an overwhelming majority the house of representatives passed a resolution. Any breach of a US patent by any person or entity in any part of the world, the resolution declared in stentorian style, is tantamount to a breach of US security. The resolution authorised US security personnel to proceed against such a person or entity so that due panishment could be meted out to him/her/it.

Consider the implications. Suppose a transnational corporation, with its principal base of activity in the US, smuggles out some *neem* or *tulsi* or *parijat* plants from India, engages researchers in a laboratory in Florida or Nevada to produce a range of herbal medicines by extracting properties from these plants, rushes to have these medicines patented with this or that branch of the US patents office, and thereafter claims to have established exclusive marketing rights to sell the medicines all over the world.

Now suppose a local apothecary in Rajamundry or Chapra, altogether innocent of the majesty of US patent legislation and the global concerns of the US house of representatives. uses in its own manner the ingredients of neem, tulsi or parijat to produce similar or identical medicines and sells them at one hundredth the price charged by the transnational corporation. According to official US punditry, the owner of this local apothecary would have thereby infringed US patent legislation. As per the resolution passed by the house of representatives, US global security was, as a result, gravely endangered. Security personnel of the great US would now move fast to repair the damage done.

At this point, a pronouncement about half a dozen years ago by a circuit judge in some remote corner of the US assumes relevance. Agents of the US government, that judgement averred, have the right to apprehend in any part of the world—and, in case necessary, even kill—anyone suspected of having conspired or acted in a manner which adversely affects US security.

Conceivably as a sequel to that judgement, US embaises and consulates everywhere, including India, had posted in alluring newspaper advertisement. All and sundry were urged by the advertisement to post information they possessed regarding individuals or groups whom they suspected to have been indulging in a conspiracy to bring down the lawfully established US government.

A cash award up to half a million dollars was promised for each such worth-while information.

As far as is known, that US promise still holds. A golden opportunity therefore could come the way of X,Y or Z in Rajmundry or Chapra to make a quick buck. He or she could duly feel tempted to report to the US embassy in New Delhi or to any of US consular offices on the nefarious doings of the smalltime apothecary in Rajamundry or Chapra, producing low cost herbal medicines from neem or tulsi or parijat extracts, thereby defying a US patent, thereby breaching US security.

Formidable legal luminaries from the US would insist that the apothecary owner was liable to arrest, on Indian soil itself, by a US security agent, who would also have the discretion to ship the accused to the US to stand trial there. Should an Indian judge or an Indian police officer intervene and arrange protection for the apothecary owner, that Indian judge or Indian police officer would be equally guilty of violating US security and hence liable to be packed off to the US to stand trial. Were he or she to resist arrest, the US agent would have the right to shoot him or her, on Indian soil, for the unpardonable offence of breaching Indian security.

No part of the above narration is a fable. It is an instance of the network of plans for global domination the world's greatest power and its cohorts have been dreaming for long and have now started to execute with a cool determination. The Marrakech treaty signed by a hundred odd country governments under US pressure in early 1995 and the new international agency it has begot, the World Trade Organisation, are intended to impose the tyranny of the US patents system on the rest of the world.

The pretest is free and untrammeled international trade. The actual objective is to ensure limitless exploitation of the resources of the poorer countries. In a regime of so called free trade, the early birds collect all the worms. The advanced industrial countries, and the transnational corporations they have spawned, have the advantage of an early start and patenting.

With their superior financial clout, they are in a position to buy outright the raw materials or biodiversities a poor country such as India possesses, process and patent products by making use of these raw materials or biodiversities, and mulct consumers by marketing these products at fantastically high prices.

Free trade is in no time to be supplemented by a grim world of monopolies and relentless squeezing of the poor by the rich. The countries which originally owned these raw materials or biodiversities would be precluded from manufacturing products based on these materials or ingredients. They could do so only with the approval of, and according to specifications set by, the transnational patentees.

Such is the new character of international slavery, otherwise known as the Marrakech treaty. The demoralised government presiding over in New Delhi at the time was in a scamperi hurry to sign the treaty. No debate was allowed to take place on the floor of Parliament, nor any consulations took place with the state governments. The Constitution, the explanation was prefered, entitles the Union government to sign any international treaty. The constitutional prerogative does not however cover the right to sign the covenant according to which decision on the range of goods the counry could produce and sell as well as the price at which the goods are to be sold would be the prerogative of external agencies.

One problem has nonetheless proved insurmountable for the love of foreign patents. India's patents legislation needs to be amended if the WTO hegemony and the suzerainty of US patents are to be firmly established over here. Our parliament has, till the date, refused to buckle in though.

In matters concerning economic policy, the new administration in New Delhi is however a carbon copy of the one it has succeeded. Hemmed in the foreign debt and by the belief that the nation's further survival hinges excessively on incurring more foreign debt it thinks, it does not have too many bargaining counters. A great many people within the administration are in fact not interested in any barganining at all. This lot certainly includes a few ministers, and quite a collage of senior civil servants.

Even as the last monsoon session Parliament got going, a senior civil servant announced to the world that the necessary amendments to the country patent laws to make them harmonious with the WTO conditionalities were ready and scheduled to be passed soon. His minister had not heard about the amendments, nor had parliament. An official press note disowned the secretary's statement. Barely two months later, yet another senior official doled out to the press the same kind of story about impending legislations Parliament. As on the previous occasion, a ministerial denial followed.

The permissive society. Secretaries speak out of turn. They are contradicted. That is all: no disciplinary action proposed against them. Meanwhile the US administration is losing its patience. So is the US congress. So too the transnational corporations. And the Federal Bureau of Investigation itching to set up office in India, so as to enable it to pick up such Indian scientists, researchers, economists, politicians, lawyers, judges as dare to defy US patent laws. The Indian media has made up its mind. It has taught itself to love US patent laws. Reports on opposition to the emasculation of our patent rights will accordingly not find mention in the press. Resistance groups will have to rely upon surreptitious notes from the underground. They will soon run the risk, even in their own country of being pounced upon by the upholders of US security.

27th November, 1996

Politic politeness

Certain things are assumed to be not discussable in polite society. A couple of decades ago, the United States authorities had doled out thousands of ground to air missiles to Gulbuddin Hikmatyar's goons for thwarting the march of history in Afghanistan. This was public knowledge, but hush hush public knowledge, not to be mentioned in polite society.

Missiles, like chickens, have however a way of coming home to roost. Speculation is now rife whether one of these missliles, perhaps sold on Peshawar's flea market by an Afghan chiseller to some psychopath of an American tourist, was not smuggled back into the US and used to down the Trans World Airlines jet passenger plane that last month crashed in the Atlantic Ocean soon after takeoff from New York. Speculations of this kind have a habit of acquiring a cutting edge with each passing day. But a code is a code is a code: polite society will debar mention of establishment follies coming home to roost.

Polite society will not discuss what took place in Russia last June in the name of free and fair elections either. A strident operational command was put on the wire: Russia must not be permitted to slip back into totalitarian communism. For forms' sake, the charade of free and fair elections had to be gone through though. To resolve the contradiction, it was essential to cut corners.

What constitutes free and fair is a matter of definition. Billions of dollars were despatched through various sources by the US authorities to fill the incumbent president's war chest. US strategists took over as Boris Yeltsin's electoral advisors. His communist opponent was even denied the right to buy advertising space in the media: each and every television channel organised saturation coverage on behalf of the incumbent president; any stray visitor to the country could not have but formed the impression that there was only one candidate in the elections and his name was Boris Yeltsin.

The task of ensuring freedom and democracy in Russia could not however be exposed to the slightest risk. According to reports, vote rigging of a genre which could put to shame the experts in this particular art in Bihar, India, was therefore resorted to. The policy of the principle, after all, is the best policy; in order to save democracy, it might on occasion be necessary to make short shrift of democracy.

The story of the impeccable march of freedom and democracy in Russia does not quite end here. That highly sophisticated, sometimes ponderous but always readable journal, the *New Yorker,* has breached the conventions of polite society and disclosed a hither to well guarded secret; even were the candidate of the Americans to lose the elections democracy would still have remained safe in Russia. Between the US state department and Yeltsin, it was pre-arranged that were he to trail in votes, a terse announcement would have been issued post haste: at this critical juncture of Russian history, hard earned democratic freedom could not be surrendered back to the abominable communists, who do not believe in freedom of choice and therefore have no moral right to come to power on the basis of free elections; in order to ensure free elections in future, it was hence important to reject the outcome of free elections *now.* Amen.

Has not the electoral verdict been made irrelevant here in India as well? The decisive mandate in the April-May elections was for the ejectment of the Congress, and by implication, the wholesale disowning of its economic policies. A common minimum programme has been drafted by the disparate political parties who find themselves constituting the alternative government. This programme, in the circumstances, walks up and down on both sides of the street: it is for compassion and greater social equity, it is at the same time also for the kind of "reforms" the World Bank- International Monetary Fund sorority talks of.

The first budget presented by its finance minister demonstrates extraordinary acumen in putting across the dominant point of view inside the government: reforms *a la* Washington, DC are perfectly legal tender as long as these are juxtaposed with token gestures towards the direction of destitute rural women and spouses of truck drivers killed in highway accidents.

Newspapers are playing up laboured analyses of how the social sectors have been swamped by generous budgetary allocations and other special measures initiated to stimulate systemic growth. These ends, it is expected, will be gratefully chewed by the humble folk who make up the overwhelming majority of the nation: at the other end, "reforms" in the financial and similar other sectors will continue in scampering hurry.

The depositories bill has entered the statute book. Import tariffs have been further brought down; export earnings already exempt from income and corporate taxation, will not henceforth even need to be repatriated within a given time interval. More industries have been delicensed, and rules for entry of foreign capital in the small scale sector further liberalised. The list of industries where foreign parties will be able to hold 51 per cent of the equity has been expanded; in quite a few industries, foreign equity will from now on be allowed even upto 74 per cent. That apart, formal approval of foreign investment proposals is to be speeded up.

Sections of industrialists may be unreasonable; they may worry their heads off over their ability to hold on to their share of the domestic market in view of the heavy accross the board reduction in import duties. Their worry will not have much purchase. It is the age of the superpower, of the only superpower we have in this modest globe of ours. Its desire and intentions need to be respected. The superpower loves to doctor the elections in Russia; it also wants to assure itself that, despite the poll verdict, India's new political Ledership will not dare to slacken the pace of West directed reforms.

India's ruling class could not agree more. Which is why its mindset is currently concentrated on making it certain that the inflow of direct foreign investment touch $10 billion every year. Whatever is considered vital to translate that dream into reality must pass muster. If China can get $40 billion each year from the foreigners, why must India remain satisfied with only plus minus one billion dollars?

The answer to such a soulful questions does not lie in fiscal exercises. A budget can neither abort nor push forward a social revolution. The incentives and inducements it offers at most lead to a redistribution of incomes and assets, securities not excluding, within the confines of the superstructure; these do not ever percolate down to the base. Equitable growth encompassing the whole society is consequently a non-starter. Since large scale development, which could expand the domestic market several times over, fails to occur, foreign investors decide to play hooky for the present; since foreign investors keep away, growth falters further.

This grim theorem of a vicious circle nonetheless bypasses a crucial truth. Investors from overseas, including from staunchly capitalist Western countries, flocked into China only after the middle kingdom attained a fantastically high rate of growth. That success was the product of a strategy of sustained self reliance reaching down to, and drawing sustenance from, the grassroots. Tokenism is no substitute for that kind of massive social engineering.

The budget in India is an irrelevance even in a narrower sense. The major resource raising exercise continues to take place away from it. The finance minister's discourse on the restructuring of corporate and income taxes as well as of import tariffs was an exercise in vacuity: fresh tax proposals in the budget are to yield less than Rs. 30 billion on an annual basis. The steep pre-budget increase in the administered prices of petroleum products, in contrast, which net roughly Rs. 60 billion, disinvestment of shares of profitable public undertakings is supposed to bring in another Rs. 50 billion.

In any event, the principal revenue raising instrument in the country remains, as it has been in the past, deficit financing. The burden of such fiscal deficits invariably falls on the dumb masses. When the slightly nondumb species, such as the trade unions, gather the temerity to holler, righteous indignation overcomes polite society; the cheek of labour aristocracy demanding unconscionable compensation for rise in prices is too much, they are thereby eroding the government's ability to do more for the helpless, unorganised sections.

Old rhetoric. For nothing changes in a moribund hinterland where, while cliches parade as great philosophies of life, exogenous forces increasingly assume centrestage. This is globalisation for you. The pressure of such external factors has rendered elections into a farce in Russia, or, in the years of yore, made available to Afghan bandicoots, almost as a free gift of nature, thousands of ground to air missiles. One or two of these missiles are now coming home to roost—so as to blast away from the sky the jet airliner which had just taken off from John F. Kennedy airport for Paris: it was, to all appearance, so tranquil, soft piped music, and the stewardesses had begun to serve pre-dinner cocktails.

7th August 1996

Buy for now

Does it not seem that "operation covering the flanks' has started in some earnest? Industrialists have a reputation of knowing fairly early which side of their bread is going to be buttered. The ensuing Lok Sabha elections, they must have concluded, are bound to usher in a change of regime in New Delhi. The irreversibility lobby, it must be equally obvious to them, has had its day: following the installation of the new administration, major-changes in economic policy are more than likely.

Chambers of commerce and industry are regarding it prudent to beam signals towards the direction of the new set of rulers, whoever they might be: please, sirs, there will be neither intransigence nor non-cooperation on our part in case liberalisation is made to go through the wringer and a harsher set of rules are proposed, for example, for the multinationals. Industrialists, it is being further hinted, were in any case a divided house on the issue of the unbridled entry of foreign capital; should the new government insist on ensuring a level playing field between domestic and foreign investors, why, that would be only an echo of what some of the stalwarts of Indian industry had been stating all along.

It is perhaps not necessary to bother too much about the industry spokesmen. Over the near half a century since independence, domestic enterpreneurs have not exactly covered themselves with glory by there genuflections. The government and Parliament offered them blanket protection, and, besides, subsidised supply of key intermediate products, courtesy a fast expanding public sector.

These advantages, industrialists assumed, were their birthright. They accustomed themselves to these advantages much in the manner a duck takes to water. They however contributed little in return to the nations's cause. All they did was to enter into lazy, sloppy collaboration agreements with foreign firms only too eager to sell them washed out patents of obsolete technology.

Our industrialists were expected to unleash their animal spirit. Instead, they lolled on the easy profits engendered by the controls and licensing system. Little interest was evinced in research and development: such dirty work was left to the public sector units and the government established research laboratories.

Winds of change began blowing since the second half of the Eighties, liberalisation, which tilted the scale further in their favour, was on the anvil. That hardly changed the mindset. Sections amongst the industrialists rejoiced that the controls were off, no irritants henceforth in the name of regulating the activities of monopolies and big industial houses and no restrictions on imports, particularly of luxury consumption goods which constituted the crucial adjunct of high living.

Once again, there was little evidence of the lurking presence of the animal spirit which, according to the script, was to accelerate the pace of industrial and economic growth in the post—"reforms" phase. Perhaps the fault lies in the ambiguity of the script itself, in the overwhelming space it earmarked for foreign investment. Globalisation was intended to be a one dimensional phenomenon: foreigners would come in and carry out the essential tasks that needed to be carried out, such as investing heavily in basic infrastructure. The role of domestic entrepreneurs was not quite spelt out, such as in what form the animal spirit was to manifest itself.

Foreign capital did come in, but neither the government nor the private sector has succeeded in concealing their disappointment at the pace and pattern of the inflow. Most of the foreign money has gone into the secondary market; with the rupee made convertible in current account transactrions, raking short term gains in the stock exchanges became the principal objective of foreign investors. Foreign investment in new productive ventures has been few and far between during the quinquennium of the so called reforms, the annual average not even touching one billion dollars, and the grisly episodes of Enron and the telecommunications tenders have left a sour taste in the mouth.

The bulk of what has passed for direct foreign investment has in fact gone for installing or expanding capacity in frivolous activities, mostly food, drinks, apparel and transporation, catering to the narrow market offered by the country's rich. More recently, institutional investors from abroad have been buying up equity of Indian units experiencing little local difficulties. Capital expenditure on the part of the government was duly cut back as per the "reforms" agenda; with foreigners too playing hooky, investment has been severely affected. Unrestricted imports of industrial goods have worsened the situation. In the circumstances, selective deindustrialisation cannot quite be brushed off as hallucination.

Heavens are therefore unlikely to fall if the new government inducted next month chooses to reintroduce a touch of illiberalism, for example, by imposing certain conditions on the inflow of external capital and specifying the areas where it will be allowed to roam. International financial and trade agencies, representing die hard interests of the capitalist West, will holler.

That will however be mostly regulation hollering, more for the sake of record. Since it is India's "political stability" which will for some time be at the top of foreign concerns, what will be considered as short term pin pricks will be taken in their stride. Once the Congress has its surcease, any alternative coalition arrangement, the foreigners must have already realised, will involve a review of the open door foreign investment policy since 1991.

Industrialists at home will fall in, foreigners do not yet count much, the principal challenge to the new government will however come from elsewhere. There has been till now little overt articulation of the major lesson from the travails of the "reforms": the country cannot yet afford to survive in a setup which has divested itself of the exchange control mechanism in toto.

The tidings are fairly ominous. Accumulated foreign debt is hovering in the neighbourhood of $ 100 billion. The annual debt service obligations now exceed the accretion of fresh external assistance; this state of affairs, the projections suggest, will worsen in the course of the next decade. The trade deficit on the current account, contrary to hollow ministerial assurances and despite the external value of the rupee being continuously pushed down, has grown and grown, crossing five billion dollars in 1995-96; should there be no restraint on imports, it is bound to bulge even more. A $10 billion service obligation and another $ 10 billion of trade deficit will add up to a formidable annual burden, the country will not have the wherewithal to meet it.

Before a stock taking is ordered to the many other things that have gone grievously wrong, the new government will need some breathing space. This space can only be provided if there is at least a temporary moratorium on the unrestricted entry of imported goods, draining precious foreign exchange. And this is going to be one of the toughest tasks facing the new regime. The influential upper and middle classes have got habituated, in the course of the past quinquennium, to sophisticated soft and hard drinks, to fine fabric to luxury automobiles, to the charms of the varied wares the satellite television channels have constantly endeavoured to make them enamoured of.

The worst of the sins committed by the government which goes out next month is the purposive creation of an illusion that this is a vastly rich country which need not bother about frugality and savings and might as well concentrate on consumption and consumption alone.

The new regime, whatever the coalition of interests it represents, will have no alternative but to tell the nation that the reality is somewhat otherwise. It will have to serve notice on the middle and upper classes: if the nation is to survive, most of the imported goodies they have got used to have to be bidden goodbye, at least for some while. These besotted classes, rest assured, will organise a storm of protest.

Whether it can ride that storm will be the litmus test for the new regime. Those who will comprise this regime have only a few weeks at their disposal; they are, besides, in the thick of the poll campaign. Even in this confusion, they must find the time to gather their wits—and to plan ahead.

17th April 1996

Joys of lesser fare

The refrain in ruling party and industry circles has a common burden : be proud, the country has been opened up as it was never opened up in the past; autarky, who does not know, is bad, integration with the global economy is good and excellent. The farm lobby, with a gleam in their eye because of the prospects of high profits grain exports might bring in, have not lagged behind either. The greater the extent of our integration with the global economic processes, the easier, it is claimed, will it be for us to reach the pinnacle of all round efficiency.

Even as we pass through the portals of the 21st century, the state of the art technology will then be our lodestar, enabling us to occupy our rightful place in the comity of nations.

The specifics of this vision do not, however, detain us. What sort of a world are we proposing to integrate with, who will be our friends, who are going to be our adversaries, what is the genre of problems we have to tackle, and tackle successfully, before we emerge as a reasonably successful economic entity—questions such as these are not even raised. Since the issues are not raised, nobody is also around to respond to them.

The factors underlying this—call it vacuity, call it disinterestedness—in the future of our international relations, including international economic relations, are not far to seek. The tacit assumption shaping our foreign policy—including foreign economic policy—in recent years is that passivity is king.

Be reasonable, the world belongs as of now to the only superpower that is around. Whether it is Iraq or Bosnia or Israel or Taiwan or Cuba or Burundi, the superpower has chosen the role of global gendarmerie. It might behave like a prize boor, such as over Iraq or Cuba, none would still dare not to go along with it.

It controls the policies of the World Bank and the International Monetary Fund; the charter setting up the new international trade body, the World Trade Organisation, reflects ambitions nurtured by multinational corporations based in the United States. We have to take as datum a world the landscape of which is painted sombre, from horizon to horizon, by the forbidding presence of the only superpower.

Contrary to the evil canards spread from time to time, we as a nation are pragmatist to the core. The superpower both proposes and disposes. The architects of our foreign policy did not take long to define their task in the circumstances. One must cultivate the timidity of one's convictions; the only initiative we can afford for ourselves is to clinch the point that we propose to be on the right side of the superpower and its major partners through thick and thin.

It is a persuasive argument, if the bosses are satisfied with us, they will be gracious enough to ensure that our land is filled with milk and honey. If only the superpower would lower its tariff wall and liberalise its import quotas, some more of our textiles and handicrafts and footwear could add to exports. Were it to give the nod to the World Bank, the flow of concessionary assistance would not get interrupted. If the US treasury secretary picks up the telephone and speaks to the IMF managing director, the pressure on the rupee would ease. If the US administration should consider seriously to defend the Pressler amendment, the pinpricks from Pakistan would have a surcese.

Why, the superpower may, in the kindness of its heart, direct the Association of Southeast Asian Nations to admit us into their fold? It has therefore boiled down to a single point venture : to ingratiate ourselves with the superpower; who know, if we keep plugging, the superpower might even appreciate our difficulties over the concept of nuclear non-proliferation and adopt a benign attitude toward our prayer for a permanent seat in the United Nations security council.

To recreate third world solidarity or to reconstruct the Group of 77, which was such an effective forum in the Sixties and the Seventies, is, in consequence, no longer a part of the agenda. Wheatever is good for the US and its cohorts is, it is taken as axiomatic, good for us and the third world as a whole. The whel has turned an astonishingly full circle.

In the period following the cessation of World War II, puny little southest Asian countries like Thailand and the Philippines were wary of dangerous thoughts unleashed by the so called Bandung nations; they felt safe under the umbrella of protection offered by the South Asia Treaty Organisation and the US military advisory group. This was even true for a relatively big sized country such as Pakistan, and, for a while, for Dudley Senanayeke's Ceylon too.

Commentators in New Delhi, basking in the sun of "Panchsilla", would have mild fun at the expense of these neighbourhood Uncle Toms. Forty odd years later, the third world is only a derelict billboard, and the conformist ethos of Thailand and the Philippines has bowled over even countries like India and Egypt; Yugoslavia has ceased to exist, and Indonesia is firmly in the grip of a hardheaded military junta who have managed to persuade the Americans to invest in the country at the rate of as much as $15 billion annually notwithstanding the smallness of its size. It is left to past lackeys such as Malaysia occasionally to give voice to anti-American sentiments on global trade or environmental issues.

A specific mindset is busily being assembled. Humble nations such as India cannot afford the luxury of an independent foreign policy. Such conditioning of the mind is contaminating. Even pronouncements from the political opposition, while full of assertion on the need to return to the processes of a self reliant economy, are silent on the issue of the contents of foreign policy which ought to be the adjunct of the strategy of independent economic development. The standard cliche ridden utterances try to draw a veil over what remains unsaid: discretion, ladies and gentlemen, is the better part of valour, or better still, what cannot be cured in the immediate period must be endured.

We therefore keep mum over Iraq, over Cuba, over Taiwan; we see no evil, hear no evil. A doubt nonetheless persists. Is there any basis at all for entertaining the theory that the US and its partners in the Group of Seven fraternity are benign patriarchs, they will keep doing us good turns in case we are on our best behaviour?

The London weekly newspaper, the "Economist", can be taken, as a safe, perhaps the safest, guide of superpower, and Western thinking at the very highest level. It shapes and reflects Western establishments' attitudes. Its haughtiness is a conscious expression of the dominance of power. The newspaper lectures to and entertains the major domos in the Western world on the stratagems of how to go about to perpetuate the hegemony of Caucasian civilisation.

It has been the patron saint of Margeret Thatcher and Ronald Reagan; it continues to advise, from the sidelines, ceaselessly, Bill Clinton, and, as an excercise in contingency planning, is currently busy drafting a catalogue of do's and don'ts for the Republican presidential aspirant, Bob Dole.

The "Economist" framework of mind, to repeat, is the quintessential Western framework of mind. It therefore needs to be read with care. In a recent editorial article discussing, schoolmarm fashion, the merits and demerits of the various presidential candidates in Russia's forthcoming elections in June, the "Economist" is dismissive of the candidate of the Communist Party, Gennady Zyuganov. The stereotyped reasons, from the solid capitalist point of veiw, for rejecting a communist ogre are of course all there. The most substantive argument for its project of Zyuganov however comes at the very end: should this wretch be elected president, the country, that is, Russia, "could fast slip third-world-wards".

The arrogance of not just power, but of ethnic superiority too. The "Economist" could not be more out-spoken. The third world is the pits. The third world is cholera, AIDS, obstreperousness, Castro, famine, chaos, terrorism, barbarity. The third world does not belong to civilisation. The third world nonetheless remains the white man's perpetual burden.

The thought process revealed by the "Economist" is archetypal 18th and 19th century imperial philosophy: this world belongs to the whites, they will run it for their own edification, the third world is there only to be exploited for its resources and the market it provides: otherwise it is pariah, untouchable. Things went wrong in Russia for 70 odd years; thank goodness, it has been finally rescued from the clutches of the evil forces that had made a captive of her. But, be on your guard, Russia under wrong leadership could once more sink back into darkness, it might slide "third-worldwards", nothing could be more calamitous.

The "Economist" is giving vent to the haughtiness of white civilisation, if such is civilisation. Those who still believe that, by behaving like slaves, we will have a greater flow of material benefits heading toward our direction are living in a fool's paradise. Slaves and cronies are treated with contempt by the world's haughty set: scan history, this has been the reality in all centuries.

The only way to bring this set down a peg or two is by engaging them in combat, which can, depending upon the exigency of times, assume any form; hauteur has to be responded to by parallel hauteur.

The poor countries may not for the present have the arms or the resources. All the greater reason why they must have a foreign policy. Uncle Toms are the last persons fit to fill the role of architects of such a foreign policy.

3rd April, 1996

Force within a farce

The Central Intelligence Agency, even a child knows, plots and plans to further the global ambitions of the United States administration. Its mission has not ended with the collapse of the Soviet "evil empire". Other objectives lie in wait. The CIA would, for example, like to destabilise, provided it had the capability, the People's Republic of China. Tibet has been on the top of its agenda ever since Chiang Kai-shek's scampering escape to Taiwan.

Unwittingly or otherwise, many Indian personalities have participated enthusiastically in this game of China baiting on the ground of that state's alleged denial of the right of self determination to the Tibetans. The dividing line between the efforts of the CIA and the Dalai Lama-loving politicians strewn across the Indian landscape has been very, very thin.

The US intelligence outfit has however found no reason to leave India out of its sphere of endeavours. Creating confusion in third world countries has been one of its respectable supplementary goals over the years. India's top leadership, servile enough where economic issues are concerned, do not find it easy to toe the American line on a number of other issues, such as on nuclear non-proliferation. Domestic political considerations perhaps sway them. Such impertinence is not permissible.

The CIA has accordingly made up its mind: India too deserves destabilisation. The recent disclosure of the contents of the blueprint of its prospective activities, and India's occupying a prominent place therein, should thus cause no surprise. The reactions to this disclosure should be predictable. Cutting across party lines, politicians over here would be aghast at the CIA's cheek. Frothful statements would issue condemning the outrageousness of the CIA's intentions.

This or that leader would demand that the National Integration Council be immediately summoned. Some of the professional Tibet lovers will, without batting an eye, join the protest demonstration before the American embassy in New Delhi's Chanakyapuri. Their righteous indignation would receive raucous support from all over the country.

And yet, how many of them would admit that, no use blaming the CIA alone, they, at least a fair lot amongst them, are equally guilty of the charge of hastening this nation's disintegration? As the French would say: "Comment?" The preceding sentence indeed needs some clarification. So here we go.

The name of David Ledger will perhaps ring a bell, perhaps it will not. Ledger was, one and a half decades ago, part of the young crowd who gathered under the banner of the Assam Gana Parishad and made things extremely difficult for the authorities in that part of the country. Many of the AGP's demands were genuine and justified; a number of others smacked of narrow chauvinism and betrayed linguistic bigotry of the worst sort.

Anyway, thanks to the uprising lunched by the angry young people, Assam went through the catharsis of a bloodbath. At a certain point, the AGP won an overwhelming victory in the assembly elections and took charge of the state administration. But its leaders soon started bickering among themselves, and the tacticians in New Delhi regained full control over the state.

Amid this confusion, Ledger, who perhaps always had half an eye on the main chance, crossed over to the Congress. He was quite a catch, and was rewarded with a seat in the Rajya Sabha.

His performance in the Rajya Sabha was no worse than that of many others. He would not speak often. Whenever he would, it would be with clarity and conviction. He represented Assam in the Rajya Sabha, "the Council of States", and he would concentrate on the problems afflicting that remote state and its disturbed neighbourhood: the pervasive economic stagnation, the lack of basic infrastructure, the horrendous incidence of unemployment. His impassioned appeal for the introduction of a saner regime of Centre-states relations in the country would be nearly indistinguishable in tone and content from what a left ideologue would advocate.

His tenure came to an end in 1995. His friends pressed for his renomination. But the Congress decided otherwise. The term of the finance minister, who too had represented Assam in the Rajya Sabha since 1991, was also ending at the same time. There was only one sure seat available to the Congress: the choice was between the finance minister and Ledger. The decision did not take long. Ledger had served his purpose in the past; now he was only a squashed lemon.

The finance minister, on the other hand, was the finance minister; his continuance in Parliament had to be assured. At least such were the specific instructions from New Delhi. So Ledger was bumped, and the only Rajya Sabha slot from Assam in the control of the ruling party went to the country's finance minister.

Did the decision makers ever stop to consider whether, by this particular decision, they were advancing or hindering the cause of national integration?

The Constitution had explicitly intended the Rajya Sabha to be a "Council of States", much in the image of the US senate and the house of nationalities in the erstwhile Soviet Union. In the American system, each state, big or small, never mind whether it is New York or Hawaii, sends exactly two senators to the senate so that the voice of the smaller or economically weaker states receives as much attention as that of the stronger or bigger states.

Similar aspirations guided those who drafted the 1936 constitution of the Soviet Union. The issue is the enshrinement of the federal principle. For a large sized, thickly populated polity marked by ethnic, cultural and linguistic diversities, it makes sense to have a built in arrangement which tries to equalise opportunities between its large and small constituents, between constituents proximate to the seat of Central authority and those that are away from it.

The ladies and gentlemen who drafted our Constitution had no doubt in their mind about the role of the council of states; the nationalities constituting this great nation must be provided with a chamber where they could give expression to their thoughts, grievances and aspirations.

Kindly go through the proceedings of the constituent assembly: in the Rajya Sabha, each state, it is clearly indicated, will be represented by men and women who belonged to that state and were acquainted with the minutiae of its problems. A member of the Rajya Sabha representing a state, it therefore followed, must be "ordinarily resident" in the state; the Representation of the People's Act gave statutory flesh to that conditionality.

Well, Ledger had been, every since his birth, ordinarily resident in Assam; the finance minister could not claim such credentials. There are ways and ways though to have one's name inserted an elector from a state even without ever living in that state or visiting it even once, for instance by procuring back dated receipts of paid out house rent or forging ration cards. The finance minister had to resport to such subterfuges to establish his claim to be an elector from Assam.

Such skullduggery cannot quite suppress uncomfortable queries though: how many days all told during his entire lifespan the finance minister has spent in Assam before his induction as finance minister, and how many days he has spent since then, what the nature of acquaintance is with the problems of Assam, and so on. So what? Not Ledger, or somebody else who was a genuine citizen of Assam, but he, the finance minister, who does not speak a word of Assamese, was picked to represent Assam in the Rajya Sabha from the only slot available to the party.

To be fair, the finance minister has distinguished company in this comprehensive demonstration of contempt for the country's Constitution and statues. The list includes a former finance minister, the chairman, till only the other day, of the Janata Dal and stalwarts of the Bharatiya Janata Party. These individuals may talk themselves hoarse on the need to protect the nation against the CIA's nefarious intentions to destabilise it; their own role as would be saboteurs of this nation's integrity is however no less potent. Just ask the disenchanted multitude in Assam.

There is of course a residual issue, that of integrity. Some of those who declare themselves to the "ordinarily resident" in Assam, Orissa or Gujrat in order to wangle a Rajya Sabha seat, even when they know in their heart of hearts that they are indulging in blatant falsehood, may happen to be clean in financial matters, but do they still deserve to be described men of integrity? According to Biju Patnaik, they do. That is precisely the trouble with the nation: these Patnaiks have emerged as arbiters of moral standards.

21th February, 1996

In the garden of Gethsamene

The government we have in New Delhi decided, as soon as it assumed power in 1991, to let foreigners take on its behalf the major economic decisions affecting the nation. As part of that thought porcess, it had set its mind to accept the Dunkel draft proposals *in toto* and join the World Trade Organisation when it came into life on January 1, 1995.

This government is also a stickler for colonial grammar. Before each member country could sign up, it—the WTO's joining rules say—would have to declare formally its adherence to the basic tenets of the charter signed at Marrakesh in April last year. Each member country, one on these tenets says, must allow within its territory the right to foreigners to patent both products and processes for an uninterrupted span of 20 years.

The Indian Patents Act, legislated in 1970, holds a different view. Foreigners, according to this quarter of a century old legislation, have no inherent prerogative to exercise patent rights on our soil. The patenting of products may be allowed by the government at its discretion. And even in cases where such rights are granted, the period covered will not be 20 years, but only 14. The patenting of processes, where granted, will be for a much shorter period, to wit, only six years.

That is to say, according to our law, while a foreign patent for a particular manufactured product may be respected, at the government's discretion, for 14 years, our scientists and technoligists are still within their rights to try to evolve a near identical product through an alternative technology or method or process at the termination of just six years.

This provision was inserted in the 1970 Patents Act to ensure that the creativity of Indian science and technology is not stifled by the invasion of foreign patents. If one would recollect, that Patents Act, passed by the nation's Parliament with much pride 25 years ago, was based on three basic postulates: (a) this nation would in no case accept foreign patents for basic food items and life saving drugs; (b) multinational companies would not be allowed to mulct our consumers on the pretext of exercise of patent rights; and (c) no foreign patents must stand in the way of the nation's self reliant growth, which is why, even in those instance where foreign patents were recognised, rigorous time limits were set for both product and process patenting.

This is a new international order. Erstwhile imperialists are once more ruling the roost over large stretches of Asia, Africa and Latin America. They propose ot resume global economic exploitation in the name of free trade. Certain expressions, it is becoming increasingly clear, are gross misnomers. In today's topsyturvy world, free competition is hardly perfect competition, that is, competition between equals on equal terms. Nor does what passes for free trade represent transactions on equal terms between equally situated parties.

The advanced industrial economies have the advantage of an early start, huge capital stock and sophisticated technology. Should all trade barriers be abolished the poor countries would simply be swamped by the products of rich nations and, as a result, denied the opportunity of their own growth. The claptrap of the Dunkel draft and the WTO has no other objective. All projections of trade and income expansion following the adoption of WTO rules suggest that roughly 90 per cent of the gains would be appropriated by the advanced capitalist countries; the third world would receive only some morsels.

The case of patenting illustrates the predicament faced by the world's poor. If foreigners are permitted the right of both pruduct and patent processing for an undisturbed period of 20 years and in all spheres of economic activity, as the WTO charter enjoins, our scientists and technologists would have to sit it out during this spell of time. There is little point pretending that scientific and technological efforts in the fields affected by the patents could be resumed once the stipulated two decades are over.

At the end of 20 years, it is bound to be a squeezed lemon situation. since the technology embodied in the old patents would have been rendered throughly obsolete, and the poor nations would once more be shut of by patents restrictions from participating in newly emerging areas of technological endeavour. The purpose of the Dunkel-WTO show put together by the Western countries is fairly obvious: one Japan was enough, Caucasian civilisation and Causasian prosperity could only survive if colonial and ex-colonial peoples, black and brown and yellow, were kept away from experimenting with, and gaining from innovative technology.

True, the Soviet collapse created the ambience for ramming the new international trading rules down the throat of the third world countries. Govenrments of these countries experienced a failure of both morals and nerves. What is worse, some amongst them, such as the present regime in India, chose to play the role of Uncle Tom to perfection. What happened a fortnight ago, on the midnight of December 31 January 1, was a clincher.

The government in New Delhi was fully aware of the doubts entertained by members of parliament about the contents of the Dunkel proposals which constitute the corpus of the WTO. Without question, the WTO treaty affects this nation's sovereignty. In terms of its provisions, an external body will have a say in what we produce and in what manner we produce it. It will have a say in what our government chooses to distribute to its people and on what terms. This outside agency is even supposed to decide whether we can subsidise food to our consumers or inputs to our farmers.

A standing parliamentary committee, which consisted of representatives of the Congress as well, unanimously expressed itself against several aspects of the Dunkel draft as now embodied in the WTO charter. The government, determined to play to the bilt the comprador role, was undeterred.

The United States, according to standard school texts, is the world's *second* largest democracy. We are supposed to be *the* largest. The second largest democracy had at least the decency to first discuss and vote on the WTO legislation in both the house of representatives and the senate. The largest democracy, the republic of India, was made to traverse differently: no discussion and no vote in Parliament, the government in its wisdom decides to join the WTO and the people are expected to accept what the government decides. It is, in other words, the authoritarian route. The government cannot even claim that, never mind Parliament, it had a direct mandate from the people on the WTO treaty: scan the Congress election manifesto of 1991, there is not even a cursory reference to such a thing as the Dunkel draft.

In view of recent developments, this government can be said to have little moral authority left to rule. To all intents and purposes, it is a tottering regime. But it had made its commitments to foreigners, the conditionalities of the WTO had to be formally accepted before December 31 January 1 midnight, including the specific provision that multinational corporations are granted product and process patenting rights in drugs, softwares, food items, fertilisers, seeds, pesticides and so on.

A technical difficulty, however, remained. Before a country joins the body, it must, the WTO charter insists, not only undertake to accept, but formally and statutorily legitimise, each of the terms of the new international treaty. That implied drastic revision of the Indian Patents Act of 1970 before the deadline of December 31, 1994.

The miserable government in New Delhi was not lacking in imagination. It dard not face Parliament. For that matter, in the circumstances that have eventuated, the prime minister of this government cannot even gather courage to face his own parliamentary party. The possibility of passing the necessary amendments to the Patents Act in Parliament was about zero. In the Rajya Sabha, the government does not have the majority to pass such a legislation. Even in Lok Sabha, it would have been dicey, given the deep reservations nurtured by many Congress MPs.

Discretion being the better part of valour, no notice was served on Parliament indicating official intention to amend the Patents Act.

Instead, like accomplished thieves in the night, the government, on the eve of the deadline for joining the WTO, forced the president to sign an ordinance enacting the called for changes in the Patents Act. Not the people's will, but the will of foreign masters, have been made to prevail by a blatant piece of authoritarianism. The ordinance, when it comes to Parliament as a *fait accompli,* is more than likely to be turned down. But tomorrow is another day. Meanwhile, the minions can inform the foreign masters that their will has been done.

Mind you, this servility was not absolutely necessary. The US congress has voted for the WTO treaty, but it has done so on the explicit understanding that the US Trade Act, the celebrated sections of Super and Special 301 not excluding, will remain unimpaired. That assertion flies in the face of a major provision of the WTO charter, which categorically disapproves of unilateral acts, or threats, of reprisal by any member country against other countries on the alleged ground of trade misdemeanours on the part of the latter.

If the US can have its Trade Act and yet join the WTO, we too could have kept our Patents Act and joined the new world body, subject to the proviso that further negotiations over aspects of product and process patenting would be undertaken during the ten year transitional period allowed by the WTO charter. This is precisely what the US administration intends to do with respect to its Trade Act. But perhaps the judgement was reached that what behoves a master nation does not behove a slave.

The WTO and the gentiles who control it should nonetheless be put on notice: sooner or later, sooner rather than later, a new government is likely to take charge in this country. This new government will not be prepared to abide by the patents arrangements as ordained by the WTO, for the simple reason the Indian Parliament will not accept these arrangements. The news ought to reach the WTO that India remains basically a sovereign country, it is soon going to install a government which would not mind reasserting this sovereignty.

11th June, 1995

All American banana split

The banana republic connotes a set of ground realities. But it also mirrors a certain frame of mind, notions are turned upside down, irrationality becomes rationality, insult is taken to be accolade. This is the state we, it would seem, have finally managed to reach.

The United States administration chose to downgrade the week long sojourn of our prime minister, Mr. P.V. Narasimha Rao, to god's own country. Unlike on all previous occations, this time it was not reckoned as a state visit; our head of state was given the treatment reserved for minor foreign dignitaries who are entitled to only some minimal courtesies. We lumped that. In order to propitiate the US administration, we chose to suspend even if, as our government claims, only temporarily—our missile test firming programme. We also rushed through a new telecommunications policy which will gladden the hearts of US transnational corporations.

Our spokesman and our media were under the instructions to make great play of the fact the prime minister was invited to address a joint session of the US congress. Between the senate and the house of representatives, the congress consists of 535 members. Of them, not even 40 bothered to be present and listen to the Indian prime minister's address; the empty seats of the chamber had to be filled by minions from New Delhi who constituted the prime minister's entourage. Even the press gallery was principally occupied by the plane load of journalists the prime minister had taken along with him.

The visit of the Indian prime minister and his perorations in New York, Houston, Boston and Washington DC were balcked out by the media. This was not deliberate, but matter of course, India was no longer the ogre leading the great nonaligned movement. There was no Krishna Menon around to license *Time* magazine by his forked tongue, and this puny visitor from a diminshed country was no Jawaharlal Nehru or Indra Gandhi.

At the joint press conference following his session in the Oval Room with the US president, Mr. Bill Clinton, our prime minister was cut to size; he was simply ignored by the media. Only one American journalist chose to ask him a question, that was on the human rights situation in Kashmir, and the answer he gave was received with unconcealed disbelief. The rest of the time the prime minister of the world's largest democracy was a mute onlooker, even as correspondent after correspondent kept targeting a barrage of questions at the US president not on US-Indian relations, but on Haiti, on China's most favoured nation status, on the domestic interest rate structure and so on.

Mr. Clinton spoke a few polite words about our country; these were obligatory for the occasion. He was however in no generous mood; he left none in doubt that the US administration would continue to harass New Delhi on the issues of nuclear nonproliferation, regional disarmament, Kashmir and human rights, there was going to be no switching off of heat following the visit.

His promise to send two special emissaries—the secretary of commerce and the energy secretary in the course of a year is not bereft of significance either. One secretary will press India to allow further market access to US goods and services; the other one is to ensure that the Indian authorities do not renege at the last moment their pledge to buy dozens and dozens of obsolete power plants from the US and additionally gurantee American investors a minimum rate of return of 16 per cent,

This is precisely where the state of the mind becomes relevant. All sensitivities are spent. The banana republic does not even realise that it is at the receiving end of the banana republic treatment. Every insult is regarded as benedication. The prime minister of the world's largest democracy misses the import of the adage that dignity is as dignity does; as he emerged from his *tete a tete* with the US president, he gloatingly informs the world press that, look, there has been no twisting of his arm. No Nehru or Indira Gandhi could have imagined that an Indian prime minister was capable of sinking to such a grovelling level.

But a banana republic has its own code. It lives in its own illusory world. The flock of press people who accompanied the prime minister would, for the next month and thereabouts, write dutiful columns on what a thundering success the prime minister's US safari was, on the umpteen points he succeeded in scoring off Pakistan, how well his speeches went down with US audiences, how US industrialists and businessmen were totally bowled over when our prime minister described to them the limitless possibilities of the market India offered, on how our prime minister's quote from Abraham Lincon had completely befuddled a nondescript US state department official named Robin Raphel.

Such is the banana republic state of the mind, or, if one were to use that state of the art expression, mindset. A banana republic assumes itself to be the centre of the universe. The reality is that it is nobody. It gets accustomed to the role of a vassal state, but imagines the serfdom to be sovereignty. Its press becomes excruciatingly conformist. We are at the moment witnessing the unfolding of the phenomenon.

Our government, if we have to go by our media, can do no wrong, and the Americans, thanks to the prime minister's visit, have shed all their reservations about our country. Even on Kashmir and the nuclear business, the Americans, it will be asserted, have been most understanding. A surrender to foreign pressure, don't you know, is not really surrender, but an act of accommodation. The lingo itself undergoes a transformation. We no longer talk of a suspension of our missile development programme, we merely "cap" it.

The banana republic has arrived, and it has brought along with it a news manual of manners and norms. The poor have dropped out of the nation's conscience. The nation itself is now defined in terms of foibles and predilections of the top 10 or 15 per cent of the social stratum.

The latter dream America and think America. Their priorities determine official policy. Thanks to the spate of economic reforms since 1991, this upper crust had never had it so good; the consumerist arcadia they have attained has therefore to be protected at all cost. The high living of the upper classes has been made possible by interminable borrowings from foreign parties; such borrowings have been contingent upon letting go, in substantial measure, bits and pieces of the nation's sovereignty. The surrender of economic prerogatives cannot but endanger political sovereignty as well, as we are increasingly likely to learn in the course of the next few months; Mr. Clinton has promised as much.

But the upper crust mindset is not disturbed. This mindset expresses itself only in cliches; globalisation is good; we must integrate with the world, the market must be free; there is no substitute for efficiency; privatisation promotes efficiency. What good globalisation has done till now to the country is a query this mindset feels no need to respond to; the fact such data as are available suggests that efficiency in the Indian public sector units as a whole, measured by the rate of return, has in the recent years been much higher than in the private sector, does not impress them. Nor do they like to be detained by such abstractions as loss of national sovereignty. Since they never had it so good, why should they worry whether their country has been reduced to the state of a banana republic and anyway, what is wrong with being a banana republic?

The prime minister and his entourage perhaps know better. But they have their private concerns. The model they have opted for, they know, is unsustainable without continuous, and rising, inflow of foreign funds. In past decades, such funds were arranged on government to government basis, with some master of ceremonies role on the part of the World Bank. The cessation of the Cold War has ended the chapter of government to government munificence. Private capital inflows now offer the only possibility of escape.

The wretched foreigners are however not coming in droves, and they are not investing in growth.

US business and industry are playing hard. India is an eleventh rate country which does not hold their interest. They will come only if their charter of demands is fully granted, and perhaps not even then. There is no evidence that the Americans have ever helped any banana republic to develop into an economically strong nations. It is the fate of a banana rupublic to continue to be a dependent territory.

The upper crust will not mind that state of being, but will they be able to hold down the nation's overwhelming majority who will get nothing, absolutely nothing, out of the emerging social and economic arrangements? The prime minister may keep visiting the US oftener, US officials may increase the frequency of their visits to our shores, the answer to the riddle however lies within the country itself.

1st June, 1994

Import of inflation

Nobody and nothing are giving the economy what the Americans call a leg up. Examine the trends in industrial production for the first three quarters of 1993-94. Manufacturing output is up by a meagre 1.8 per cent over the corresponding period in the pervious year. This despite the supposedly extraordinary surge in demand for consumer electronics items. The production of capital goods continues to decline steeply. Mineral output too is down.

It is only because power generation, mostly under the aegis of the much maligned, much berated state electricity boards, has advanced by seven per cent that the over all index of industrial output shows a rise of 2.4 per cent over the year.

The finance minister's claim of a four per cent industiral growth will therefore be, rest assured, a bit of a non-fancy free exaggeration. So too his projection of the inudstrial production index rising by six per cent in the current year. The arcadia promised three years ago obviously remains a far distant dream. Even according to prim official circles, vast expansion in public outlay alone can dispel the pallid gloom that has descended on Indian Industry.

With the budgetary and fiscal deficits as high as they already are, and the International Monetary Fund breathing down its neck, the government is in some difficulty in deciding upon its next step. Does it ignore the frowns of the IMF and pump some more money into the system to tackle, even if partly, the problem of industrial recession? But if it does that, would not double digit inflation receive a further spurt?

Towards which direction should the authorities dare, or should they not dare at all? Are the electoral prospects of the ruling party going to worsen in case it dares? On the other hand, what is the gurantee the electorate would not turn viciously hostile should the ruling satraps toe the line of the washington concensus all the way, even if those presiding over the concensus seek to assure the natives that their government is doing wonderfully well. Besides,the hefty sum of $ 15 billion in the foreign exchange kitty is a reality even logical positivists will vouchsafe for.

Whenever ministers and their acolytes are afflicted by a blue mood, they could seek solace in the bosom of the exchange reserves. That is their entitlement.

Here too, though, the dialectics does not quite resolve itself. Life without foreign exchange reserves is unthinkable, but living with a stockpile of such reserves is a it seems no less hazardous.

There is flip side to the story of the exchange pile up. Once foreign exchange of any magnitude comes in, the Reserve Bank of India has to dole out an equivalent amount in Indian currency. This adds to internal monetary resources.

As much as $ 9 billion dollars, the authorities boast, have come in the course of the past one year. Purely on account of this occurrence itself, money supply must have gone up by something like Rs. 280 billion. Other things remaining the same this should mean a 20 per cent monetary expansion over the year. Leave aside the government's fiscal polices. Its monetary management too would appear to have gone haywire.

Double digit inflation, it thus follows, is not an act of nature. It is what the government brings upon itself and the helpless people over whom it rules—by its doings and misdoings. Its anxiety to deport itself as an activist regime aggravates the problem. It is under pressure. The accretion of exchange reserves, it has been told, has to proceed beyond the phase of borrowed plumes. The country must either export or perish.

Matters are hardly easy. Despite all the "front loading" of our tariff concessions to propitiate them, the wretched Americans have slowed down their purchase of our textiles, our leather manufactures, our carpets and handicrafts. And they have begun to talk of labour standards.

The government still knows its mind. Export earnings have been freed from the shackles of income and corporate taxation. Prometheus is unbound. The clarion call is on—concentrate on agricultural exports, sell cotton overseas, sell sugar overseas, sell oilseeds and foodgrains overseas.

How unreasonable. This noble initiative too is not devoid of complications.

For instance, in case the *basmati* variety of rice is exported in large quantities, its price shoots up. If the price of basmati rice goes up, the price of superfine varieties of rice too rise. If the price of superfine varieties rises, the price of fine varieties follows suit. If the price of the fine varieties rises, common quality rice experiences a similar escalation. If the price of the common varieties of rice moves up, the price of the coarse varieties too are caught in the rising spiral.

The sequence does not end here. For if the price of rice zooms upwards there is bound to be a sympathetic movement in the price of wheat, in the prices of *jawar, bajra* and other so called inferior foodgrains as well. If foodgrain prices rise, the sympathy factor goes on the rampage, farm prices rise across the board. Industrial prices naturally fall in line. A general inflation of impressive proportions ensues.

The government is in a jam. Because of the fiscal policies thrust upon it, there is a halt in public investment in the farm sector. Infrastructural facilities built over the decades, such as irrigation networks in the northwestern parts of the country, are exhausted. Agricultural output has in consequences tended to level off.

Farm exports can therefore be raised only at the expense of current consumption. Should official preference be for export of foodgrains as well?

After all, since foreign exchange accretion is adjudged to be highest here in terms of units of effort put in, the objective can be ensured only by reducing the domestic per capita availability of grain.

An extra element of uncertainty therefore enters the picture. Were the rains to fail this year, and yet grain exports not to be cut back, the government would have a major internal crisis on its hand. So much so that the jargon export or perish would undergo a mutation—it would be a case of export *and* perish.

Things have been going awry for quite some months now. The provisional index of wholesale prices shows an increase of 10 to 11 per cent over the year. Cross over to the retail price index and food prices have actually gone up by almost 50 per cent. Bland facts of such nature may not immediately disturb the tranquility of the highminded ones who administer the country from the ramparts of the nation's capital. But events have a way of catching up with them.

The inter-relationship between exports and commodity prices is not—it cannot be—a phenomenon confined to foodgrains alone. Ask the hundreds of thousands of handloom weavers who have been without any source of livelihood in recent months because of the shortage of hank yarn induced by the policy to export cotton and cotton yarn. The price of hank yarn has jumped fourfold in the course of the past four months.

The government has a look of injured innocence. Why, it is fully seized of the developing situation. It has decided to allow imports of cotton, oilseeds and sugar. That will take care of the turbulence on the price front.

The authorities concerned know their obligations and will not mind running down the foreign exchange reserves and import essential commodities so as to discipline domestic prices. Please also note how generous the government can be. It is allowing the imports to take place at zero or nominal duty.

No question the authorities are being generous. Their generosity is however toward the traders who are being urged to import under the open general licensing scheme. Private trade raises prices. The same private trade is being offered the opportunity to import stocks of sensitive commodities as part of anti-inflationary policy. The authorities will clearly have no control over the imported supplies. It is entirely up to private trade to decide what to do with the imports, or whether to import to the extent the government wants them to.

The class interests of traders may still dictate them not to release extra supplies in the market. That could spell trouble. The government should not complain, it created the trouble in the first place. Globalisation and trouble constitute a perfect example of joint supply.

4th May, 1994

Tiger and pussy cat

We cannot recreate history. Castigating *expost* men who have since passed into oblivion is such a wholly pointless exercise too. Should we not nonetheless confess obscurantism is something which runs deep in the Indian temperament? Fundamentalists—as they are known to be—are of course the easier targets. Are not there however others who show about the same traits?

We have to get used to China's role as the major Asian power. To many in this country unable to get out of the 1962 syndrome, this hurts. Some amongst them would dearly love to keep holding conventions where pledges will be taken to liberate Tibet, please do not ask how.

But this sort of game China can play with much greater finesse and with a greater order of confidence: the moment some Indian politicians take up Tibet, the Chinese find a way to mix up their signals over Kashmir. In other words, the cards are heavily decked against us.

We may gloat over our foreign exchange holding of $ 13 billion. But once the stock exchanges start sliding, a large chunk of these holdings is bound to disappear, courtesy the foreign institutional investors, courtesy our noble non-residents.

One does not want to hurt the finance minister's *amor propre* by reminding him that in his budget speech he forgot to mention one basic datum. Our debt repayment obligations over the next three years could exceed $ 30 billion. China, in contrast, is running up an export surplus of $ 15 billion annually. Its total foreign exchange earnings are likely to be in the neighbourhood of $ 60 billion.

Our finance minister prays to the rain gods. Simultaneously, he prays for the advent of foreign investors not so much to play ducks and drakes in the share market but to sink their funds in productive activities. The Chinese do not have to do any such entreating. They do not have to chase foreigners. Foreigners, instead, chase them : please, would you kindly allow us to enter your market and share a minor slice of it; we promise to behave, we promise not to infringe the rules you frame for us, barbarians. The multinational giants appreciate the compulsions of the situation.

A time lag, however, affects the understanding of the state department of the United States, which finds itself in its newfound unfamiliar role as champion of human rights. This latter fact has indirectly helped India at Geneva.

We were bailed out not just because Iran, a Shia state, has few friends within the Organisation of Islamic Conference and would dearly love to set up a counterpoint. But without China, the last minute salvaging of India's honour would have beet impossible. China had its specific reasons. It has had enough of the US secretary of state, Mr Warren Christopher, and the clutch of visiting US senators lecturing it on Tibet and human rights. Of course, it signed on the doted line of the General Agreement on Tariffs and Trade treaty. That is because it promises, over the next six or eight years, something like $ 40 billion worth of extra annual trade for China. Even in this matter though, the Americans nurtured ambitions to be a spoilsport. The domestic economic problems are overwhelming. The US administration would for dear life like to shut out textiles and footwear and consumer electronics originating in low wage Asian countries to save employment at home. At the same time, it would keep trying to gain entry into the lush and wide Japanese and Chinese markets.

The tension in their relations with Japan the Americans are experiencing will, rest assured, give way in the next few weeks or months to greater tensions with China. The Americans, therefore needed to be told off. They needed to be told off as much on the trade issue as on the human rights issue. In any case, US congressmen would love to link up the two. The Chinese would not mind giving the Americans what they asked for.

We have been caught up in this China-US situation. The nitty gritty of the *realpolitik* is simple enough: for taking the heat off Kashmir, we have to accept the oblique patronage of China. Such a development would, in addition to causing heartburn even amongst many in the opposition ranks, ensure sleepless nights to the minions in the ministry of finance who think Bank-Fund, dream Bank-Fund and do Bank-Fund.

These are problems the prime minister is nonetheless seemingly learning to handle with skill. Beyond a point, the International Monetary Fund cannot be obliged on the size of the fiscal deficit, and the Americans have generally been, for his government, great bailers out.

But the constraints of parliamentary democracy are not easy to escape from. Elections have to be fought in the states. The overall picture looks gloomy. The kind of last minute salvaging in Himachal Pradesh and Madhya Pradesh need not automatically repeat itself in Andhra Pradesh and Karnataka. The results of the stray byelections are hardly encouraging.

Should the two southern states slip away in the elections later in the year and the empress of Tamil Nadu remains as inscrutable as ever and the

Muslim League in Kerala continue to be riven with dissensions, the honourable members of the Lok Sabha who defected towards the direction of the prime minister's party would find ways and means to defect in any other directions.

In any event that conjuncture of circumstances would be such that the elections for Lok Sabha would perhaps have to be brought forward by at least a year.

The minister for commerce would stick to his claim that, after all, only two persons in the country are qualified to comprehend the GATT treaty, namely himself and his secretary, and therefore none else better interfere with his decision to write the deeds of this particular surrender to foreign interests.

But even the GATT treaty would have electoral implications. Were the US to keep insisting that we must "frontload" our concessions to them while they would only offer a hypothetical promise of "backloading" concessions at the end of 10 years or thereabouts, the resulting arrangement would not only fuel double digit inflation but further deepen the crisis in agriculture and industry.

Human rights in Kashmir would therefore not be the only issue involved. Whether the Indian upper classes have been prepared for the switchover or not, it is altogether possible that we would need to increase our political distance from the US.

This would mean simultaneously increasing our economic distance. What we lose on the swings of moving away or towards the US might or might not be won back on the roundabouts of a rapproachement with China. Our leaders have however little choice in the matter.

For, in terms of domestic politics, a major setback over Kashmir would be much more damaging than even the failure of industrial output to rise or the inability of exports to maintain their momentum or prices soaring beyond the level of 15 per cent per annum.

The border dispute with China has therefore to be put on the backburner. This is tragic news for professional Sinophobes. At the end of 30 years of hot air and prodigal defence expenditure, the country would have nothing to show as net gain. Meanwhile, according to our own admission, we have decisively lost the competitive battle for economic development to China. We have, in other words, wasted the timespan of a generation and a half.

The rest of the population never really mattered, but the top 10 per cent of the nation is anxious to make up for this lost time. The model they have chosen, or has been choosing on their hehalf by the ruling party, is too full of contradictions though there is no instance in history where a country of India's size and complexity has grown economically strong through reliance on external support.

We may set up little *entrepots* of growth here and there; they would be like the foreign settlements in Shanghai in the late 19th and early 20th centuries, with no nexus with the realities of the hinterland. National income growth would be halting and unevenly dispersed, engendering regional discount. An enfeebled central regime, forced to fight too many domestic bushfires, could then, be even more enfeebled, so much so that the republic would be in danger of actually withering away.

Were we to lump our ego and accept China as the big brother in Asia, we would have saved Kashmir. That would not by itself give us economic development. Large scale social engineering, more or less of a drastic nature, would be called for. The ruling politicians and tycoons, who assume they are as wisdom worthy human beings as they pretend to be, are full of precepts from China's so called market socialism.

They have to be told the basic fact of life: market socialism did not drop out of thin air, it has a prehisory, a prehistory of disciplined, egalitarian living. If that is considered strong medicine, then of course we always have the last alternative with which we started. That is to say, we can simply continue to plod along in the manner we have been for the past 40 odd years.

Even that choice, cynics would say is soon going to be closed up if we fail to ensure the wherewithal to pay back $ 35 billion in debt services in the course of the next three years,—so what can be new, pussycat?

23rd March, 1994

World's only flower power

The follies of the Vietnam war are not quite a quarter of a century old. The manner the United States establishment continues to treat its own black citizenry is no shining example of observance of the provisions of the universal human rights charter laid down by the United Nations. None of this however prevents the US administration from lecturing the rest of the world on human rights.

That the US has emerged as the only superpower and therefore jolly well has to be indulged is not exactly the reason for this incongruity. The superpower has umpteen other preoccupations. Where human rights are concerned, cocking a snook at it would not have been a difficult exercise in ordinary circumstances. Unfortunately for us, this particular issue has become a part of Mr. Bill Clinton's domestic compulsions.

The underpinning of the president's support base is still the Rooseveltian coaltion of urban liberals, ethnic minorities—including the blacks, and the trade union lobby. A hilly billy from a half southern, half midwestern state does not merge easily into the image of this coalition. He must therefore try and, in the language of the advertisements for the car rental agency, try harder.

The role of bully boy in international relations, especially in matters pertaining to trade, has a lot to do with the persistence of recessionary conditions back home. Jobs are scarce, inventories are high, both investment and production are at a low ebb. For dear life, demand for goods and services must be revived.

If domestic demand refuses to pick up, foreigners better be pressured into buying more US goods. Should the pursuit of this objective mean riding roughshod over third world susceptibilities, well, that cannot be helped. Other considerations follow.

Liberalism is fine as an abstrat doctrine. But it cannot be preached to a home crowd severely feeling the pinch of unemployment. The Dunkel treaty notwithstanding, the US administration is therefore unlikely to allow generous entry of foreign goods into the country.

At the same time it would not hesitate to use strongarm methods when it is a question of pushing US goods into foreign markets. Hard epithets do not break bones. Mr. Clinton will not mind if, in the wake of Dunkel, the

Americans are called names in international fora. Besides, despite the disaster of the Russian elections and the funny goings on in Belorussia and Ukraine, it is most improbable east Europe will not continue to be docile for some more while.

Unfortunately voters back home, and especially the traditional coalition sustaining the Democratic Party, are clamouring for much more. The callow youth who constituted the vanguard of the campus demonstrations at the time of My Lai have now reached middle age. Their concerns cannot be wished away. They are, for example, vocal on environmental matters. For articulating their views they have their man right inside the administration, the vicepresident, Mr Al Gore. He has in fact authored a book on biodiversity and sustainable development.

It ought also to bring wry smiles to third world faces that the US administration, ceaselessly preaching the virtues of wholesale privatisation to aid seeking poor countries, is moving toward the directrion of a comprehensive state supported health insurance programme for its own citizens.

The administration has little choice in the matter. One of the major themes repeatedly heard during Mr Clinton's election campaign was health security. The president's wife herself, no less, is a leading luminary of the health lobby.

The White House is more or less in the same bind with respect to human rights. Howsoever odd it sounds, ensuring and expanding human rights across the six continents is now an essential component of the US domestic agenda. The Vietnam generation is long on memory. It would perhaps like to atone for the bestialities in that little far eastern country.

One way of doing so, it must have been decided, is to take multiple pledges to protect human rights on a global scale. This would be an excellent strategy too for neutralising recalcitrant backwoodsmen within the Democratic Party such as the black pastor, Mr Jesse Jackson. These people would otherwise harangue and harass the president on the allegedly slow pace with which the retrograde civil rights record of the Republicans during their long 12 years of rule is being reversed.

Have no illusion, the US administration will therefore keep breathing down our neck on the human rights business. In any case, even thought the Cold War has ceased to be no particular reason exists for it to dispense with the tilt forward Pakistan. The fact our government has prostrated itself before the US on crucial economic matters is hardly a consideration. For that has rendered India into only one of a species. All third world countries these days prostrate themselves before the Americans.

We also need occasionally to look at our face in the mirror. On both Kashmir and Punjab it will be difficult to rebut the proposition a conspiracy of silence exists within India's political establishment. Even so we have, it is now tacitly accepted, few legs to stand upon in Kashmir. The wailing of the Pandit community expelled from the valley provides a mild divertissement. But it is not enough to blot out the follies perpetrated one after another in the valley since the summer of 1948.

Besides, Mr K.P.S. Gill may have emerged meanwhile as a local here among India's urban elite much like in the manner Mr. T. N. Seshan has. But as the Buta Singh episode suggests the ground reality in Punjab is something else. The waywardness of the Khalistanis is an indisputable datum. Nonetheless, sooner or later this nation will have to answer if not to the world at least to the US human rights lobby for the encounter deaths engineered in Punjab and associated other shady doings over the years.

There is a further irony in the situation and which adds to our embarrassment. Our present ambassador to the US, Mr Siddhartha Shankar Ray, is about the most inappropriate person to defend the counry's plaint on human rights. This gentleman happened to be the chief minister of West Bengal when in the early Seventies the Research and Analysis Wing, actively collaborating with the local constabulary, patented the Indian version of encounter killings. It extensively put it into practice for liquidating Marxist radicals. His expiation of the pristine state of human rights obtaining in India can only be expected to be greeted with considerable hilarity.

The offensive against us will be relentless. The demand will be pressed that the human rights commission recently legislated in this country be armed with more teeth. Going by indications, the commission as proposed to be constituted is intended to go the way of the inter-state council. It is to be there in name but only as an inert body. The government's general calculation, one suspects, is it should function more or less in an Uncle Tom fashion.

This scheme of things could now come under some threat. The well heeled Khalistani and Kashmiri lobbies operating in the US will of course have a nuisance value. But our government's principal worry is going to be the radical fringe of the Democratic Party. This group will refuse to be swayed by the mellifluours prose embellishing the chapter on the directive principless of state policy in the Indian Constitution.

Groups such as Worldwatch and Amnesty International will persist in being pests. They will be egging on domestic human rights groups in the US to concentrate on Assessing the objective conditions prevailing in India and in the subcontinent as a whole.

The logic of economic liberalisation will trip us up here. The economic reforms programme is not clicking. Prices are shooting up, the fiscal deficit cannot be contained, jobs are being lost evry week and compensatory employment opportunities are not created elsewhere. The only way the government, according to its light, can wriggle out of the dilemma is by throwing itself in an even more humiliating manner at the mercy of the Americans. Importuning them for a gushing flow of direct foreign investment.

It is in pursuit of this will-o' the-wisp that, on the eve of his departure for the world economic fourm at Davos, the prime minister, Mr P. V. Narasimha Rao, chose to raise the prices of petroleum products, rice, wheat and sugar. And emulating Mr Boris Yeltsin's rule by decree he issued the ordinances to privatise the country's skies as well as the banking industry. These ordinances were not much of a gesture. A *de facto* regime was merely made into a *de jure* one.

However, every little thing counts—or so it is being thought. The US administration, given the domestic pressures upon it, cannot but play hard to get. Market friendliness is fine, but it would still keep demanding major concessions from us on Kashmir, some gesture of contrition on Punjab, and perhaps a climbdown on the issue of signing the nuclear nonproliferation treaty. In case we fail to behave it might even threaten us with suspension of the benediction from the World Bank and the International Monetary Fund.

The wages of sin are death. The wages of IMF-World Bank supported economic reforms could well be the death of our daydreams woven around Kashmir. For the king is in the counting house.

9th February, 1994

Capitulation and decapitation

The rebuff to the Bharatiya Janata Party apart, on at least one other matter the verdict of *Aryavarta* is not encumbered by ifs and buts. For the first time, a proposed international treaty was made an electoral issue in this country.

The nation's largest politcal party, now ruling at the Centre, had chosen to defend before the electorate its decision to accept the Dunkel draft. The implementation of the General Agreement on Tariffs and Trade proposals, its election manifesto sought to say, would be a great boon to the Indian peasantry. The government should cherish no illusions: the Dunkel draft has not received Aryavarta's mandate, and particularly not the mandate of the Uttar Pradesh farm belt.

Perhaps that will not bother the government too much. Decisions on crucial economic questions have for some while ceased to be made on the basis of any objective assessment of the predilections and interests of citizens. Discussion in Parliament on the implications of the GATT document has been carefully avoided for as long as possible.

Negotiating an international agreement, the prime minister, Mr P. V. Narasimha Rao, has obliquely suggested, is the prerogative of the government. Were the final signed document to turn out not to the liking of the representatives of the people they could, seems to imply, move a vote of no confidence against the government. It would now perhaps be claimed on behalf of the prime minister that just as the assembly elections were not a referendum on the performance of his government, they constituted no referendum on the Dunkel draft either.

The prime minister and his party would clearly be caught in a bit of a contradiction here. The backtracking would, however, be understandable. Politicians, at least those who are without ideology and have assumed politics to be not dissimilar to any other random profession, have to survive in power, which compulsion necessitates occasional dissembling.

The issue will still not go away. The Dunkel draft is not like any other ordinary international treaty dealing with this or that aspect of external relations. It is going to interfere with India's internal economic processes.

Under the guise of ushering in an international trade regime untramelled by tariffs and other restrictions, it would restructure production, distribution and pricing arrangements in country after country, including in this one. The government would be on extremely vulnerable grounds were it to suggest the effects of such restructuring on the people is no business of Parliament.

Provisions in the draft concerning the pharmaceutical or software industries, biodiversites, finance and communications aside, two matters stand out. The consequences for the country's public distribution system including the system of food and necessity subsidy, and the vulnerability of agriculture if farm products from overseas were allowed entry into the country.

The government, faithfully adhering to the notes furnished by the GATT secretariat, has sought to laugh away the possibility of any post-Dunkel upheaval affecting the existing public distribution arrangements. Its point of view is deceptively simple. Subsidy in the case of a foodgrain distributed by a government agency, the draft says, must not be more than 10 per cent of the prevailing market price of the grain.

In no year in the past decade, it seems, has the subsidy for publicly distributed wheat or rice exceeded this margin. What has not happened in the past is unlikely to happen in the future either, the government argues. The apprehensions of economists and Opposition politicians, it suggests, are altogether unfounded. The discretionary margin allowed by the draft agreement is sufficiently wide for the power to distribute subsidised food to the weaker sections of society to be left unimpaired.

But will it? No major crop failure has taken place in the country during the past decade. The demands placed on the public distribution system have naturally been modest and the gap between the market price and the price in ration and fair price shops for the main cereals had been relatively narrow.

However, if the rains fail in some year in the proximate future this will change. And this could well happen as the country has had good rains successively for five years. The resulting crop failure might then lead to a steep decline in market supplies. Foodgrain prices could skyrocket.

Going by what was experienced in the mid Sixties, it is by no means certain that a price rise of 200 to 300 per cent would not take place in the event of a mere 20 per cent drop in output. The market price for the principal cereals could shoot up to as much as Rs. 20 per kilogram—if not everywhere, at least in some parts of the country. Were the Dunkel proposals to become the law of the land the government would in that eventuality be precluded from distributing rice or wheat at less than Rs. 18 per kilogram.

Few of the nation's poor would be able to afford this price. In case the government were to announce, as part of famine relief operations, the free distribution of grain to distressed people, nothing would stop a free market zealot from requesting the GATT authorities that penal action be initiated against the Indian authorities for distributing farm products at a 100 per cent subsidy.

What is more, once the draft is signed, the government will have to allow the import of any and every agricultural commodity to the extent of 3.3 per cent of its domestic output. This is not as harmless as it sounds. Economic textbooks are full of examples of the violent price fluctuations of a farm product that could be brought about by a marginal increase or decrease in its supplies.

Once expectations are queered in a particular manner, and speculators and buyers are conditioned in their behaviour, even a marginal augmentation of supply is capable of bringing down prices by as much as 50 or 60 per cent, and thereby ruining the peasantry.

This clause inserted in the Dunkel proposals in not necessarily an innocent academic proviso. Some years ago, a group of strategists ensconced in the World Bank had floated a trial balloon. Global efficiency of production deserved to be maximised, including farm output. Agricultural productivity in the united States and Canada, as is common knowledge, is way ahead of productivity in other parts of the world, including of course Asia, Africa and Latin America. If the objective is—as it shhould be—to raise global resource use to its most feasible level, would it therefore not be sensible to concentrate all farm activity in the US and Canada alone?

The strategists ensconced inside the World Bank were not deterred by piffling little details. They did not care to spell out the alternative occupation or livelihood the poor peasatry in the inefficient countries could switch to if they surrendered their right to cultivate their land and became wholly dependent on imports.

Though the peasants of the poor lands would be without any occupation or income, it might nonetheless be insisted upon they pay for their imports at proper North American prices. It would be too bad if they failed to pay such prices. Imports would stop and they would be welcome to starve and die.

What is apocalypse to some is milleinium to others. Th Dunkel draft incorporates in itself the vision of a millenium thought up by the world's rich. Should the agriculture of a poor country collapse, the multinational monopolies could comfortably move in and do whatever they wanted with the county's food and agricultural policy.

It is a beautiful scheme. Once the signatures get appended to the Dunkel proposals, it would be binding on the government. The latter has for months on end refused to face Parliament on the issue, and it would be furiously denied that the verdict in UP is in part an expression of the people's wrath at the endorsement of the GATT final draft. Cheered by Western governments and the multinational lobby, it would proceed to arrange the noose around the nation's neck, nor would it feel ashamed at being present at its own beheading.

15 December, 1993

Efficiently chained slaves

Liberalisation is contaminating. Market economy *per excellence,* members of families controlling closely held private corporate units are fiercely fighting amongst themselves. Whether it is soft drinks or textiles or shaving blades or fertilisers, the turmoil of internal dialectics is affecting industrial unit after industrial unit.

Some members of the family have a gleam in their eye. This or that multinational corporation is promising them vastly profitable global markets provided they merge their firm with the multinational body or, alternately, agree to sell to it the bulk of the firm's equity. Why not then give in and enjoy tranquil living ever after?

Other members of the family disagree. They are determined to hold out. An expanding foreign market is only a hypothetical prospect. If they succumb to the bait their home market too, they fear, would be gobbled up by the multinational corporation. In the circumstances a few among them have gone to the extent of invoking the revolutionary chant, *no pasaran.*

The genesis of the recent bit of theatre jointly enacted by Doordarshan and the Cricket Association of Bengal, a little analysis will show, was not altogether different. The minister for information and broadcasting was simply chucking a googly in the direction of the minister for finance—oh, enlightened colleague, please delineate for our benefit the limits of globalisation. The finance minister, Shastri Bhavan could well maintain, is issuing ambivalent signals.

Public undertakings are supposed to be on their own. They must either generate surplus or go to the wall. Television in India is however still an infant industry. How can it generate a surplus or break even if it is exposed to open competition from sophisticated operators arriving from the United States, Japan or Hong Kong? Since a categorical answer to the query was not forthcoming, the ministry for information and broadcasting might have felt justified to play the role of spoilsport. Thus it moves to deny the cricket mad gentlefolk the pleasure of watching live Brian Lara's different strokes or the unbelievable catches Jonty Rhodes has made it a habit to accomplish.

Shastri Bhavan has at least succeeded in establishing an incidental point. Irrespective of whether and how far liberalisation has penetrated the other segments of society, its impact on the government presided over by Mr. P. V. Narasimha Rao is devastating. The principle of collective responsibility is evidently for the birds, the ministries are engaged in fierce competition against one another. Each of them have their separate philosophy and *praxis.*

The phenomenon has strong resemblance to the conditions obtaining in families feuding over the control of closely held corporate units. Some ministers are keen to go flat out for external collaboration. A handful of other ministers prefer, *a la* Mr. K. P. Singh Deo, to keep their Odissi.

It is truly a free for all. No private blighters, local or foreign, should be allowed to infringe the Indian Telegraph Act 1885 argues Shastri Bhavan. The right to use the wireless in its various forms, including its state of the art electronic manifestations, belongs exclusively to the government of India. No uplinking of the signals of the Trans World International with satellites stationed 10 or 12,000 miles away were to be permitted unless due obeisance was first paid to appropriate quarters.

Were you to walk into the ministry of civil aviation you would hear a different tune. There is no ambiguity in the Air Corporation Act 1953. It imposes an absolute ban on passenger transport on a commercial basis within the country by private air carriers, whether foreign or domestic. The ministry has chosen to ignore this unequivocal piece of legislation and allowed private airlines to crowd the nation's friendly skies.

The letter of the Air Corporation Act, it has however assured, Parliament, has not been infringed. Private air carriers have been instructed not to publish regular flight schedules. Whether this is an attempt at exploring the higher reaches of Indian philosophy or the lower depths of Indian hypocrisy should be left to research scholars from overseas.

It is easy to pick other examples of anomalous behaviour within the government. The ministry of fertiliser and chemicals orders closure of running units of Hindustan Fertiliser Corporation Limited. It also postpones indefinitely the commissioning of a new HFCL plant at Haldia. Manufacturing capacity built in these public sector units over the years at the cost of millions of taxpayer's money is not to be used. Globalisation ordains fertilisers should be imported from foreign lands.

Workers at these units need not worry. They will continue to be paid wages. Despite World Bank nagging, the exit policy—sorry, the national renewal policy—cannot be made operational. The wretched democratic elections stand in the way. Workers, their families and their relatives and friends constitute a sizeable vote bloc. They are also pestilentially a vocal lot.

A Kind of *via media* is therefore worked out. Allegedly inefficient units are shut down but the workers are not disturbed. Foreign financial agencies and multinational corporations are pleased because imports are liberalised and production in domestic units is stopped. Workers are mollified because they are promised wages. Perhaps this is what jargon loving economists describe as optimisation in decision making.

Ambivalence has its advantages. Every now and then official spokesmen give the line. Should workers of incorrigibly sick public undertakings be agreeable to accept the challenge, the government would be more than willing to hand over the management of such loss making units to their care.

But official spokesmen know their oats. They stay away from dotting the "i"s and crossing the "t" of the proposed arrangement. What would happen to the outstanding liabilities of the units concerned. Whether the government would ensure with the banks that working capital continues to flow to the units following their takeover by the workers. These receive no answers.

It is not much news that in this milieu the index of industrial production is behaving like a mule. Despite homiles from the finance minister and his retinue as well as professional cheerleaders from distant captialist nations, industrial output in the country refuses to move up. Production cannot rise if factories close one after another.

Foreign investors, it is equally worth noting, are illustrating a pattern of stylised behaviour. They are more interested in taking over old units, either directly or through shenanigans in the share markets. They are not interested in adding to capacity. Their contribution to national production or employment generation can therefore be only minimal.

With little addition to employment and public investments rudely cut back, it is fullscale industrial recession. No detailed data is yet available of the regional breakdown of jobs lost in organised industry as a consequence of the great new economic policy on the anvil for the past two and a half years.

As industrial activity contracts in a particular region, commerce too contracts, aggravating distress in the region. Mandarins in New Delhi are not in the habit of stirring out of their fortress capital. They are therefore unacquainted with the realities unfolding in different parts of the country as a consequence of the measures they have imposed.

Because mandarins do not travel is no reason for nature and economics to stop in their tracks. As inflation has climbed back to double digits, intense discountent is building up within the system. It is a dispersed—one can almost say decentralised—discountent. How and when it will explode in the form of violent unrest and whether it will be exploited by fundamentalists of different hues can only be speculated on.

Some surprises are bound to be in store. The chief minister of Assam, Mr. Hiteswar Saikia, is a famous loyalist. He serves the rulers in New Delhi with a fidelity that should serve as a shining example for would be aspirants to full fledged toadyism. Lest it be forgotten, he also arranged for the finance minister's safe passage to the Rajya Sabha.

Even this chief minister is perturbed by the emerging implications of liberalisation. Planning for all practical purposes has ended. Central investments have been pruned drastically as per directive of the credit giving international financial institutions. Market forces are supposed to shape the nation's economic destiny from now on—and the destiny of the constituent states.

Market forces could not care less for Assam though. The state does not have the infrastructure. It is infested by insurgents and would be insurgents. Private capital, not without reason, continues to steer clear of Assam. The outcome will inevitably be the state's further economic retrogression and further encouragement to insurgency.

Never mind, efficiency is not all. The finance minister considers the inefficient working of the state electricity boards to be disgraceful beyond words. Subsidies for these loss making units must be stopped.

It is a different matter with private foreign parties who are being invited to set up power plants in the country. They are being guaranteed a rate of return of 16 per cent in foreign exchange for all times. If they are unable to reap this rate of return, the government will arrange for a subsidy, again in foreign exchange. Globalisation is nothing if foreigners are not in command. We live to serve them. And that is efficiency.

1st December, 1993

Foreign fingers in our pie

By all means let India condemn the United States state department for its neo-imperial and neo-colonial attitudes. Also let it condemn Washington for being pro-Pakistan in all seasons. Our politicans and bureaucrats have travelled a long way from the Krishna Menon days. We have for the past two and a half years deported ourselves wholly in the manner of a pristine banana republic. Then why do the Americans love Indians less than they do Pakistanis?

Let us not wear blinkers. Let us stay away from accusing the US administration of inconsistency. If its spokesmen have stated in October that Kashmir is "disputed territory", they said so three months earlier in July as well. They had then, gratuitously or otherwise, added the rider that the dispute needed to be sorted out by the governments of India and Pakistan "in consultation with the people of Kashmir." Occasional variations in nuances notwithstanding, this has been the US position since the Fifties.

The Concurrent point India has whiningly stuck to is that Kashmir is a dispute exclusively between India and Pakistan to be resolved by the terms of the Shimla agreement and must never be internationalised. There are two obvious difficulties with this.

First, a treaty or agreement between two nations has sanctity till as long as both allow it such sanctity. Unfortunately, the Pakistan government is in no mood to keep the spirit of the the Shimla agreement which it claims was imposed upon it following its ignominous defeat in the Bangladesh war. By all means let India's emissaries at international fora condemn Pakistan for going back on its pledged words.

However, India can hardly make a song and dance about this complaint in the international Court of Justice. Even if we do that would not affect the reality which is that, on Kashmir, India has been pushed to the wall.

This is so on account of the second, much more important, aspect of the matter. India on its own internationalised the issue 45 years ago. Whether the skulduggery of Lord Louis Mountbatten the viceroy or the clawing charm of his wife trapped Jawaharlal Nehru into taking the decision is of zero relevance at this distance of time. It is the consequence of that decision that now constitutes the basic datum. Nor can we deny India's initial enthusiasm for a resolution, sponsored by members of the United Nations security council and passed the general assembly, recommending a plebiscite in Kashmir so as to ascertain the wishes of the people there. The only rider was that conditions, on both sides of the line of effective control, should be conducive to holding one.

That bit of ancient history is not without continuum. We steadfastly maintain Kashmir is an integral part of India which no meddlesome outsider can take away from us. Yet the country has not formally or explicitly repudiated the general principle of a plebiscite.

Please consult the record book. Whenever the issue has subsequently cropped up India has each time fallen back on an alibi of conditions not being conducive to the exercise. We may or may not now agree to put our neck into the noose. Nonetheless Indians cannot dispute the proposition that it exists because we had agreed to its being placed there.

But even forget about such technicalities. For a nation which takes pride in a logo that flaunts the philosophical abstraction of truth prevailing in all circumstances, it is time to put hand to heart and admit a few other blunt truths.

It is not Hari Singh's precious signature on the Instrument of Accession that bequeathed to India the moral right to exercise sovereignty over Kashmir. The Nizam of Hyderabad did not sign an Instrument of Accession to India. He had done quite a different thing. That did not stop troops from marching into his erstwhile territories. India was armed with the knowledge of the overwhelming approval of its action by the people inhabiting those territories. The story was the same in the case of Goa.

In Kashmir too, the authentic base of our support was provided by Sheikh Abdullah and the National Conference he led. That support was a short lived phenonmenon. Perhaps Nehru could not put up with the Sheikh's presumptuousness. Perhaps it was the other way round. A breach came.

Following the breach, the supposed umbilical cord linking Kashmir with mother India has been an illusion of the Indian mind. The sheikh was thrown into prison and over the next 20 years occasionally brought out. Bakshi Ghulam Mohammed rigged elections on behalf of the Indian National Congress. That was his only contribution to the cause of national integration. No credible alternative to the National Conference could be forged by the hammersmiths sent out every now and then from New Delhi to Srinagar.

Finally, a sort of capitulation to the Sheikh took place in the mid-Seventies. The National Conference swung back to power, the restiveness in the valley subsided for a while. Even the most pertinacious elements in Pakistan, still holding onto far out dreams of an annexed Kashmir, were about to give up.

But trust the leaders in New Delhi to make a proper hash of things. Sheikh Abdullah shuffled off his mortal coil and there was a rekindling of ambition in North and South Blocks. Nehru's daughter was in her conduct and bearing a bit of a die-hard. Kashmir, according to her lights, was real estate to which she and her family retained ancestral rights. Besides, with the Sheikh having passed from the scene, his son would be putty in her hands.

Things once again began to fall apart. Dr. Farooq Abdullah proved somewhat obdurate and refused to play second string to New Delhi. He squarely defeated the Congress in the subsequent election and formed the state government in his own right. He also as happenstance gathered a set of advisors who counselled him to cultivate an understanding with the mainstrem political parties in the country ranged against the Congress.

This latter act sealed his fate. A civil servant who had built his reputation as the marauder of New Delhi during Emergency, and who has of late blossomed as a Bharatiya Janata Party dignitary, was flown to Srinagar as governor. He was asked to organise defections from Dr. Abdullah's ranks. The Sheikh's son was dismissed in a manner which went against the grain of all civilised norms.

The folly was compounded when an inexperienced Dr. Abdullah, restless at being stranded outside the citadel of power, was won over by the bait of restoration to office. He immediately ceased to be, at least in the judgement of the valley's people, a true son of Kashmir. The National Conference too forfeited its claim to their loyalty.

The state of insurgency in Kashmir in effect commenced right then. It has only assumed the form of armed civil uprising in the course of the past four years. From time to time befuddled grey eminences safely dwelling in the national capital have dwelt on the need to resume a political dialogue over Kashmir.

Most of them are unwilling to admit the harsh truth. The valley is now an occupied tract and Indian forces are maintaining physical control over the people there by the exercise of brute military power. The grossness of this occupation has dispelled whatever chances there ever were of a negotiated settlement.

The slaughter of innocents last year at Sopore and a fortnight ago at an Anantnag suburb has incensed human rights groups. It has not led to any largescale revulsion across the length and breadth of this country. This lack of sensitivity itself has clinched the issue. Kashmir obviously does not belong to India any more and shall not one add *vice versa.*

The Hazratbal episode has merely emphasised the depth of Indian isolation. The money contributed by taxpayers has over the years been deployed to add to the might of the army and security forces. These forces, we have been told, keep constant foolproof vigil in every nook and corner of the valley. Such vigil it has to be assumed also covered the approaches of the Hazratbal shrine.

If despite this the militants could enter the shrine and entrench themselves inside, culpability devolves on none except India's army brass.

There are grave international implications for any major—for that matter even minor—incident occurring within the precincts of the mosque. Thus the balance of advantage from the Indian point of view could still lie with letting the militants melt away in the crowd.

Judged from the same point of view, it is indeed irksome that the crisis had to reach its climax during the month the electorate was going to the polls in *Aryavarta.*

Irrespective of how the denouement works itself out, one particular outcome is almost inevitable. The US state department will henceforth insist on having a finger in the Kashmir pie. The logic of economic liberalisation must work itself out. India's ministers and bureaucrats cannot seek benediction from the masters in Washington for shoring up the tottering Indian economy and yet expect the US not to take a direct interest in the shaping of our defence and foreign policies.

Compartmental globalisation is a contradiction in terms. India has to pay a price for the close to $ 8 billion worth of foreign balances it has built up through mostly US munificence. It will be demanded of us that we abide by global advice on Kashmir. Thanks to the way the valley has been messed up, India has no defensive chips at all.

17th November, 1993

Encounters of the non-resident kind

One species, belonging to the general category of non-resident Indians are the non-resident academics, the more prominent amongst them being the non-resident economists comfortably ensconced in Western universities. From December till the middle of March, the climate is cool and bracing in this otherwise wretched country. Our expatriate scholars find it congenial to visit their once-native land, especially its capital, for a brief week or ten days during these months. More often than not, their expenses are covered by some outfit or other funded by foreign foundations.

Nostalgia is an understandable attribute of the mind: revisiting the land which once raised them is an activity that can hardly be objected to. The problem only arises when, while on their few days sojourn, they take it upon themselves to freely dispense advice about what this country must or must not do.

Let us try to be fair. In this particular matter, these eminent persons are sometimes more sinned against than sinned. The organisation which invites them usually insist on a talk or a paper as compensation for payment of cabin class or first class return ticket and hotel bill.

It is not so much their pontification as its content that provokes irritation. One such visiting dignitary is rattled no end by recent developments in the country in the wake of the shame of Ayodhya. This gentleman snapped his links with India more than 20 years ago, and is now a permanent non-resident. But, because he has established himself in the academia in the United States and west Europe, he thinks, in true colonial style, he has the right to dole out advice on policy issues to our people and government. Again, in true neo-colonial tradition, the advice he renders, howsoever predictable and cliche-ridden, is given wide coverage in our newspapers.

This expatriate academic is a great believer in free trade and refuses to accept the proposition that market signals can occasionally go wrong. He has been an enthusiastic supporter of the liberalisation measures the New Delhi administration has been per suaded to embark upon since the middle months of 1991. He applauds the whole works: devaluation of the rupee, the lifting of industrial controls, the scrapping of trade restrictions, and the emasculation of the regulatory legislation concerning foreign investment.

A passionate lover of that nondelightfully vague will o'the wisp economic efficiency, he is, inevitably, in rhapsody over the policy. According to reports last heard, he has been an adviser to the secretary general of the General Agreement on Tariffs and Trade, archiect of the notorious Dunkel proposals intended to keep the poor countries in Asia, Africa and Latin America in a permanent state of underdevelopment. In view of his philosophical position, economic planning has always been anathema to our NRI. Now that the World Bank and the International Monetary Fund have insisted our government to abandon the five year plans, his joy knows no bounds.

He would not dream of returning to this wretched country, but that need not prevent him from deriving an intelectual satisfaction should it become marginally less wretched.

The consequences of the economic policy measures launched 18 months ago have, however, not been nearly as excellent as forecast by this gentleman. Devaluation has hardly had any impact on exports, but has, at the other end, raised import prices and therefore the domestic price level across the board. Since it is an integral part of the structural adjustment programme ordered by the fund and the bank to have, whatever the circumstances, unbridled imports, the trade deficit has tended to widen. The excess of imports over exports during the first seven months of the current fiscal year has been more than three times what it was last year.

While we have been made to liberalise our imports, the rich Western countries have not relented from their practice to shut out our goods to the maximum extent possible. The fund-bank policy is evidently to keep India on a short leash. They will it seems, dole out loans each year which will its allow us to cover the trade gap. But our total external indebtedness will, in any case, continue to go up. As no other means are to be available to meet the resulting increase debt service obligations, our government will be compelled to seek further foreign loans, which, if granted at all, will be under increasingly more stringent conditions.

The other elements in the situation are equally unpropitious. Despite massive imports of equipments, spares and raw materials, the rate of industrial growth has remained inordinately depressed, and more and more workers are being laid off. With the shrinking of plan funds, rural employment too is going down. In the pervasive gloom following Ayodhya, things are bound to turn much more difficult.

The assumption that private foreign investors and multinational corporations will invest loads and loads of funds in India following our government's headlong rush towards liberalisation has proved horrendously wrong: against the expectation of a capital inflow of $6 to 7 billion every year, all we have been getting is the relatively paltry sum of $ 200 million or thereabouts. The events of December have now evaporated the residual hopes for any sizeable foreign investment consignment by internecine conflict reminiscent of medieval savagery is unlikely to be the number one choice of prospective foreign investors.

If the present drift continues, the only way our economy could possibly survive would be by contracting more and more external loans on most exorbitant terms. There is, however, no guarantee foreign institutions like the World Bank and the IMF would not, one fine morning, declare India was a country beyond redemption, and that they too have decided to wash their hands off it.

The bankruptcy our government is praying to somehow avoid would then emerge as a stern reality. Its consequences would be many times more severe than the problems we would encounter were we to retrace our steps right now, return to a policy of planned self-reliance and reclamp rigid restrictions on imports, particularly of luxury goods. After all, our annual trade deficit is barely three per cent of our national income. This is not an unbridgeable gap. We have rich reserves of physical and mineral resources, we have an economic infrastructure capable of producing a comprehensive range of industrial goods, including most sophisticated ones. We have, besides, after the United States, the largest stock of scientific and technical manpower.

By harnessing our own efforts, skill and resources, and by, at the same time, undergoing a measure of self sacrifice, it should not be difficult for us to dispense with imports equivalent to three per cent of the national income, thereby putting an end to continual external horrowing.

The problem of meeting the servicing obligations on account of outstanding foreign loans would not, of course, disappear. But we can follow the example of the Latin American countries—and of Russia—and seek a rescheduling of our repayment obligations. A dose of cynicism will stand in good stead here. Should we fail to meet our servicing instalments, there is little the fund or the bank or the rich foreign countries could do. It is most improbable that they would send in their troops. The fund and the bank have no troops in any case. At most, they would threaten to stop further loans. But since we would no longer be interested in their loans, the threat would not work.

It is this prospect of the country returning to dignity and self reliance which has apparently unnerved the visiting non-resident economist mentioned earlier. He sounds frenetic. True, India's exports are not increasing, but one must not lose heart, export pessimism must be avoided at all costs. Look at him, he has exported himself; if only the country were able to produce products of appropriate quality, exports would be no problem.

This academic, otherwise so learned, fails to appreciate a pretty simple point: the US administration will not mind allowing the entry of a stray academic from India such as him, but the moment we try to export thousands of migrant labourers, or large lots of our textiles and handicrafts and footwear and engineering and electronic goods, the resistance will be fierce.

Undeterred, the non-resident economist veers off in another directrion. He is worried no end that, in the aftermath of Aydhya, there could be a reshuffle within the Central government and even a new prime minister who might choose to dispense with the present finance minister. This must not be allowed to happen, implores the non-resident pundit. the incumbent finance minister has become, to the Western world, a symbol of India's willingness to be submissive and faithfully carry out instructions issued by foreign institutions and governments.

Remove him and, the wise man warns, all foreign aid will dry up. He draws the analogy of Russia. Mr Yegor Gaidar as prime minister is the best guarantee to Westerners, the Russians would play ball with them. Which is why Mr Boris Yeltsin has insisted on retaining Mr Gaidar in his post despite severe internal press lure to have him sacked. So with our finance minister: dislodge him, and foreign aid is bound to taper off.

Well, the non-resident scholar has been travelling too much, and has been unable to catch up with facts. In Russia, Mr Yegor Gaidar has been removed from his post. So the analogy does not quite hold. Besides, there is a convincing case for arguing the only way to yet save this country from total devastation is to dispense with the fatal combination of foreign loans and interminable imports. What is a calamity to the non-resident economist is actually a godsend to the nation.

Dear nonresident wisdom-dispenser we can do without our present finance minister, and also without the fund and the bank. We can, in addition, do without you.

3rd December, 1992

A million mutinies to come

Let us indulge in some ruthless, but not altogether unreasonable, arithmetic. According to a recent newspaper which has gone uncontradicted, armed personnel in active duty in Punjab number close to 115,000. Ground forces deployed to cope with the insurgency in Jammu and Kashmir should be at least half the number engaged in Punjab, that is, around 60,000. Troops posted in Assam, where the army has just initiated a fresh operation against the young rebels belonging to the intransigent wing of the United Liberation Front of Assam, are likely to be in the neighbourhood of 20,000.

The army has also now been called in to flush out Veerappan, the sandalwood smuggler from the rough shrubbery-laden terrain along the Karnataka-Tamil Nadu border. In addition it is known to have, for the past 20, if not 40, years, maintained specially trained detachments in Nagaland, Mizoram and Manipur, where the threat of internal uprising never quite dies down. The latest North-eastern state to discover army help to be indispensable for the enforcement of law and order is Meghalaya.

It thus involves little exaggeration if the number of troops currently used for non-defence purposes around the country is suggested to approximate 225,000 or thereabouts. Since the strength of the nation's standing army is estimated to be 1.1 million, more than one-fifth of our soldiers are being employed to put down what will be defined as civil disturbances. The top brass in the army, if credence is to be again given to newspaper reports, are not exactly happy with this state of affairs. In the view of one school of military strategists, the placement of army personnel for secondary activities such as administration of law and order impairs their operational efficiency.

Even so, the prospects of the army getting disengaged from anti-insurgency duties do not look too bright at this moment. A marauder like Veerappan may soon be expected to be captured once the army swings into action. But it is likely uncertainty will continue to loom large in the North-eastern states, making it imposible to dispense with the use of army personnel in the near future.

With regard to both Punjab and Kashmir, we may keep quoting Percy Bysshe Shelley and nurturing hope, but whether hope will create from its own wreck the thing it contemplates remains an open question. The situation is near-intractable in both states and unless a dramatic transformation takes place in the political arena, it is probable that the army would be asked to stay put.

In fact, doesn't the likelihood of the domestic scene getting further clouded and the military getting more embroiled in internal operations deserve serious consideration? A number of central trade union organisations have stated in quite explicit terms that they will physically resist all attempts on the part of the government to enforce the exit policy in the industrial sector. The international financial agencies will have little time for the local difficulties the Narasimha Rao administration might encounter in the course of implementing their directive to lay off half a million organised workers from plants and factories.

Once New Delhi has satisfied itself neither it nor the nation could survive without periodic ingestion of loans from overseas, it will have to conform to the wishes of these institutions and therefore squeeze out the workers. But it is not going to be a gentlemanly process.

Those who are to be retrenched will, according to the government's scheme of things as now disclosed, belong to the age group of 35 years or below. In other words, the demobilised workers will be almost exclusively made up of full blooded youth. They will be offered no golden handshake, nor is there any proposal to impart any training to help them adapt to alternative occupations. It is proposed that they are to be left entirely to their own devices.

This could lead to an explosive situation, particularly if prices continue to rise, despite the tepid official claim of a decline in the *rate* at which they rise. Such sophistry will not impress those who are thrown out of their jobs. Should one or two major central trade union bodies reach the decision that the circumstances warrant a show of militancy on their part, major disturbances could ensue over large parts of the country. With only one state government in the country possessing left credentials, no paritcular inhibition need be felt by the trade unions about stirring up trouble to the maximum extent possible.

The resulting turbulence is not going to assume a vegetarian hue either. It is quite on the cards the protest movement will escalate into widespread violence and destruction of public property. The precedent of the so-called IMF riots in a number of African and Latin American countries should provide our government with some idea of the primordial forces that tend to be unleashed in the wake of externally imposed structural economic reform which further immiserise the poor.

It is a dead certainty that troops would then have to be called out. How many troops would have to be commandered and over what period of time are impossible to estimate precisely at this point of time. But since army strength cannot clearly be depleted in Punjab and Kashmir, it would involve a net further drawing of personnel from the army pool. After all, once there is disruption of law and order on some issue or the other, it becomes a matter of prestige for many chief ministers to demand the induction of not just para-military forces but of one or two companies of army personnel as well. *Noblesse oblige*: the centre straightaway responds favourably to the demand.

But aren't there ample other signs too of the polity hurtling itself towards a general breakdown? Half a dozen years ago, to improve its political prospects against the Left Front which goes on forever in West Bengal, the party ruling at the centre decided to shore up Subhas Ghising and his Gorkha National Liberation Front in Darjeeling. The experiment has had mixed success. Obviously, the temptation to repeat the experiment on Lalu Prasad Yadav's goose could be properly cooked, has proved irresistible.

But fomented agitations of this nature have a way of going out of hand. The Jharkhand movement, once blessed by central support in some form or the other, is bound to spill beyond Bihar and could provoke civil disturbances in Madhya Pradesh, Orissa and West Bengal. It might even provide a fillip to the semi-dormant agitation for Uttarkhand in Uttar Pradesh. And a Bansi Lal, unused to the state of being long out of power, could be tempted to resuscitate the claim for a Vishal Haryana.

Down South, an outfit like the Pattali Makkal Katchi might feel the times propitious for trying out a version of Tamil Eelam right in the indian Deccan itself. These agitations would after some while, begin to receive nourishment from one another and the embers of anger and ambition would not quite die out.

Besides, if the economy gets globalised, can the polity be far behind? Espionage agents from countries far and near are likely to flock in. An additional complicating factor is the lull in the civil war in Afghanistan. The slack in the demand for arms from the landlocked country will be largely made up by the requirements in Central Asia, where the erstwhile Soviet republics will keep splintering and fighting among themselves. But some of the sparable weaponry could well infiltrate the borders of India. Such weapons would be put to use in the cause of Jharkhand or Uttarkhand or Vishal Haryana or Autonomous Chhattisgarh or Swadhin Tripura.

It would then truly be a festival of civil unrests all over the country. The actual nature of the restiveness would hardly be civil though. The army would be much in demand. Were the pace of things ot accelerate, our entire standing army, consisting of 1.1 million jawans and officers, could then be fully occupied in dealing with blockades, riots and insurgencies.

The increase in defence spending could be either at the cost of economic development or met by imposing further levies on the people. Either alternative could be expected to create fresh waves of discontent, to quell which more troops would be called for, necessitating a further rise in defence spending, and, therefore, a further shrinkage in development outlay or, alternatively, a further impost on the people.

Ruling politicians are a happy lot. They can do without the long view, a faculty which enables them to sleep without worry and enjoy sweet dreams.

23rd September, 1992

The illegal hand of US Law

With the collapse of the Soviet Union authoritarian communism is supposed to be dead. A few conspirators allegedly wanted to revive it in Russia late summer last year. They were put down with a heavy hand. Along with the Western media, our newspapers went to town to celebrate the event. A grand euphoria set in. The world was finally safe from the totalitarian menace. Stray irritants like Cuba were best ignored.

The moral influence of the world's only superpower will henceforth ensure freedom and liberty for all in the nooks and corners of the six continents. As you approach the US from across the Atlantic, the first thing that greets you is the noble Statue of Liberty. Freedom and the US are synonymous. Now please read on.

In the fading montsh of 1989, a judge presiding over an obscure circuit in Texas handed down an extraordinary judgment. The law of the United States of America, he said, has global jurisdiction. If an individual in any part of the world, never mind his nationality, is suspected of having committed a crime which is culpable according to US law, agents of the US government have the right to arrest him even in a foreign country and ship him to the US to stand trial. No permission of the government of the country where the person is apprehended is required.

Moreover, should a US government agent be compelled to commit a murder in this line of duty, it would be regarded as justifiable homicide. No prosecution would be maintainable against the agent.

The US is a big country, with its quota of cranks and megalomaniancs. That cricuit court verdict tgwo and half years ago did not therefore create much of a ripple accross the globe. Some judges, it was commented, are indistinguishable from made hatters, so why bother about the Texas judgment?

Those offering such soothing observations spoke too soon. Last month, the US Supreme Court, the highest judiciary in the land, upheld the Texas judge's decision by a 6.3 margin. It is now authoritative US law: the administration and its agents are entitled to kidnap, at their sweet will nationals of any other country on any ground whatsoever, unless there is a bilateral treaty between the US and that country barring such kidnapping.

This then is what freedom is about. Might is right. Since the US is the only superpower left in the world, its writ will prevail everywhere. Its agents can arrest, maim, kill any individual whom they hold to be guilty of contravening US law, or whom they imagine is engaged in a conspiracy to bring down the US government. And please do not assume for a moment the Superme Court verdict is going to be a dead letter, one that could be simply ignored.

Following the supreme Court judgment, a citizen of Mexico, doctor by profession, has been kidnapped from his native country and handed over to the US justice department. The doctor is alleged to have been involved with the torture and murder of an American narcotic agent in Mexico in 1985. Mexican law is obviously not good enough for the US. The US administration did not consider it appropriate to move the Mexican courts seeking prosecution of the doctor for the alleged offence. That would be *infradig* for the world's only superpower. The Mexican had to be physically seized and carried across the border so that he could receive his just desserts from a US court. It would be pointless to quote international law in this context. US law, that Supreme Court judgment says, supersedes international law.

We are thus back to the 15th, 16th and 17th century world of piracy and pillage. No one dare question the US's overlordship. The US is the leader and the master of the free world. It has the liberty to act, much in the manner of the brigands of yore, exclusively according to its own whims. If they fancy, US agents can murder people in any part of the world, and they will have the full sanction of their national law. Lest some of us had forgotten, two years ago, the US armed forces, without any fuss at all, invaded Panama to bring back General Manuel Noriega to stand trial in Florida.

Citizens of the sovereign democratic republic of India would be living in fool's paradise if they thought the list of countries whoses overeignty the US would contemptuously brush aside stops with Mexico and Panama and a few of the other banana republics.

In early 1990, the US embassy in New Delhi and the US consulates in Bombay, Calcutta and Madras issued a public notification: if anyone knew anything about a person or group of persons conspiring against the lawfully established government of the US, he or she should, *pronoto,* either past this information to a New York address or get in touch with the embassy in New Delhi or the nearest consulate. He or she would receive a hefty reward.

Before issuing the press notification, members of the US diplomatic mission did not consider it necessary to clear it with the Indian government. To our eternal shame, Indian authorities did not have the courage to lodge a formal protest with the US. This is the epoch of pragmatism. Any such protest could lead to the cutting off of IMF-World Bank loans.

In other words, the Americans have made themselves at home in India. And there is ferther confirmation to that effect. A US bank, with branches in

New Delhi, Bombay, Bangalore, Madras, Calcutta and may be a few other places, has been financing the purchase of cars by its customers. The loan advaned for the purpose are supposed to be recovered, along with the interest, in instalments. Some of the bank's clients have been unreasonable. They have defaulted on the payments. The bank has evolved a rough and ready method to deal with such defaulters. It has employed a few musclemen in the cities where the misbehaving, borrowers reside. The musclemen have sought out the addresses of the defaulters, and physically repossessed the cars.

Since the bank is American, it is perhaps oblivious about having violate Indian law. Under the Indian penalcode, no one is permitted to take the law in his or her hand. If a party defaults on contractual payments, the proper procedure for the aggrieved party is to file a suit in the appropriate court with jurisdiction over the alleged offence. The law then takes is own course.

Slowcoach justice obviously does not suit the US bank. It is in typicarry, and it has a healthy contempt for laws that restrain its pace, especially if these do not happen to be American laws and are only statutes of good for-nothing countries like India. The bank has therefore chosen to go about it in its own way. Its hoodlums have been delegated the task of meting out instant justice, which they do with commendable speed and efficiency.

As far as is known, no one has ventured to protest against the bank's deliberate flouting of our laws. Newspapers, inveighing in season and out of season against totalitarianism and so jealous of freedom and sovereignty, have refrained from indulging in any righteous indignation. No bar association has spoken out either. Not one member of Parliament has raised the issue on the floor of the Lok Sabha or Rajya Sabha.

But this is perhaps only a quiet beginning on the part of the US and its representatives. Greatly fortified by the Supreme Court judgment, they might gradually decide to be out on a spree to administer retributive justice all over the world.

If a wayward politician in Satara, Maharashtra, should go on record against US imperialism, or a flippant journalist make a rude remark about President Bush, the guilty party might be airlifted from his house at day of night, economy class, all the way to Washington to answer charges. If he or she should be foolish enough to resist arrest, US agents might even shoot him down. The government of India would presumably, all the while, look the other way. There is safety in overlooking the indiscretions of the world's only superpower.

1st July, 1992

Do not ask for facts

Intolerance in the air, journalists in Bombay had a taste of it. But are the Shiv Sena—and those of its ilk, such as the Vishwa Hindu Parishad—the only threat to freedom of opinion in the country? The right to know is complementary to the right to the untrammelled expression of views; the two together constitute, or so we have been told, the base of a true democratic edifice. The manner the Shiv Sena has gone about to sabotage the cricket match at Wankhede Stadium—and subsequently to bully those who have condemned its action—is beneath contempt. An indirect spin-off of the episode is however the baring of facts concerning the country's cricket establishment. The tales about the annual jamboree at Sharjah now being narrated in the aftermath of Pakistan's decision to call off the tour are indeed staggering. Sharjah has meant money to players, former players, commentators, and the cricket control board and its members. Free travel, free hospitality and some easy private pickings were apparently enough to keep the conscience of our cricket administrators quiet even where the nation's honour has been involved. The Cricketers Benefit Fund Series took full advantage of the Indian avarice for easy lucre. It was outrageous on the part of the CBFS to insist on the continuance of that final league match between the Pakistan and Indian teams even after the street lights had been switched on. Even more outrageous was the extraordinary hush-hush maintained by our cricket bosses; the CBFS must be kept in good humour, otherwise the flow of money would dry up. The Pakistanis too needed to be kept in good humour; once they came and played the five one-day matches, both the circket control board and the associations affiliated to it would build a nice nest-egg. The policy of the principle was therefore to swallow all insults; that these insults demean the nation did not bother the cricket control board, even though its president happened to be a member of the Union council of minister, no less. It is only because the Pakistanis have now refused to come, on account of the Shiv Sena's flexing of muscles, that the veil of silence is off.

The story does not quite end here. The Pakistanis were not touring, the cricket bosses were tearing off their hair in despair, their dream of a augmenting their revenue had come a cropper. Never, however, say die. After decades of waiting, the apartheidpractising South Africans have just been readmitted to the international cricket circuit. They are sort of on trial; it was important, according to one widely held body of opinion, to make sure that racial discrimination in sport had, really and truly, ended in that country before our team started playing cricket with them; besides, it is for them to convince us of the correctness of their conduct. Instead, it was once more the avarice for money at work. Our cricket authorities did not stand on dignity, either of their own or of the nation's. Pretences of seemliness were thrown to the wind. A small group of representatives of the South African Board of Control were visiting India on a preliminary public relations mission. They were the subject of round-the-clock private importunings; please, oh noble ones, you must agree to send a team to India at the shortest possible notice, to play three one-day matches, so that our cricket associations could compensate themselves for the pecuniary loss they have suffered on account of the non-arrival of the Pakistanis. The erstwhile racists have overnight been rendered dearest to the heart of our cricket bosses; even the Shiv Sena, who mind the Pakistanis, would not mind the racists.

Money contributed by the ticket buying public fills the coffers of the cricket associations, but their behaviour repudiates all notions of public accountability; ordinary people, it is assumed, do not have the right to enquire how such bodies function. The free market principle is at work: the cricket bodies will do as they like, and, privatisation being what it is, no information is to be leaked out on the shenanigans they indulge in. To question their conduct is just not cricket.

But, then, is not this attitude very much in harmony with the general ambience? It is, it appears, equally not cricket to ask of our government what, for instance, is the updated magnitude of the country's aggragate indebtedness the items included, or excluded from, this estimate, the break-down of this total into its short, medium and long-term components, and the annual and quarterly burdens of debt servicing the indebtedness entails. Even were some members of Parliament to ask for the information, the government would find a pretext to fudge the reply; disclosure of the data asked for, the representatives of the people would perhaps be primly told, might harm the country's credit rating in the international money market. Nothing could be more fatuous, for foreigners do not experience any difficulty in laying their hands on such data. Every now and then, some foreign journal or other puts together and publishes estimates of India's external debt; the veracity of these estimates is neither confirmed nor denied by officialdom. There is no deviation from the basic doctrine: our own people are not to be told what is what. It is on account of the accumulation of the huge foreign debt and the serviceing obligation it has entailed that the government has surrendered its prerogtive of independent economic decision-making to the international financial institutions. The constituents of the nation are not considered mature enough to know the facts underlying the reason for their loss of economic sovereignty.

Liberalisation so-called has actually gone hand in hand with an increasingly illiberal attitude toward economic policy dissenters. A massive media campaign has been on since last July in support of the new economic measures. Those disapproving the government's headlong rush to open up the economy have been subjected to fierce ridicule; their right to continue to express views contrary to what the government and the international financial institutions are propagating have been openly questioned. The browbeating is straining to proceed beyond the bounds of decency. The *Economic and Political Weekly* of Bombay, without question the best known social science journal to be published from Asia and commanding enormous prestige around the world, has taken a sardonic view in its editorial pages on the recent happenings in the country in the name of economic liberalisation. It is under pressure to reform its editorial policy, or else.

A last, related example again of keeping the news away from the people. The collapse of socialist regimes in the East European countries, including in the Soviet Union has been celebrated with great eclat in the western Press. The media in our country have faithfully followed suit. It has been a long season of jubilation. Capitalism has been restored, free enterprise is back, statues of Lenin and Stalin and the rest of the disreputable characters have been pulled down over there, what could be more gladdening to the heart of pure liberal souls, hallelujah.

But do we have enough information on the nature of happenings in these lands following the demise of socialism? In country after country, the Communist Party has been made to pay for its past sins and blunders; off with its head. But, with the restoration of capitalism, along with free expression, have milk and honey resumed their flow? The western media are not interested, our newspapers too are, therefore, not concerned with that sequence. If, close on the heels of the end of socialism, full employment has been replaced by joblessness for more than half of the country's working force, prices have risen ten times, the ration shops have emptied, the social security arrangements have crumbled, criminals and cardsharpers—and, in some instances, neo-Nazis have taken over the city streets, why, these are unimportant details not to be communicated to the world.

Poland was the first country in East Europe where large chunks of public opinion were mobilised against the communist regime, the Solidarity movement was lionised in the West, its leader was rewarded with the Nobel Prize for Peace. The anticommunists have now administered Poland, in their own manner, uninterruptedly, for five years. The western governments again in their own manner, have been exceedingly accommodating; 20 billion out of 50 billion dollars of Poland's outstanding external debt have been written off, promises have been unending about investments to be undertaken by the multinational corporations. Nothing has apparently helped. If hearsay is to be believed, Poland is in a deep economic and social mess. The solidarity has splintered. National income has more than halved in the past five years. Both prices and unemployment have kept soaring at a frightening pace. Social discontent is threatening to tear the nation apart.

In this setting, the first 'free' elections were held in the country last month. A bare 40 per cent of the electorate cared to vote. The Solidarity lost heavily. Only that wing of the movement which had in the past entertained the prospects of a working arrangement with the communists fared relatively well. The Communist Party, now known as the Democratic Leftist Alliance, nonetheless trailed it by hardly a few hundred votes. The people of Poland, having gone through a certain gamut of experience, would not evidently mind too much to repose back their trust to the votaries of socialism, they had enough of the paradise of the free market.

And it is not Poland alone. Whether it is East Germany or Hungary or Romania, ordinary men and women, chastened by the nightmare of the past few years, have been freely airing their views: they were far better off under socialist rule, economic liberalisation has spelled disaster for them.

True, such snippets of one-sided reporting are just that; there are reports from other parts of Eastern Europe where trends of public opinion are different. What, however, causes concern is the scrappy nature of information in our country of developments over there. Now that our government too has decided to cross over to full-scale liberalisation, the experience East Europe is going through would have the acutest relevance for us. But scan the pages of our newspapers; according to their version, there is and can be no further history beyond the already formally pronounced death of socialism. Maybe they are right; maybe they are not right. Why not let the people judge from the facts? That is, why not, in the first place, let them have the facts?

13th November, 1991

Already in the world bank's territory?

Why not say it, the government in New Delhi has reduced itself to a burlesque. It will, in all probability, still continue. The feeling of dislike the leading participants in the bawdy goings-on harbour toward one another is intense. But they will stop short of perpetrating the ultimate act of folly. They can expect, they know, no forgiveness from the people should they break up the government and thus frustrate last year's mandate.

The government will continue, but is not the mandate in fact already a faded chapter in history? The country's external indebtedness has touched Rs. 1,20,000 crore. There is very little of concrete evidence that the government is overly concerned with the problem. It has endorsed every one of the previous administration's policies and practices which were instrumental for the five-fold increase of our foreign debt in the course of a single decade. The National Front manifesto had pledged a return to an integrated programme of economic self-reliance so as to extricate the nation from the ignominy of the debt trap. That pledge, it now appears, was exclusively for the sake of pledge-making. Advisers who played a crucial role in policy formulation under the previous regime remain undisturbed. Some of them have even received a lift or two under the dispensation of the new set of ministers. These advisers know their mind; the ministers do not.

Those currently protesting against growing Fund-Bank influence inside government might thus have arrived on the scene a trifle too late. For, consider the following narration. The Reserve Bank of India has recently released the report of an Agricultural Credit Review Committee it had set up some time ago. The country's central bank can certainly order periodical appraisals of the working of the monetary mechanism and modalities to ensure credit to the different sectors of the economy. So there is nothing unusual in the Reserve Bank's constituting an Agricultural Credit Review Committee. What is however extraordinary is the composition of the committee. Apart from the chairman, it had six other members, of whom as many as three were foreigners nominated by the World Bank. We have, after the United States and the Soviet Union, the largest reservoir of scientific and technical manpower. There are any number of competent economists and monetary experts in the country. And yet one-half of the Agricultural Credit Review Committee had to consist of so-called foreign experts, placed on the Committee at the explicit suggestion of the World Bank. How this came about is revealed in the report itself. The Reserve Bank of India subsidiary, the National Bank of Agriculture and Rural Development (NABARD), has been utilising since 1975 a foreign exchange loan—in the jargon, a 'general line of credit'—from the World Bank. The total amount NABARD received from the Bank was as much as US $875 million till 1985. A further loan of $375 million was then promised. But this was subject to conditions. One stipulation was that our government must agree to carry out an 'in-depth' review of the country's agricultural credit system, and this review must follow guidelines laid down by the World Bank. He who pays the piper calls the tune. Since it has given us a hefty loan, the World Bank claims it as its right to decide in what manner our agriculture credit system is to operate. The committee set up to advise on this matter must therefore bear the impremature of the Bank's approval. So that is how it goes. We are a sovereign nation, the Reserve Bank of India is the central bank of this sovereign nation. It has however, little effective say in the composition and terms of reference of the committee to review the country's rural credit system; that prerogative has passed on to the World Bank.

Does not the issue deserve a little further probe? What was the earthshaking need for a foreign exchange loan for our agriculture? Close to 90 per cent of our agrarian population is abysmally poor. They seek credit to pay for seeds, fertilisers, pesticides, and irrigation water; very often, a great number amongst them are in need of consumption loans to buy in the market foodgrains they are short of. For non of these purchases they are called upon to pay in foreign exchange. Affluent farmers conceivably seek credit for one or two additional purposes, such as for buying a tractor or a harvester combine. But even these are ordered locally. The foreign exchange loan extended by the World Bank to NABARD has thus little to do with the actual financing of agricultural projects; whatever funds NABARD needs to advance credit to our farmers could have been placed at its disposal by the Reserve Bank, and no foreign borrowing was called for. The Bank loan is obviously being used for other purposes, such as for importing spares and components for Maruti-Suzukis or for paying instalments on account of the purchase of German or American technology for our colour television sets.

The World Bank has its own theology. It has little confidence that the majority of this nations's agrarian population, the landless workers and small peasantry, can play any significant role in effecting improvements in farm production and productivity. Land reforms and provision of credit for the poorer cultivators are anathema to it. Our government has borrowed funds from it to improve farm credit. It being the paymaster, its ideas must therefore be the ideas of the

Agricultural Credit Review Committee the Reserve Bank of India was instructed to set up; to ensure this, the composition of the committee must also be decided by it. One major recommendation of the committee, for example, is abolition of the differential interest rate scheme under which poor farmers and artisans are offered loans at a subsidised rate of interest. Advances disbursed under the DRI scheme do not constitute even one per cent of the total bank advances in the country. Principles are however principles. Farm subsidies may be all right for the United States and the west European countries; they may be all right for Japan. But they are not all right, the World Bank has ordained, for the countries of Asia, Africa and Latin America. Subsidies for the poor are a waste, off with them, says the Bank. Off with them, echoes the faithful committee.

A few months ago, even as the new government at the Centre was announcing its resolve to write off outstanding farm loans upto Rs 10,000 crore, a curious side drama was being enacted. Several states avail of NABARD's farm credit refinancing facility. One or two state governments, such as of Andhra Pradesh and Karnataka, expressed their intention to reach this credit to their farmers at a rate of interest lower than what was recommended by NABARD. That is to say, these state governments wanted to offer an interest subsidy to the farmers *out of their own coffers.* Under our Constitution, agriculture is a state subject, and the state governments have the absolute discretion to decide whether agricultural credit ought or ought not to be subsidised. But no, NABARD chose to interpose with a fiat of its own; it did not believe in interest subsidy; unless the decision to subsidise the interest rate was reversed, NABARD would refuse further refinance facilities to the states.

Three aspects of the controversy struck one at the time. First, since the Union government itself was writing off entire loans, what was wrong if some state governments offered a mere interest subsidy? Second, from where did NABARD get its clout which enabled it to challenge the views of democratically elected governments? Third, why did the Union government not intervene, and rap NABARD on the knuckles for its misdemeanour?

These puzzles are now answered. He who pays the piper calls the tune. NABARD owes its allegiance not to the Government of India, but to the World Bank, whose views it faithfully reflects. The Government of India is aware of this reality: it does not dare attract the ire of the Bank of pulling up NABARD for indiscipline; foreign exchange loans from the Bank might then stop.

Have not those economists and politicians who are exercised over Fund-Bank penetration in the government arrived somewhat late on the scene? We are seemingly already a dependent territory of the World Bank. The Bank's will is to be done; the nation's dignity and interests are no longer relevant considerations.

25th July, 1990

Food or ballistic missiles?

With all the fudging of statistics, officialdom finds it difficult to conceal the fact that at least two-fifths of the nation subsist below the minimum nutritional level, and close to three-fifths are unable to sign their names. At least in one-third of the country's village, there is not even a single source of potable water. Irrigation is yet to reach 70 per cent of the traditional rain-fed areas; survival in the chronically drought-prone areas remains as dicey as it was forty years age.

Priorites are however priorities. Life, it has been decided, is not worth living without Agni, the intermediate range ballistic misslile we have been trying to send hurtling into the sky from Chandipur in Orissa. Twice in the course of the past month, announcement were made with great eclat about its impending launch and villagers were unceremoniously herded out of a vast expanse of area around the launching pad. On both occasions, the effort failed because of hitches developing at the last moment in this or that sub-system. Police and other incidental *bandobasts* alone on account of the two failed efforts, have reportedly cost a total of ten crores of rupees. There is however such a thing as single-minded devotion. Money is no consideration; money has been spent, and will be spent, like water, on projects such has Agni. There will now be a third attempt later in the month to launch the missile. And no wretched foreigners have any right to criticise our activities in this direction. Is not Agni one hundred per cent indigenous, what business do outsiders have to poke the nose into our domestic affairs? As that country saying goes, since it is our goat, it is our prerogative to decide whether we chop it at the neck or at the tail.

Ballistic missiles of the kind our scientists have been asked to experiement with have only one purpose. They are integral to a successful delivery system, a euphemism for 'delivering' nuclear bombs on other people's territories. We are determined to prove ourselves in this area. While we continue to be one of the poorest nations on earth and cringe for development assistance from all and sundry, we nonetheless go ahead with our space and nuclear programmes. Grave issues of principle are here involved. We are against the emergence of monopoly in any sphere. Why must a handful of nations, such as the US, the USSR, Britain, France and China, have the nuclear monopoly? We have to break into it. That apart, in our little corner of the globe, we must be seen to be the cock of the road; we must stay ahead of the wretched Pakistanis in the armaments race; that includes the race to develop the 'delivery' system too.

We resent the nuclear oligopoly of a small group of countries and want to smash it. We do not show a similar quality of resentment against the monopoly of affluence enjoyed by the same set of countries. The asymmetry could not be more striking. Unlimited budgetary resources are allotted for nuclear and other defence-linked reasearch; there is hardly any accountability, of how these resources are spent. We, it will perhaps be argued, have no option: foreigners will not help us in this kind of research, we have to be on our own. Foreigners are supposedly somewhat more understanding about financing purely economic projects, and there is a steady generous inflow of foreign funds to boost our development effort. Which is a good thing, for resources we thereby save we are able to put into nuclear and space programmes. If, instead of doing so, we had chosen to invest *all* our available resources on development programmes and succeeded in accelerating the rate of economic growth, we could have been a better-off nation, less hungry, better educated, happier, healthier, and well on the way of penetrating into the monoploy of affluence of the select few nations. But first things first. We are the most ancient of human civilisations; there are some concomitant obligations to being such. We may go hungry, or be claimed by pestilence, but pride must have precedence. Smashing the nuclear monopoly and developing a delivery system we call our own have to come first. Therefore, whether we can afford it or not, money will be spent like water on projects such as Agni.

We are a sovereign nation, and others cannot sit on judgment on our government's priorities. A residual problem however, exists. On November 27, 1986, our Prime Minister signed, along with M. Gorbachev, General Secretary of the Central Committee of the Communist Party of the Soviet Union, a 'Declaration for a nuclear-weapon-free and nonviolent world.' It is a lovely document, full of nuggets of wisdom. Bits and pieces from it are worth quoting: 'Nuclear weapons threaten to annihilate not only all that man has created through the ages, but man himself and even life on earth.' 'It is necessary to change the existing world situation and to build a nuclear weapon-free world, free of violence and hatred, fear and suspicion.' 'The expansion of nuclear arsenals and the development of space-weapons undermine the universally accepted conviction that a nuclear war should never be fought and can never be won.' 'On behalf of the more than one billion men, women and children of our two friendly countries, who account for one-fifth of mankind, we call upon the peoples and leaders of all countries to take urgent action that would lead to a world free of weapons of mass destruction, a world without war.' 'Only disarmament can release the enormous additional resources needed for combating economic backwardness and poverty.' 'All nations must work together to solve urgent humanitarian problems and cooperate in areas of culture, the arts, science, education and medicine for the all-round development of the individuals. A world without nuclear weapons and violence would open up vast opportunities for this.' 'Solutions must be found to global problems such as shortage of food, the growth of populations, illiteracy and environmental degradation through the efficient and appropriate uses of the resources of the Earth.... A termination of the arms race would create better conditions for this purpose.' 'International security can be guaranteed through the adoption of integrated measures in the field of nuclear disarmament using all available and agreed measures of verification, and confidence building; just political settlement of regional conflicts, through peaceful negotiations; and cooperation in the political, economic and humanitarian sphere.' 'A nuclear-weapon-free and non-violent world require specific and immediate action for disarmament. It can be achieved through agreements on complete destruction of nuclear arsenals before the end of this century; banning of all weapons from outer space, which is the common heritage of mankind; banning of all nuclear tests; prohibition of the development of new types of weapons of mass destruction; banning of chemical weapons and destruction of their stockpiles; reducing the levels of conventional arms and armed forces.' '....mankind has the power to prevent a catastrophe, and to pave the way for a nuclear-weapon-free civilisation. The gathering strength of the coalition for peace embracing the efforts of the Nonaligned Movement, the Six-Nation Five-Continent Initiative for Peace and Disarmament, all peace-loving countries, political parties and public organisations gives us reason for hope and optimism. The time for decisive and urgent action is now.'

General Secretary Gorbachev can put his hand to his heart and claim with all sincerity that in the two-and-a-half years since the Declaration was signed, he has moved in some considerable degree toward the direction suggested by it. We do not belong to the same league as the Soviet Union. Even so, the contrast in behaviour is glaring. We signed the Declaration, our Prime Minister, however has little, very little to show that we took it seriously. We have continued to strain every effort to put a ballistic missile in the sky so as to strike terror in the neighbourhood; the rest of our nuclear and related space programmes have not been cut back either. Our protestations that all such programmes of ours have a 'peaceful' intent have evoked wide-spread derision.

It can of course be claimed that our sovereignty vests us with the prerogative to practice hypocrisy too. But the broader question remains beyond fudging: should playing with nuclear and space toys have precedence over food and education and shelter for our people? Since we are still a functional democracy, it is ultimately for the people themselves to decide on it.

Normally, one would expect such issues as the repeatedly aborted efforts at launching Agni to be raised and debated on the floor of Parliament. A cultural transformation has however taken place. Parliament has been persuaded to evolve a new code regarding which issues are of central concern to it and which are peripheral. As much as two thirds of the Union Budget is therefore passed without any discussion. The demands of even the ministry claiming the largest appropriations—the ministry of defence—are guillotined; there is hardly any outcry at this extraordinary development. All the greater reason why, even at the risk of being at the receiveing end of accusations of unpatriotic and treasonable conduct, one must keep raising inconvenient questions in other forms, and invite the political parties to debate these questions during the campaign for the coming Lok Sabha poll. According to one story making the rounds, the discomfiture the poor scientists have faced consequent to the fiasco over Agni was forced on them; the ruling politicians in New Delhi badly want a ballistic missile hoisted to the sky so as to impress the electorate on the technological heights the nation has been able to climb under their inspiring leadership, thereby ensuring maybe at least half a dozen crore of extra votes in their favour. It is a matter of putting it. Let the matter be put starkly before the people: food or ballistic missiles?

17th May, 1989

Fend for Yourselves

Budget day has come and gone. This year's Budget, without questions, is of extraordinary import. Its significance however does not lie in what it contains, but in what it does not. The Budget does not include any serious revenue proposals. Direct taxes are barely touched, the minor adjustments have little revenue implications; if anything, some more concessions are being allowed on income tax, thereby further inconveniencing the states, who are entitled to receive the bulk of the proceeds of this tax. There is some playing around with excise and custom duties, but the net additional yield is a piffle/or trifle compared to the government's total requirements. The Union finance minister is not at all concerned though. And his lack of concern has its own tale to tell.

The 1988-89 Budget in effect confirms the emergence of a new fiscal philosophy : henceforth, the government will make its draft on the community not through the Budget, but through extra-budgetary sources. The government is in bulk control of either the production or the distribution or both of key consumer articles and industrial inputs, including foodgrains, sugar, petroleum products, coal and iron and steel. It is the sole arbiter of the price to be charged for public utilities. So the normal budgetary course need no longer be traversed. From time to time, this or that set of administered prices will be raised, including the price of post cards, telephone calls and railway tickets. True, to enlarge its funds, the government, in author of raising administrated control author have made extensive use of the device of raising excise duties. In that case, however, the proceeds, the wretched Constitution says, would have to be shared with the states, which the Union government is most reluctant to do. If state governments want money, they must come as supplicants to the Centre; depending upon its own mood—and their political colour—the Centre may then decide whether or not to satisfy them.

But, as this year's Budget has made it particularly obvious, it is not even the hefty, exclusive revenues collected through continuous increases in administrered prices which will from now on be the main filler of the government's coffers. That role is being fully assumed by the printing press. The tally of budgetary deficits for the past three years is impressive beyond measure: Rs. 6,565 crores in 1985-86, Rs. 8,285 crores in 1986-87 and an estimated Rs. 6,010 crores in 1987-88. Practice maketh perfect: the government has gone ahead and planned a deficit of Rs. 7,484 crores for 1988-89. And, given the experience of the past years, the actual deficit could well be comprehensively larger.

The message comes filtering through. The nation has been put on notice that it is going to be henceforth standard practice to cover between 10 and 15 per cent of the government's total disbursements by note-printing. Such deficit financing is also going to be by far the most important measure for additional resource mobilisation.

For the government, deficit financing is the easiest method of raising money. All it has to do is to print the money, and it is there. It holds out the illusion of being painless: unlike direct taxes, no slice is seemingly taken from anybody's earnings; unlike in the case of indirect imposts, no price increase takes place for any particular commodity. But the immediate impression is a bit of a fake. For budgetary deficits, by adding to the quantum of money in circulation, soon lead to an across-the-board increase in prices, and each and every one's earnings are reduced in real terms. When there is a general price rise, the prices of essential articles rise more than in proportion. The poor are hence hit much harder by deficit financing. They are also hit harder because they have no protection at all against the price increase. The bulk of the rich and the affluent, in contrast, are either big manufacturers or major agricultural producers or traders, and their profits tend to go up, invariably, when prices go up.

Budgetary deficits are therefore a fiscal instrument biased against the weaker sections. A government which chooses deficit financing as the major device to bridge the gap between its income and expenditure betrays a deliberate insensitiveness towards the state of the nation's poor. The poor are asked to fend for themselves; the government tells them, elliptically or not so elliptically, that it could not be bothered how they fare, it is overwhelmed by its own problems, so the poor better live by their wits. Otherwise, let them disappear silently.

This of course is the big presumption, namely, that the poor, faced with the consequence of unbridled deficit financing, will go down silently. They may do so, but they also may not. They may decide to rise in revolt. Here the government perhaps banks upon the relatively under-developed mobilising capacity of the poorer classes. They may be discontented, but they may be in no position to articulate their discontent. There is also the other, not altogether unrealistic, assessment: in the case of such a huge, big country as ours, riots and uprisings are unlikely to synchronise, they will be sequential events, and the authorities will have the resources and coolth to be able to tackle them one by one.

The pros and cons of hefty doses of note-printing have been duly taken into account, and the government, which knows which side its bread is buttered, has taken the plunge. It requires quite a gumption to print year after year additional notes amounting to close to three per cent of the country's national income, more so in the current year, since, on account of the drought and for other reasons, wholesale prices have already risen by 10 per cent over the past eleven months and most retail prices by more than 20 per cent.

Prices are bound to increase further. The actual order of increase is at this stage largely a matter of conjecture. In case the rains fail again this year and our stock of foodgrains deplets rapidly, inflation could take wings. But if the authorities have received private assurance from the US administration that, should worst come to the worst, quick shipments of wheat would take place, the price increase need not then assume devastating proportions.

The basic issue cannot however be shoved aside. Whatever the magnitude of the price rise, it will affect more adversely the weak and the unorganised. The organised workers, including employees in government and mercantile firms, will perhaps upto a point be compensated for the price increase, even if the compensation is with a time-lag and also less than one hundred per cent. The small farmer and the share-cropper, who have little surplus to dispose of, will be badly hit, as they will have to pay heftily for non-food items. The agricultural worker, specially in regions where little political and social consciousness has spread, will be the most vulnerable, along with millions who are unemployed and under-employed.

But that is the intention, to put the squeeze on the nation's poor and lower middle classes. Their real income will erode, much the larger proportion of their earnings will have to be spent on acquiring bare necessities. And this is precisely where a social crisis could threaten to rear its head. For the Budget has another facet too. It also throws out several lollipops, inviting the community at large to indulge in the sin of at least minor luxuries. It is an open society, the allurements reach out as much to those who cannot afford as to those who can. The government in fact is hoping for an upsurge in the demand for industrial products to boost national output and thereby, contain inflation. Here, then, will be the latent irony: the nation's vast majority, who are poor, will have even less money than before, as a direct consequence of the Budget, to spend on industrial goods.

The open society's enticements will keep blaring to each and all, to the affluent, to the somewhat less so as well as to those who are altogether without means. The desire to reach out to the goodies will be kindled in equal measure in the hearts of the poor, but, not having the resources, they will burn up with frustration. Some amongst them, particularly those who live on the urban fringes, will be a more determined lot. Inflation has pinned them down, they must monetheless somehow acquire a few of the accoutre ments of the consumer society, so they must come to extra money. In case they are unable to do so by straightforward means, never mind, they will take the lawless road, and indulge in extracurricular activities. Such activities need not necessarily be confined to blackmarketeering tickets for the performances of *Shahenshah.* Smuggling and dope peddling may well be included on the agenda, along with snatchings and knifings. A weak, disorganised working class can be taken advantage of by the government and inflation sought to be rammed through. But, since it also fosters a milieu where each one is for himself or herself, it provides a romping ground for the generic tribe Karl Marx had so picturesquely described: 'vagabonds, discharged soldiers, discharged jailbirds, escaped galley slaves, swindlers, mountebanks,....pickpockets, tricksters, gamblers, procurers, brothel keepers, porters,....organ-grinders, rag-pickers, knife grinders, tinkers, beggars.' Such specimens are a resolute lot, they are determined to survive, and equally determined to partake a slice of what the rich and the well-placed are partaking, inflation cannot deter them, inflation in fact further stokes the fire of their desire to get even, whether by hook or by crook, with the luckier ones.

The Budget-makers in New Delhi have assumed an awesome responsibility by planing fiscal deficits of elephantine proportions for ever. By their decision, they are unleashing a virus of social anarchy which might in no time liquidate the nation's residual hopes and values. Who know, that could well be the purpose.

9th March, 1988

Are we really on the same boat, brother?

Almost coinciding with the non-aligned movement's four-yearly fireworks in Harare something of grim significance to the developing countries took place, without fuss or fanfare, in late August in Washington, DC, where the International Monetary Fund is located. The executive board of the Fund decided to declare Peru 'ineligible' for fresh loans because she had defaulted on her schedule of repayments to it. It was a major decision. The Fund, along with the World Bank, consider themselves responsible for enforcing discipline in the world economy and in the international monetary system. Whoever defies them does not deserve to belong. Peru, they have decided, must cease to belong; that little insignificant South American nation along the Pacific coast, consisting of barely 20 million people, will be tought the lesson of her life for daring to defy the Fund-Bank establishment.

Peru is in a bind. The country has piled up debt obligations to foreign private banks, international financial institutions and multinational corporations to the extent of nearly 15 billion American dollars, or roughly 750 dollars per capita. Interest charges are by themselves of the order of 1.5 billion dollars each year. Annual export earnings, on the other hand, do not exceed 3 billion dollars, and foreign exchange reserves are only a little more than 1 billion. The country's young new President, Alan Garcia, is no leftist. He has steered clear of Fidel Castro's exhortation to the Latin American countries to repudiate all repayment obligations for past external borrowings. On being installed as President last year, Garcia took what many had then considered a bold, but reasonable, stand. Yes, Peru's economic problems are in part the result of past errors on the part of politicians and policy makers: land reforms has lagged behind, impending agricultural growth; high per unit costs and low productivity continue to haunt the industrial sector; trade and tarrif policies have lacked both rationale and consistency; the upper income groups, who have traditionally controlled the levers of power, have indulged in indiscriminate and frivolaus imports. But, then, was not the International Monetary Fund equally responsible for the debacle in Peru's balance of payments and for her huge external indebtedness? Has it not insisted on certain 'conditionalities' which have made the country's economic plight worse with every day? Has not the Fund kept on demanding that imports be liberalised, subsidies to agriculture drastically reduced, employment generating programmes slashed, bank credit drastically cut down, and coordinated economic planning increasingly substitued by the free play of so called market forces? Finally, how do you expect Peru to honour its repayment obligations when the international terms of trade have tilted sharply against its products and its export earnings continued to shrink?

So President Alan Garcia took a decision about this time last year. No, he would not go as far as Fidel Castro, but the international financial institutions, the private commercial banks and the multinational corporations would not be allowed to have the pleasure of their full pound of flesh, Peru would not go under, she would limit her external debt repayments to 10 per cent of the country's export earnings, or at about 300 million American dollars per year for the present. Because the world's rich have a stranglehold over the international credit structure, they have no business to sqeeze the poor nations out of existence. Let there be a thorough restructuring of the world monetary system; let there be a major increase in the flow of concessional credit to the economically distressed nations; let there be an international commodity fund to protect the poor exporting countries against the ravages of a declining terms of trade; let the advanced western countries do a little retrospection and bring down the protective walls of tariffs and quotas they have built to shut out exports from the poor nations; let them reduce significantly the interest they charge for loans advanced to the latter. (For example, even a one per cent lowering of the rate of interest charged by foreign banks and international institutions will save the developing countries at least 10 billion American dollars each year.) Until these reforms are undertaken, Peru served notice, she would not pay the foreigners, as debt repayment, more than 10 per cent of her current export earnings; if she were to pay more, no resources would be left for development.

The International Monetary Fund was scandalised. The international monetary system was in danger; the hegemony of the rich nations was under attack. If the revolt was not crushed right at its incipience, there would be greater trouble ahead. The fund decided to act. At the beginning of the year, Peru owed the Fund 72 billion dollars in outstanding interest obligations. An ultimatum was served on the Peruvian government to settle accounts by April 14, Peru paid 35 million dollars, and told the Fund that enough was enough for the year. The Fund wanted to send a mission to Peru to enforce further drastic economic 'reforms' on the recalcitrant nation, including perhaps a dose of devaluation. The Peruvian government turned down the demand for a mission, informing the Fund in no uncertain terms its resolve not to countenance any more Fund-imposed 'conditionalities' which invariably reduce the poor to even further penury.

Retribution was swift to come. The executive board of the International Monetary Fund met in August. Peru's insubordination was intolerable. If Peru got away with her doctrine of meeting repayment obligations only up to 10 per cent of export earnings and nothing beyond, other debtor nations too would catch on to the idea. What a calamity would then befall the Western capitalist countries, their private commercial banks and their multinational corporations? So the executive board of the Fund acted: Peru has been made ineligible for further loans until it learns to behave.

The developing economics are represented on the Fund's executive board, even though they have only a minor voice in it. India is the foremost of the poorer countries among the Fund's member-nations, and she has a permanent executive director on its board. According to reports, representatives of the developing countries, led by India, supported the resolution to suspend Peru from the Fund; they too were against countenancing international monetary indiscipline.

Within a bare fortnight of all this happening in Washington DC, the NAM countries met in Harare. A long, ponderous statement was prepared, debated and finally issued inviting attention to the intolerable external debt situation faced by the member-countries. The resolution was full of right phrases and appropriate sentiments; it talked of the need to restructure the world monetary system, the desirability of working out a more liberal repayment schedule for the poorer nations, the importance of defending the terms of trade of primary goods producing countries, the inequity of the interest rate structure in the international money market, and all that. There was however not one reference to what the IMF has done to Peru, nor any demand that it reverses its decision. And, barring you know who, everyone was polite to everyone else, none was there to raise the query: pyrotechnics apart, comrade delegates, how did you and we vote on the Peru resolution at the meeting of the Fund's executive board?

It is a remarkable cocktail of cowardice, self-seeking and hypocrisy. The affair of Peru had provided an opportunity to the Fund's members representing the developing nations to take a stand on a principle. Here was a country which openly admitted her past mistakes in economic policy, she was making honest endeavours to reform her internal structure so that production and productivity could pick up, Peru could not be held reponsible for her declining terms of trade, all development activity in Peru would come to a full stop if the repayment burden is not re-sheduled, Peru's predicament only invited pointed attention to the imperative need to restructure the international monetary and credit arragements, including interest rates. The poorer nations, with India providing the led, could have said in unison that Peru was not alone, Peru's problems were indivisible from their own, Peru's protest was symbolic of their qwn agony, so Peru, the brave one among them, must not be an outcast. But, no, not a squeak; the developing countries, with India's executive director leading the clauqul, enthusiastically voted for the resolution, Peru, out, out. The government of each developing country makes its little calculations, oral solidarity in the cause of the poor is all right, but, when the chips are down, given the life style and class background of our leaders, we jolly well will have to stay on the right side of the World Bank and the International Monetary Fund, of the United States and United Kingodm, of Chase Manhattan and Bechtel. So we vote against Peru on our knees.

Having done that, these representatives of the poor countries hop in and fly to Harare. It is another meeting and another season. The fire-eating resolution, running down the International Monetary Fund, the multinational corporations and the quasi-racial white hegemony lording over the international monetary system is passed with wild acclamations, this time the delegates voting with their feet.

Thank heavens for at least one Muammar Gaddafi who was not found wanting in tearing to shreds this abominable hypocrisy. Need one also wonder that the capitalist governments of the West treat resolutions of the nature passed at Harare with derisive indifference, they already have the full measure of those who draft such resolutions?

8th October, 1986

To talk of sacrilege

Trust her to be always equal to the occasion. Shrimati Gandhi has provided the philosophical under-pinning for the obscene splurge of funds which is the Asiad. It is going to bring, we have been informed, the young people of Asia near to one another. Have a heart, she could not possibly have declared that it is going to bring lucre and her dear ones near to one another.

The total outlay which Asiad has involved will perhaps remain forever a well-guarded secret. The expenditure has been borne under many heads, and the accounts must be all fuzzy. Asiad was, after all, only an alibi. Despite Madam Prime Minister, the important motivation for this gigantic spree of expenditure in the government sector was to spruce up the nation's capital, and, in the process, augment the income of certain groups of people proximate to the centre of power. New Delhi must be rendered into a showpiece. Nothing but the very best for it. In appearance and amenities, it must compare well with the leading capitals of the world. A conservative estimate places the aggregate liability for Asiad at Rs. 1,000 crores. Some others, who have totted up the different columns of disbursements, including those by the banks and public financial institutions, will lay a wager around Rs. 2,000 crores. It would be foolhardy to go on record, that the true figure must lie somewhere in between; we simply have no way of knowing.

What is not in doubt is the Government's order of priorities. Nobody in charge has even once complained of shortage of money for the Asiad. Men and *material* may have been scarce, but not funds. The Union Government had underwritten to provide the entire sum needed, and it has done so. When requested to arrange for the extra expenses which the delay in the construction of the second Hooghly bridge has made inevitable—a delay for which the Union Government can be squarely held responsibile—the Union Finance Minister blandly pleaded lack of funds. The second Hooghly bridge is a public utility, but, sorry, no money is to be made available to complete it. The outlay on the Asiad could hardly be justified as an essential category of expenditure. But the Union Finance Minister would have been shown the door by his employers at Number One Akbar Road and Number One Safdarjung Road were he to plead lack of funds for it. He did not, he dared not. No interdict from the International Monetary Fund would have operated here either.

The problem however remains. If total resources cannot be increased, and printing of notes is to be frowned upon, the huge chunk of expenditure which the Asiad has called for can be only at the cost of some other proposed head or heads of expenditure, which now have to be chopped. A thousand crores of additional outlay here means a thousand crores less of outlay somewhere else in the economy; two thousand crores more here implies two thousand crores less somewhere else. The entire gamut of decision-making about the areas where to enforce the cut, and by how much, has to be the exclusive concern of the Union Government. And it would be altogether outrageous if the Centre tries to economise by drastically reducing the amount to be released to the States for redressing the distress caused by the drought—or, for that matter by the flash floods in Gujrat.

Having centralised the major sources of revenue gathering, the Centre can hardly pretend that the States must themselves generate the extra funds necessary for drought or flood relief. The States are in no position to raise the kind of money called for when emergencies of such a nature arise. Successive Finance Commissions have held differing views about the manner in which the States are to be provided with funds for the purpose; nonetheless, they have been unanimous that the onus of arranging for such funds belongs to the Centre. A State Government can at most supplement the remittances from the Centre to the extent of five or ten crores of rupees, but the major chunk of money has to come from New Delhi.

It would be dangerous folly if, exhausted by the Asiad, Shrimati Gandhi's Government would now try to prune expenditure on drought or flood relief. If the polity is to be held as sacrosanct, should not the Centre, in its search of economy, travel elsewhere, and take a look, for instance at the size of defence expenditure? It is no use stating that defence outlay cannot be touched, that has an over-riding priority. There cannot be two sets of over-riding priorities at a given moment. If the outlay on the Asiad, as claimed, has the topmost priority, defence expenditure, quite obviously, cannot claim the same status.

This is an awkward territory to traverse. In an open democracy, which is given to elections on the basis of adult suffrage at periodic intervals, populist sentiments carry exceptional weight. And the issue gets inextricably mixed up with the mythology of love and hate. The defence of the holy motherland is the most sacred of all obligations. If China is conspiring, we cannot afford to fall behind, that would be akin to treason. Once such a syllogism has been enshrined in the people's psyche, continuous mindless increases in defence expenditure becomes the easiest of things to bring about. The tribe of contractors and commission agents soon arrive on the scene. Since Pakistan has *that* how can we afford not to have *this,* since China has purchased aircraft of this particular specification for its air force, for dear life we shall have to go for additional aircraft of an indubitably superior specification offered by country x, y or z, otherwise we are bound to fall behind. It is not simply a matter of the by-now-standard idiocy of maintaining the so-called balance of deterrence. Wheels begin to operate within wheels, deals begin to be matched by other deals. At least in part, the story is no different from the Asiad's contractors and commission agents, the foremost amongst partiots, take over, they know their way along the intricate corridors and catwalks of the Ministry of Defence, as also elsewhere, including Number One Safdarjung Road and Number One Akbar Road. Transnational links too are forged in no time. No qestions are to be asked; parliamentary surveilellance over the outlay on defence is less than perfunctory; the Comptroller and Auditor-General is politely told that the concept of performance budgeting can hardly apply to defence expenditure; in other words, the ability to spend funds is itself the criterion of performance, otherwise our certified enemies will steal a march over us. Every now and then, polite suggestions have been made that the chiefs of staff in the respective services themselves be asked to analyse the 'cost-effectiveness' of the money being spent each year within their service, and perhaps they could themselves evolve ways and means of reducing the outlay by 5 or 10 per cent. At such junctures, newspapers have been conveniently flooded with disquieting news about what Pakistan is up to, what the Chinese army brass is up to, 'cost-effectiveness' received a very short shift.

Year after year, we have thus been spending five to six thousand crores, supposedly to shore up our defence. Year after year, we have been unable to have an outlay of even two thousand crores on building new irrigation facilities which could come in the form of multi-purpose barrages, against floods too. Year after year, a large proportion of the defence expendituure takes the form of outlay in foreign exchange, for import of equipment and spares is involved, causing a further strain on the balance of payments. Sleek new fighter planes are bought, sleek new missile-carrying planes are bought too. They add to the stockpile, year after year; and are accordingly replaced by sleeker planes, the latest marvels of technological advance. In lieu of *one* such plane, we could have perhaps bought *two thousand* passenger buses for the road, but this is idle thought, the metaphysics of national defence has to have precedence.

Meanwhile, irrigation facilities do not expand, essential roads and bridges are not built, the ballasts against the threat of drought and floods do not come up, public transport all but breaks down. Will it be a sacrilege to suggest that maybe we should take another look at our system of values? A poor nation cannot have everything, it cannot have the Asiad, high defence outlay and, at the same time, adequate expenditure for economic growth and social amenities. Some thing has got to give. The problem, admittedly, is tough. Ensconced as they are in New Delhi, it will be difficult to convince the decision-makers that we are poor; New Delhi, with its splendour, does not belong to a poor nation. So, along with the Asiad, defence expenditure too will continue to have over-riding priority. The cut, when it comes, will be on expenditure in times of natural calamities. Cut out the dole, it is bad for the morale, don't cut the outlay on the fifth swiming pool at the Talkatora Gardens.

Fourteen developing nations, along with Rumania, the headline says, have asked for a reduction in military budgets. You can wager more than even money that India does not belong to the fourteen. Vacuous idealism goes ill with a nation whose spiritual father, allegedly, is Mohandas Karamchand Gandhi.

24th November, 1982

Please pay for non-development

An outrage has to be called by its appropriate name. Were not we told a while ago: there are at most five hundred hardcore terrorists who are creating all the mischief in Punjab, and they could be easily taken care of? And yet, consider what the government has now bulldozed through Parliament. The circumstance in Punjab is the alibi; because of it, we have to put up with indignity of our letters being opened at will by those in authority. One or two faint voices of protest by this or that member of Parliament, but no massive, collective anger rent the sky, even the parties belonging to the Opposition did not bother to come together and counsel with one another on how to evolve a strategy for resisting the extraordinary measure the government has proposed. National security is a most useful scarecrow; politicians and political parties, who may otherwise be dead set against the government, are frightened out of their wits the moment such issues as the need for defending the polity against internal and external subversion are invoked. Therefore one or two routine speeches are made against the non-desirability of opening the mail of private citizens even when the nation is not formally engaged in a war; the government is advised to be adequately circumspect in exercising the powers it has taken upon itself; it is admonished not to bite more than it can chew. Once these homilies are delivered, the passion is spent. The government gets the hint. Little by little, with a seeming casualness that demands, and receives, grudging admiration, those who consider the Articles in the Consitution begining with Article 14 a load of rubbish go about with their demolition job. The Opposition parties can marshal their forces when the occasion is, say, our failure at the Seoul Asiad. Otherwise, their sense of priorities fetters out fairly early. What even the foreign masters were not permitted to do when we were under imperial shackles, the government of free India can now enforce with ease. Shri M. G. Ramachandran and the Speaker of the Tamil Nadu Legislative Assembly are mistaken, they should ask the Union government, the Constitution *is* for burning.

In the area of communications, the decision to empower themselves with the legal right to steam open mail is not however the only outrage the authorities have perpetrated in recent weeks. Consider the matter of remitting money from one part of the country to another. Bank charges have been raised, most unreasonably, in recent years. Even so, the service charge debited by a bank for encashing an outstanding cheque, unless it be for a relatively small amount, remains modest; for cheques of relatively higher amounts, the cost of encashing the cheque in fact comes to barely 0.2 per cent or thereabouts. In the case of bank drafts, the charge is, almost uniformly, one-half of one per cent of the amount. But, in our country, the poorer sections do not generally avail of the facilities of the banking system to remit money from one place to another. Most of them will be scared stiff of even approaching a bank office. And yet, many amongst them must send money from their place of work to their families.

Millions of our working people travel away from home in search of livelihood. Barring perhaps the north-western states, in every other region grim symptoms of unemployment and under-employment stalk the countryside. Landlessness marks at least a quarter of the nation's agrarian population, another quarter can perhaps lay claim to a plot of land, but the average size of their holdings will not exceed one acre. Considerable numbers amongst them are therefore on the move. They walk, they load themselves in trucks and trains, sometimes they use camels or other animals, millions and millions of them travel, every year, in search of jobs. Some of them travel perhaps fifty miles, or perhaps five hundred miles or even more, across the borders of more than one state. Many find work in the fields in the relatively more prosperous areas, or they get absorbed in irrigation projects or rail projects. Some get absorbed in plants and factories in the more advanced industrial states. Yet others drift into distant towns and cities, and join the so-called informal sector, picking up whatever work comes their way, or learn to ply a trade or sell a ware.

These millions have left their families behind in their villages. They visit their families once a year, or not even that, possibly once in two to three years. They however send remittances home, every month, or every two months, or once a quarter. These money-remitters include clerks belonging to the lower echelons of the middle class, but they also include agricultural labourers, factory workers, hawkers, railway gangmen, itinerant trades people of diverse description. They all remit money home at regular or irregular intervals: twentyfive rupees, fifty rupees, a handred rupees, two hundred rupees, two hundred and fifty rupees, five hundred rupees. They are major users of the facilities offered by the postal department: almost the whole of their remittances they send by money order.

To a large extent this country is in fact held together by money orders. Border quarrels go on between state and state, linguistic fissures rear their head, there are assorted other tensions between the different peoples who constitute this great nation, but the labour market is still remarkably integrated, the periodic slogans favouring jobs for sons of the soil are mostly aimed at the organised sector in industry and commerce; they are yet to affect, in any part of the country, employment in farms or in informal trade or services. This inchoate community of quasi-migrant workers are hardly aware of the banking system. The vast majority of them have no banking accounts. The vast majority of them are probably unable to sign their names. They encounter difficulty in maintaining even postal savings accounts: everytime sums have to be withdrawn from such accounts, they run into problems. There is no question of their writing crossed cheques which their families could encash, or to send a bank draft. The families depend on their remittances, and these remittances, almost invariably, are through money order.

The relevant data are always somewhat cut of date, and always less than complete. But—here one bases oneself on whatever information is officially available—at least 150 million money orders are sent through the post offices every year, and the aggregate sum remitted will come to anywhere around three to five thousand crores of rupees. For the families who receive these remittances, it amounts to as much as 50 per cent of their total annual income, or even more.

In state after state, it is usually the most wretched of the earth who move out of the villages in search of livelihood elsewhere. A fair number of the money orders therefore originate with, as well as are destined for, some of the nation's poorest households. These money orders are truly their life belt.

Our Parliament in its last session was not only cajoled to agree to legislatiion which will permit interference with the mail; there was a second piece of legislative measure which raised postal rates, including the rates for money orders and postal orders. The upshot is that while bank remittances do not cost more than 1 per cent, and progressively less and less as the amount of remittances increases, remittance by postal money orders will cost at least 3 per cent, and, for the majority of the cases, 4 per cent of the amount remitted. The government, we will be told, had to follow in such matters the World Bank's instructions. The Bank wants the price of all public utilites to go up. Bank remittances are a component of standard banking service, they do not according to the World Bank, constitute a public utility. Money orders however do. Somebody or other has to pay for the nation's development—or nondevelopment.

A certain insensitivity has entered the official soul. Or, for all one can surmise, it is not insensitivity, but a calculated cynicism. The millions who send money through the post office are economically weak and unorganised.

There is no specific constituency to which they belong. The authorities felt reasonably confident that no major outcries were likely to follow the enhancement of postal rates. They have been proved right. The opposition in Parliament registered a token protest, a few political parties issued a token statement of indignation, and there the matter has been allowed to rest. With effect from the first day of the New Year, the new rates have come into operation, and the nations's poor who depend on remittances are to experience further erosion in their earnings.

The government is unable to match its accounts. It is determined to lower taxes for the rich. It therefore does not mind charging higher rates for money orders and postal orders in case that would yield it even 10 or 15 crores of rupees on an annual basis. There are a hundred other different ways the government could have arranged to raise this amount of Rs 10 to 15 crores, or a hundred different ways it could have curtailed its expenditure by Rs 10 to 15 crores. It will not do either; it is the nation's poor who are to be made answerable for the government's woes.

The air is thick with talks of economic liberalisation and open competition. In an altogether free competitive system, it would have been inconceivable that banks could charge around 0.2 per cent or less for their remittances while the government charged 4 per cent for postal remittances; there would have been an evening out of the rates. It is about equally absurd that, in our country, where the banks are under the government's total control, this anomaly—an anomaly which grossly discriminates against the poor—is allowed to continue. But, then, it is the government which is actually promoting this anomaly. You know who have inherited the government and therefore inherited the earth. And the country's Opposition will duly advise you that it is not the season for righteous indignation.

14th January, 1981

The other Americans

"America! America!/ God shed his grace on thee,/ And crown thy good with brotherhood/ From sea to shining sea./ ...America! America!/ God mend thine every flaw,/ Confirm thy soul in self-control/ Thy liberty in law."

These are lines from the anthem children in the United States of America learn to sing full-throatedly. The same anthem refers to America as a "thoroughfare for freedom". The Bushes and the Rumsfelds have made heavy weather of these pious expressions. That does not extinguish the radiance of the legacy which the US can, legitimately, lay claim to. It may now sound bizarre; even so, it would be cruel to forget that a war of independence, severly fought, ushered in the American nation-state. This war was fought on the basis of an ethical principle which, by universal acclamation, constitutes the bedrock of democracy: "no taxation without representation". The doctrine propagates a message both solemn and simple: to rule a nation, one must have the sanction of its majority.

Nor can another hard datum be slurred over. Their nation-state was roughly three-quarters of a century old, the American people again went to war, a civil war, this time to assert the nation's belief in another equally precious moral principle: no human being has the prerogative to exploit other human beings. The civil war led to the decisive defeat of the segregationists, and the American nation can justly take as much pride in the contents of Abraham Lincoln's address at Gettysburg as it does in those of the Declarations of Independence at Philadelphia. True, racial prejudice dies hard; it took the Americans almost another full century before the emancipation of the blacks could be both codified and ratified through effective administrative action.

The surcese of racial discrimination, some will say, is far from complete, one just has to compare the average US per capita income and the average income of its black minority, or the average holding of wealth of the two respective entities. The Contrast stretches to health, education and housing facilities as well. And on the issue of defending freedom and democracy, the US global record in the recent period makes a mockery of the two concepts.

Such contemporary history still does not make mince-meat of what passes as the American legacy. Throughout the 19th century, immense waves of migrants found their way to the US; they were escaping from European misery of various description, including economic distress, religious pogroms and Czarist and other forms of tyranny. Later, in the 20th century, they fled from Nazi persecution. They arrived at the land of opportunity, and, at least as far as the white citizenry is concerned, the opportunity they discovered was enriched by the imprimature of equality. The US prospered, economically and otherwise, the liberal tradition became firmly established in the American psyche, all radical causes were accorded an open hearing: one could preach the cause of the blacks or of other ethnic groups, or campaign for the liberation of women or for the socialist millenium or for Seventh Day adventists.

Cast your mind back to the first decades of the 20th century. Radicalism was, for large sections in American society, the beacon of the future. The socialist movement was taken seriously; in the 1912 presidential elections, Eugene Victor Debs, the socialist leader, was regarded a major contender, so much so that a first-generation Russian immigrant couple from Rostow named one of their two sons Eugene Victor, the other one was named after the great American revolutionary poet, Walt Whitman. History played one of its random jokes. Walt Whitman Rostow grew up to be an averagely good economist and happened to be the closest confidant of President John F. Kennedy in the early Sixties. He could not care less for the radical lineage of his name; he egged on Kennedy and, subsequently, Lyndon Johnson, to carpet-bomb Vietname.

But that does not detract from the lustre of the other America. The US has always been in the habit of springing surprises. At about the time Debs was charming the American radical crowd, Paul Marlor Sweezy was born to a rich East Coast family. Wealth makes for snobs; wealth, however, stimulates liberalism, rationality and independence of thought too. The mind of Paul Sweezy was blessed by each of the latter traits. He grew up into a gentle, kind, civilized human being, whose natural instinct was to defy one's class moorings and cross over to the side of the dispossessed. In a manner of speaking, he provided an empirical proof of a precept expatiated on by his teacher in the Harvard economics faculty, Joseph Schumpeter. Schumpeter held the view that the Marxian tenet about the secular decline in the rate of profit apart, capitalism would collapse also on account of the rapid spread of rational ideas amongst the rich capitalist progeny, who, aghast at the ugly asymmetry of capitalism, would migrate into the enemy's ranks.

Sweezy, along with the other Paul, Samuelson, were the brightest and the best in Schumpeter's class. Samuelson travelled to neoclassical fame. Sweezy, went, in the nadir of the Thirties' depression, to the London School of Economics. At the LSE, Hayek's anti-communist hectorings only made him a more devout Marxist. It was in London that he decided to write a tract in English which would present Marx's economic construct in a non-obscure readable form to the Anglo-Saxon clientele. The outcome was *The Theory of Capitalist Development,* unsurpassed till today not just as an explicator of Marxist economic thought but also as its defender and annotator.

At the end of World War II, Sweezy returned to Harvard as a member of the faculty. The Cold War philosophers were, however, spreading their tentacles fast. Very soon, it was the turbulent days of Joseph McCarth. Hounded out of Harvard, Sweezy had to face charges of treasonable activities in New Hampshire. He was a proud, noble American; he did not chicken out and fought the accusation tooth and nail; it took him years to be fully vindicated by the US Supreme Court.

As Lilian Hellman said, it was scoundrel time, it did not upset Sweezy's equilibrium though. He was confident that his Marxist belief was in total harmony with his American patriotic passion. That passion spelled democracy, Equality and the brotherhood of man. The ill spell turned out to be good for him in the long run, good for American society and good for humanity at large. Denied a teaching slot, Sweezy instead founded the *Monthly Review.* Economics, Sweezy told the world through the *MR,* was neither obfuscation nor skill-fetishism; economics is a science whose aim is to advance human welfare and serve particularly the cause of the poor and the downtrodden; economics without idelology is a sterile, empty box.

Not that scholarly work in search of Marxian trough was ever suspended: *Monopoly Capital,* written jointly with Paul Baran, bears evidence of that steadfastness. Even so, to heck with academic recognition. Sweezy was an activist. *MR* got shaped in his ideological image and was always in combat against the world's several ills. It carried to American society and to its global readership a number of specific messages. Once its initial spurt of creativity is over capitalism stifles human progress. In fact, it becomes a twin menace, for imperialism is only an extension of the capitalist cancer. Therefore, the fight has to be on all fronts, domestic as well as international. The *MR* has always believed in calling a spade a spade. If it suffered from cerebral deficiencey, so what? It has been consistently in the forefront of battles against capitalism, colonialism and imperialism in the different parts of the world and has been a thorn in the side of US imperialism. Whether the cause was Cuba or Vietnam, Rwanda or Iraq, Brazil or Venezuela, the Fund-Bank structural adjustment programmes or the World Trade Organisations' Colonial designs, Sweezy and the *MR* were there to give the trumpet call: expose—and resist.

Comrades, or the calibre of Leo Huberman and Harry Magdoff, were there to help him, but everybody knew where the principal source of inspiration lay.

Until infirmity claimed him, Sweezy never stopped being vocal on global issues using his sober, persuasive, straightforward prose. His review of the month and the monthly commentary in the *MR* were compulsory texts for successive generations clinging to radical beliefs in country after unfortunate country. Was it ironical, or just natural, that, in the week Sweezy died, the US administration publicized the latest edition of the outrages it has become furious for: the ousting of Jean-Bertrand Aristide in Haiti? The battle against injustice, Sweezy would tell his admirers, is never adjourned.

He was forced to give up teaching in the Fifties, but he remained a great teacher for the next fifty-odd years. Nature's law is nature's law; now he is gone, but the *Monthly Review* survives and promises to survive all future vicissitudes. That too is a typical Sweezy-esque reflex: adversities are opportunities.

22nd March, 2004